MARATHON MAN

MARATHON MAN

One Man, One Year,
370 Marathons

Rob Young
with Dustin Brooks

**SIMON &
SCHUSTER**

London · New York · Sydney · Toronto · New Delhi

A CBS COMPANY

First published in Great Britain by Simon & Schuster UK Ltd, 2016
A CBS COMPANY

1 3 5 7 9 10 8 6 4 2

Simon & Schuster UK Ltd
1st Floor
222 Gray's Inn Road

The [author and publisher] have made every [e]fforts
to c[...] and [...] apo[l]ogise
fo[r any omissions or errors in the form of credits gi]ven.
[Corrections may be made in future printings.]

[A CIP catalogue record for this book]
[is available from the British Library.]

Hardback ISBN: 978-1-4711-5287-0
Trade paperback ISBN: 978-1-4711-5300-6
Ebook ISBN: 978-1-4711-5289-4

Typeset and designed in the UK by M Rules
Printed and bound by CPI Group (UK) Ltd, Croydon, CR0 4YY

To Joanna, Olivia and Alexander.

And to my second family, the running community.

'Sport has the power to unite people in a way that little else does. It speaks to youth in a language they understand. It can create hope where once there was only despair.'

NELSON MANDELA

'If you're going through hell, keep going'

WINSTON CHURCHILL

Contents

Prologue

Dad punched me again and I could hear my heart beating fast. Then I slipped and fell onto my knees and his foot came up fast as lightning into my stomach. The force of it flipped me onto my back. He had blood on his knuckles which he noticed for the first time now. I think it came from my cheek.

The sweat was pouring off him, but he looked energised, not tired. He rolled up his sleeves and came back for more, punching and kicking wildly. I stayed down. This had been going on ever since I could remember, an almost daily occurrence. I'd learnt the best thing was to not to put up a fight. Just to wait it out.

Then he started shouting at me, telling me what a useless good-for-nothing I was. 'You're no good, boy. You're no good!' he screamed. 'You can't even defend yourself!' I could see his face so angry and creased, I remember thinking he looked more like a monster than a human being.

Crazy as it sounds now, this was all pretty normal for me. It was just a part of life, the only one I'd known anyway. And scary as it was, it was bearable, unless he was really drunk and then he didn't know exactly what he was doing. Then he'd hit me too hard and I'd be a wreck for days and have to stay in my bedroom.

Usually the beatings took place in the living room and

when we were alone in the house. Or my little sister would be up in her room doing God knows what. She never came out when Dad was beating on me, though. I imagine she just kept quiet and prayed he wouldn't get bored with me and come visit her.

He grabbed me by the ankle and dragged me to the bottom of the stairs. I knew what that meant. The panic rose up in me. My heart was beating fast and I felt really hot by now. I grasped the stair rail, desperately trying to get away, but his fist came down hard across my arms, breaking my grip.

What was coming next was the thing I hated the most. So I got ready, going deep inside myself to a place that was all mine. The volume would go down on his shouting, like it was a TV turned down low. Inside I was preparing to endure something. It needed all my focus to do it right or I'd be in trouble. I had to get control of myself and not be overcome by my fear. I couldn't afford to get dragged in. By now I was in a state I call 'locked-in'.

He pulled me by my feet to the top of the stairs, my head hitting each stair on the way up. It didn't matter too much because I was ready now. I was ready for his sick little game. It was going to start very soon and I was prepared.

I was only five years old.

CHAPTER ONE
All for Twenty Pence

13–14 April 2014

I woke up at about 9.30am in Isleworth, south-west London, a bright blue sky peeking through the crack in the curtains. I could hear my missus, Joanna, next door playing with Alexander, our son. Now she was telling him off. He was only a year old, but he was always getting into trouble with her, almost as much as I was. I stumbled next door to join them. Alexander looked upset as he didn't like getting told off, then his face broke into a great big smile and he rushed over to me.

'Put the telly on, Joanna,' I said. 'The marathon's on.'

'We were trying to eat breakfast,' she said, her hands on her hips, as I switched on the TV.

'I'd love some toast,' I said, smiling at her. She looked exasperated: two naughty boys to look after, it wasn't easy for her.

The wheelchair marathon was already underway. David Weir was in the leading group, a real competitor. I'd met him a couple of years earlier at a school fundraiser and he seemed like a really nice guy, but tough with it. He'll take some beating, I thought.

I played with Buddy (the nickname we have for Alexander) but kept my eye on the marathon in the background. Mo Farah was running his first marathon, and all eyes were on him: the double Olympic gold medallist from two years earlier, at the 5,000 and 10,000 metres. Mo was class, a world champion, but could he handle the marathon?

Joanna came over and stood in front of the telly and tried to talk to Buddy and me, as she wanted to go out somewhere. 'We can't stay in all day,' she said. I wanted to watch the marathon, though.

'Buddy and I want to watch the race,' I replied. 'Come on, join us. We can go out later on.'

Unimpressed, Joanna disappeared to do some chores, leaving me with Buddy and the race. I'd find a way to make it up to her later. It was almost 10am now and the runners were gathered at the start of the race. It was a warm and beautiful day, uncommon for April in London. You could see the professional runners, all skinny and fit-looking at the start line. The indefatigable Kenyans looked serious, as though nothing in the world mattered more than this race.

Behind them was the sea of club and park runners that make up most of the 40,000 entrants. Wearing their colourful charity vests or fancy dress, they *were* the marathon to me. Most had a heart-rending tale to tell of someone they knew who'd had cancer or dementia, and they were the reason they were running. Every year Joanna and I would cry a few tears hearing someone's story. All these people putting themselves through something tough to help someone less fortunate, it made you feel good to be part of the human race (no pun intended).

I'd find out later that £53 million was raised on that day. A big pile of money that would keep charities going, buy life-saving medical equipment, fund research, pay for nurses and more. Money that would give people hope and change lives, save lives even. It's pretty awesome when you think about it!

Joanna marched in from the other room. She'd clearly finished the ironing and was ready to do something. Anything. 'Why are you watching this, Rob, when we could be doing something? Buddy needs to get out to get some fresh air. Let's get some exercise, not watch other people getting some.'

'I'm going to run a marathon,' I said. 'So I need to watch this a bit more, get some advice.' That wasn't exactly true. I had no plans to run a marathon any time soon, but I did want to watch the race.

She relaxed and smiled. 'You'll never run a marathon,' she said with such certainty.

'I will,' I said, standing up. 'You just watch me.'

She shook her head. 'You're too lazy to run one, Rob. You can't even take your family to the park.' She was baiting me, but I didn't care.

'I could run fifty marathons,' I said. I have no idea where that number came from.

'Fifty marathons!?' Joanna laughed, shaking her head as though it was the most ridiculous idea she'd ever heard.

'I'll bet you twenty pence I can,' I said, offering her my hand to shake. We were always doing 20p bets back then, usually over silly things. She took my hand without hesitation.

'You're on,' she said. And then she stared at me, her beautiful blue eyes becoming more serious now. I think it was dawning on her that I might not be joking.

And that was how it all began: no huge forethought or

preparation, no great intentions. Just a little bit of banter and a girl laughing at her fiancé's plans. Ladies, be warned!

That bet quickly turned into my attempt to run more marathons in a year than anyone had ever done before. The year that followed would be tough on our family and there'd be times Joanna would deeply regret having challenged me. Marathon running would turn me into an absent boyfriend and father, our money would dry up and eventually we'd be forced to leave our home. But we got into this together and we'd come out the other side together, too. Happier, wiser, richer even.

Well, two out of three isn't bad.

The rest of the day is a bit of a blur, to be honest. We did get out the house and to the park, but my mind was elsewhere: something had clicked in me, since that conversation. A light had switched on in my brain and rusty cogs had started to turn. I was motivated. The idea of running 50 marathons had turned into a bigger idea. How many marathons could I do in a month? How many in a year? What are the world records for these kinds of things? Looking back, this all seems quite ridiculous when you consider I was just a 31-year-old office worker who hadn't run his first marathon yet.

Though that's not strictly true. I had been in the Army in my twenties and I was always the one who could march the furthest and the quickest with a heavy pack. Then I was a pro cyclist for a while and represented Britain as a junior triathlete, so I knew I had some sporting ability and a talent for endurance. That kind of thing doesn't just disappear – even if it had been lying dormant in me for the last seven years. Add to that a dream that had been dancing around in the back of my mind for ages now, a vague idea, entirely without focus. I had always wanted to do something inspirational, involving sport, to raise money for underprivileged kids. I didn't know what exactly, or how, but still the idea kept nagging away at me.

So that evening was spent online, learning about those who'd gone furthest, discovering the world-record holders and those who claimed to be the record holders. The crazy ones. It turned out to be a little complicated. The *Guinness World Records* held American Larry Macon's 157 marathons to be the most run in a single calendar year (2012), and he went on to complete 239 marathons in 365 days in 2012–13. It was impressive in its own right, but doubly so when you realise he was in his sixties at the time. They were all official organised marathons, the kind that are usually just held at the weekends. He must have had to do a lot of flying around the US to make it work (think of the airmiles!).

Then there were other, unofficial marathon records. Ricardo Abad from Spain ran 366 consecutive marathons in a year in 2011, which meant running at least one every day for a year, with no days off. They weren't all official, sanctioned marathons, so Guinness wasn't interested. But I was – it was a real challenge, and one you didn't need to be rich to take on.

I also looked into the history of the marathon: why was it 26.2 miles long, for example? Everyone knows the first marathon was run in Greece, but it wasn't originally 26.2 miles, as it is today. In 490BC, Pheidippides, a Greek soldier, ran approximately 25 miles, from the battlefield in Marathon to Athens, to report victory over the Persians. Then he keeled over and died.

Some 2,400 years later, in 1896, the organisers of the first modern Olympic Games decided to celebrate the story by recreating the race, this time with a 40km (24.85 miles) course from Marathon Bridge to the Olympic Stadium in Athens. Twelve years later, in 1908, at the Olympics in London, the length of the course became extended to 26 miles and 385 yards (or 42.195km), so that the race from Windsor Castle could finish in front of the Royal Box in the White City Stadium in Shepherd's Bush. In 1921, this distance was determined by the International Amateur Athletic Federation to be the official distance of a marathon. And it has stuck ever since.

So, now I knew the history and the records, my next problem was how to get started? And where? It was 8pm by then. I was tempted to head off into the night there and then, to find a signpost to a place 26 miles away and set off there, but I figured I'd wait until the morning and run my first marathon before work. That kind of thinking is what counts as patience and restraint in my world.

To be taken seriously, I knew I needed to run official marathon courses, even if they weren't being marshalled at the time. The only local marathon I knew about was one held in Richmond Park each year. This leafy royal park in southwest London had an official course you could follow, and I used to do the occasional 5k park run there at weekends. After a bit of digging around online, I found a map of the course and printed it off.

My next concern was getting verification for my achievements. How would anyone know that I'd actually done the marathons? I needed witnesses to verify my story and, as soon as I could, GPS tracking. I read different versions of this online, but most said I needed at least two people to sign off as witnesses of my runs. I asked Joanna to come down and then called a friend, Eva, and asked if she could come out to witness me running.

'Why are you running a marathon on your own?' she asked.

'I won't be alone,' I said. 'You're coming.'

No doubt she thought I was crazy, but that was something I'd just have to get used to. I packed a rucksack with a towel, my work clothes for afterwards and some fruit, then I set my alarm and got into bed beside Joanna who was already fast asleep.

My alarm went off at 3.30am and I was up. Joanna stirred but didn't fully awaken. My head had been whizzing all night with a hundred thoughts, mainly about charities, as I wanted to raise money if I was going to take on this challenge – I wasn't just doing it for 20p. I had been trying to remember an advert I kept seeing on the tube on the way to work, with a picture of a child crying. Disturbing and motivating, it had stuck in my head, though what charity it was for I still couldn't remember. I'd decided I was going to make a difference to kids and running was going to be my passport. It was all clear now, before I had even set foot on a marathon course. It's funny how life can give you that kind of clarity sometimes. The rest of the time we just muddle around in the dark. I realised then that I had been looking for this sort of opportunity for years.

I crept out of the bedroom and peeked inside Alexander's room. He was sleeping serenely as children do. I never get tired of seeing him sleep. Then I pulled on my running gear and my worn-out trainers. I had a good look at the map of the Richmond Park marathon route I'd printed off the night before. It was complicated, but I knew where every point was. I tucked it in my shorts just in case.

It took only about 20 minutes to cycle to the park, so it

was about 4.15 when I got there. If you don't know Richmond Park, then you should visit when you have the chance. It's full of wildlife, including deer, as well as kite flyers, dog walkers, runners and the like. There's nowhere more beautiful in the world.

And right now I had it all to myself. I realised I'd have to be careful running in the pitch darkness, with only the moon and stars to light the way ahead, as the path was strewn with roots, rocks and deer poo. I put my bag down at the start of the route, took a deep breath and set off. I knew what I wanted to achieve over the coming months, but I had no idea what to expect, or whether I'd get anywhere near the targets I had started to set myself. I was literally heading out into the darkness.

I don't remember any problems during that first run, which wouldn't always be the case. I'd come to run this route more than any other and have all kinds of mishaps and mini-adventures. The 750 deer in the park don't always behave themselves, I'll tell you that. It's particularly unnerving when there's a thick early morning mist and you can't see more than a couple of metres away. Then the sound of the deer braying all around you can be a little intimidating. They like to pop up out of nowhere and surprise you just when you least expect it. Many a time I'd almost literally run into an angry stag on the path who looked ready to charge. But I would never actually be harmed by them and we'd grow to know each other like old friends over the coming months

The route is almost all on a path called the Tamsin trail, which circles the park's perimeter. It's a complicated route: a 3.1 mile loop, followed by a 9.1 mile loop, then lastly two 7.2 mile laps of the perimeter. There's not too much overall elevation, 340 metres in total, including a couple of small hills.

You've got to watch your footing in parts, especially on the downhills (and in the dark). There are four or five water fountains on the course, all of which I'd need today. The route comes back past the start point at Sheen Gate four times, so leaving my bag there, full of snacks and drinks, would become my routine.

After a couple of hours, the sun came up but I still felt pretty good. My breathing was heavy and the mileage was a shock to my system, and my feet in particular, but I was bearing up. I was so focused that my body just followed my intention. It was one of those moments when I knew I was in the right place, doing the right thing. I fitted. I hadn't felt like that since I was cycling and even then only intermittently. The ease was only temporary, though, I can assure you. It wouldn't last and soon I would find that pretty much everything hurt.

As I ran that morning, I realised how bizarre the whole thing was. The idea of Rob Young the runner is hilarious to me. Let me explain why: when I was 17 years old I was a triathlete for Great Britain. I'm a decent swimmer, so I could hold my own in that, splash around with the best of them and finish up there with the leaders at the end of that first stage of the triathlon. Then we'd get on the bikes and I was in my element. I was born to cycle. Ever since I was a teenager, racing banged-up, broken-down old bikes against men on their expensive road bikes, and beating them, I had a way on two wheels. I was fast and I had the lungs to push.

So the second stage of the triathlon was a breeze. Well, it would have been, only I couldn't afford to just be fast – I had to be super fast. I had to bomb off and build up a big lead, come in in first place (and by some way) to have a chance in the race overall, because my running was awful. I was slow:

Mr Plod, Dr Dawdle. Which meant coming off the bike was the beginning of my race. It was only a matter of time before I could hear someone breathing down my neck and then, more times than not, going past me. I couldn't hold them off. So running was always associated with defeat and failure for me. And now here I was running around the park with dreams of world records and helping charities. You couldn't make it up.

The second half of the marathon was tough going; I was red-faced, sweating and struggling. I walked for some bits but soon began running again. I saw Eva at Sheen Gate, just as I was about to start my final lap and I stopped to tell her about the bet and how it was all Joanna's fault for getting me going. The last lap was difficult. There was no 'wall' (the moment some runners discover when it becomes almost impossible to continue) to get over, but it wasn't easy as I finished in 4 hours 7 minutes. Hurray! I had lost my virginity. Now I just needed more practice. A lot more.

Joanna and Buddy turned up at the end to see me (and feed the ducks). She looked at me as if to say, 'What are you doing?' I'm sure she really didn't believe I would do this, but by now it was too late to go back. I was a marathon runner, though I didn't have the medal to prove it yet. And I needed to complete only 49 more marathons to win that 20p.

I changed into my work clothes in the park before cycling off to Richmond to get the train to work. I was tired and hungry but still felt fresh. This wasn't going to be too bad, I thought, though I might have to run quicker or get up earlier in future as I was going to be late.

I worked up in Hampstead as a manager for a car parts company. My boss was a gentleman called Ken who has been something of a father figure to me. Over the years, he'd taken me under his wing and showed me a few things about life. In return, I'd helped make his business considerably more profitable. We got on, but we didn't always see eye to eye.

I decided not to let Ken know about my running plans yet. He's old-fashioned and I sensed he wouldn't want me taking my eye off the day job too much. I was pretty sure he wouldn't understand why I was doing it. Through the day at work I felt fine – empowered, really. I think I probably grinned a fair amount, alone with my secret: I ran a marathon this morning while the world slept.

In fact, I felt so happy about what I'd done that morning that I began to develop a new plan: maybe I should run another one after work? I knew I had to run more than a marathon a day to beat Abad's 366 in a year, and I thought it was probably best to get ahead early, while I'm fresh. So I rang Joanna and told her my plan, saying I'd be back late that night if that was OK? There was quite a long pause before she laughed.

'Rob, what are you doing?' she asked.

'It's OK,' I answered. 'It's just a bit of running.'

At about 5.30, I left work and took the train back to Richmond. Then it was off to the park and into Richmond Gate where I'd arranged to meet up with Eva again. We cycled down to Sheen Gate together. I locked my bike, dropped off my rucksack at the log by the start point, and chatted to Eva. She'd agreed to cycle to various gates at various times in the next four hours to see me run past (I was ever mindful from the beginning of the need to be witnessed by third parties in order to verify my runs). I necked a bottle of Lucozade followed by a can of Red Bull and off I went again.

I wanted to get a shift on so I could get home before it was too late, so I pushed it a bit. My body knew how far it had to go now and there was no mystery left. I enjoyed the early part of that run and initially it wasn't as tough as I thought it would be. I could barely hear my muscles complaining, as my head was spinning with so many related ideas: I needed a fundraising page, a Facebook page, a website. And what would I call the website? Towards the end of my second ever marathon, some 18 hours after I'd begun my first, my muscles screamed for rest – it was the only way they could draw me back from my dreams. I felt a bit sick at one point and I thought I was going to throw up. But I got through it and finished in 3 hours 28 minutes – a personal best and still there was no 'wall' to climb over.

It was nearly 11pm by the time I got home, exhausted. I came in and lay down on the carpet in the living room in front of Joanna. I was playing it up a bit, but of course I was knackered for real. She laughed and took a picture of me. We chatted for a bit and I reminded her it was all her fault. She told me what she and Buddy had done that day, while I lay on the floor, unable to move. Then I got up, went into the kitchen and ate everything I could find before crawling into a hot shower. I set the alarm for 3.30am and slid into bed. I was exhausted. Physically, I was in a state of shock, but in my mind as clear and focused as I've ever been.

Tomorrow couldn't come around quickly enough.

CHAPTER TWO
Marathon Man UK Is Born

15–26 April 2014

Marathon Man. That's a good name: easy to remember and does what it says on the tin. That was my first thought as the alarm dragged me to my senses at 3.30am. I'd be lying if I said I felt fully rested. I had a couple of small blisters on my right foot, but thought they were nothing to worry about. My legs felt tired but that was the new normal. They'd get used to things soon enough – I just needed to show them what to expect and who was boss.

I ran the marathon quickly, finishing in 3 hours 19 minutes. In fact, I had been too quick and I was hobbling around all that day. I realised that if I was going to take on this challenge, I had to pace myself better; it was an early lesson for me.

I know that for many this isn't the case, but I should state that running times aren't very important to me. I'm never going to be that fast and it's not that interesting to me. I've described myself plenty of times as a plodder, which is what I am. OK, I have some athletic pedigree, but I'd never consider myself a good runner. I know others think that's funny, but I think my times show I'm no greyhound. It's the endurance element of long-distance running that interests me, taking the body to the limits, going further for longer and without much rest. When you do that, it becomes a test of the mind and that's where I think I have the edge.

That first week carried on like that. I ran two marathons on the Thursday, before and after work, and two on the Sunday, too. Joanna, Eva and other friends came out to watch me when they could. I was trying to get as much corroboration for what I was doing as possible, though I knew I was falling short. The thing about me is I like to dive into things. If I get an idea, I like to just do it and try to piece it all together as I go along. Other people have to keep up if they want to come along. I've always been like that.

As the year progressed and a team eventually built up around me, necessary and appreciated, it became harder to be spontaneous like that, which made things a bit of a struggle for me. I'm not one to worry about the details too much, which has its good and bad sides. It's hard to fight with your nature, though.

Having realised that I was able to cope with the demands of running at least one marathon a day, I knew I had to spread the word about what I was doing and did some research into which charities I wanted to help. I began to use my spare time to start working on my website. Part of my job is to design and set up websites for the business, so I was at home with code though my initial effort was a bit basic. I liked how it looked: it had a chimp logo with the words 'Beat the Beast' on it, which is still part of my new brand, Run Wild. I love to play around with Photoshop so I enjoyed designing the logo. However, later on, we got a bit grander and a company called Terra Ferma Medi@ offered to build me a more professional site.

When I was looking into the charities, I stumbled across Dreams Come True. I love children and still feel like a bit of a child myself. I knew I wanted to do something to help kids who needed a break, so DCT sounded perfect. It is a small UK charity that makes wishes come true for children with life-threatening illnesses. I love that idea of bringing happiness into a child's life who would otherwise face so much difficulty. They may not have long to live, but we can make their lives better while they are here. Reading the stories on their website and seeing all the smiling faces made it an easy choice for me.

I had it in my head that I would represent three charities, and Great Ormond Street Hospital was the next obvious choice. A friend of mine, Damo Creed, had a child who'd been in there and everyone knows what amazing work they do for children. Now I was on the lookout for a third.

I bought the web name marathonmanuk.com and started a Facebook page. Then I started a Just Giving page and registered Dreams Come True and Great Ormond Street as my charities. Things were taking shape, offline and online. I was committing to the crazy idea I'd had, putting things in motion. There was no going back now.

As my plans grew more concrete, I realised that up until that point something had always been missing from my life – the great adventure, I guess you'd call it. I couldn't be that office worker any more, or at least not *just* that office worker. I needed to find out what else I could do, what challenges I could overcome.

Marathon Man UK was officially born on 16 April 2014 when I started the Facebook page in his name, but he was naked to begin with. Not literally – the world's not ready for that yet. Marathon Man UK was missing something because he didn't yet have his kilt.

In those early days I was trying to get noticed. I'm naturally very shy and I don't much like meeting famous people, and I certainly wasn't doing this to try to become one myself. But Marathon Man does. He knows you don't raise a lot of money for charity hiding behind the sofa. You have to stand out, be seen, be recognised. Which brings us to the kilt.

As I've mentioned, I'd done the occasional 5k park run in Old Deer Park and Richmond Park for quite a while before my challenge. They're always a good experience – the social side of running is what I love, the shared experience, the fooling around and the encouraging one another. Parkrun.org.uk is an organisation that puts on free, weekly, timed 5k park runs all around the world. They aim to get regular people of all ages to take a bit of exercise together at the weekend. It's a great concept and I love running in their events.

A few months earlier, I got chatting to some kids and asked them what I should wear to the next run. They all said different things – fairy wings, a scuba mask, a kilt. You know kids; I think one suggested an Incredible Hulk outfit, which I am still trying to track down. Anyway, the next week I turned up in the kilt, scuba mask and fairy wings and the kids went nuts.

'You can't wear your trainers, though,' one of them said. The rest of them shook their head in agreement.

'But I have to wear the shoes. I need them to run in,' I said.

They continued to shake their heads.

'OK, let's negotiate here,' I said. 'If I give you each fifty pence then can I wear them?'

No deal. Damn, those kids were tough. Obviously 50p

isn't what it used to be. We ended up settling at £2.06 each and I got to wear the trainers (an expensive arrangement on my side, but fun for the kids). With my eye-catching outfit, everyone wanted to talk to me. I became a celebrity in an instant and I loved seeing the smiles on everyone's faces.

So I remembered this and dug out my kilt on the first Saturday of my challenge, for my eighth marathon, just six days into my running. That kilt was one I'd bought and worn to the wedding of a Scottish friend of mine, Chris. It's a big old woollen one, not exactly designed for ultra-running, but it got me noticed – as well as refreshing you in parts other running shorts can't reach. (Truth be told, I wear shorts under my kilt when I run. I'd be arrested otherwise.)

It's amazing how much attention I got wearing the kilt that first time, which made me a bit uncomfortable. But it also prompted a few discussions with other runners, broke the ice so I could tell people what I was up to and why. I wore a t-shirt which I'd had printed at a local print shop to promote my world-record attempt, but it was the kilt that got tongues wagging.

Since then I've had dozens of conversations about the kilt, most of which revolve around whether I'm Scottish or not, and if not what's an Englishman doing in a kilt. I'm English as far as I know, which isn't very far. There could be some Macintosh in me for all I know.

I sometimes tell interested parties, or vociferous Scots, that the kilt was originally invented by an Englishman. According to Wikipedia, we can thank Thomas Rawlinson for it. Sometimes I don't share this information, mind you. It depends on the height and build (and state of inebriation) of the Scot I'm about to educate. Anyway, I think it's served its purpose getting people's attention and making me stand out.

The other thing I wore to draw attention to myself was Wacky Sox, a brand of very colourful, knee-length sports socks favoured by rugby players. They aren't ideal for marathon performance, but I love the way they look and go for the orange ones or the green ones (as originally picked out for me by some kids in the shop, to match my running vests).

Since starting to wear my kilt, I've tried wearing an 'athletic kilt', but they just don't feel right, flapping about in the wind like a lettuce leaf. I like the heaviness of the woollen one and the way it feels as I run. However, I was soon to discover that my chosen piece of identifying equipment had a serious design flaw. The kilt buckle quickly began to dig into me and that, along with the rotation of the coarse material against my skin, gave rise to some painful cuts on my midriff. They got really bad at times and gave me some deep cuts and a couple of infections in the first few weeks. Nothing too terrible, though. If I wasn't game for a little discomfort then I'd have been feeding the ducks instead of running multiple marathons. A little discomfort I can deal with. After all, I'd had worse.

I was born on 18 October 1982 in the seaside town of Portsmouth, England. My parents were there on holiday so I can only assume I arrived ahead of schedule. To most new parents their first baby, a healthy baby boy, would be a cause for celebration. But I don't think any champagne got drunk that night. Maybe a little whisky, though.

I later learned my dad didn't want a son, he wanted a daughter. So I was in his bad books from day one. According to my mum, he tried to push my pram in front of a car on one occasion in those first few weeks. Anyway, they named me Robert, after my dad: Robert Harvey Paul Young.

We soon returned home to our detached three-bedroom house in a small village somewhere between Wakefield and Barnsley, Yorkshire. I don't know the name of the place, and I don't have any photos to remind me of my childhood, but I do have a few vivid memories.

The Young family was comprised of my dad, my mum, me and, a year after I turned up, my sister, D. Oh, and the family dog, while he lasted. Unfortunately, I can't tell you any stories of birthday parties and holidays, or time spent at the park flying kites. I don't think I can remember anything really nice happening at all. I don't recall ever getting a birthday or Christmas present, except once when my dad bought me a colouring book, though I didn't have any pencils to colour it in with. So in effect, it was just a very dull picture book. Still, that was the best gift I'd ever had and I enjoyed flicking through it and having something to look at. My sister, however, always got presents. So many a day I would sit in the living room, feeling sad and lonely, watching her playing with her new toys.

Instead, my earliest and most vivid memories from that time are of getting beaten by my dad or waiting for a beating to begin.

Anticipating a beating was the worst thing. I remember Dad would come home from work and I'd be upstairs in my room. He worked as a fundraiser for a children's charity, I think. I'd hear him at the door fumbling around for his keys, swearing and muttering to himself. Usually he was drunk, which meant I was pretty much guaranteed a beating unless he fell asleep first. So I'd sit in my room waiting, hoping he wouldn't come looking for me.

I got beaten almost daily, as I remember it, and it was just something I got used to, as much as you can get used to that kind of thing. He'd punch and kick me, or hit me with whatever came easiest to hand. Often he'd shout things at me. I was young so I didn't understand some of the things he said, but his anger was terrifying. His raised voice would instantly send chills down my back and give me a lumpy feeling in my throat. We had an outhouse in the back garden and sometimes he'd go in there to get a big stick. And I mean a really big stick. I knew I was in for a very nasty beating then.

There were many terrible things that happened back then and I don't see the point in going into every last detail. But at the same time I think maybe what I experienced then is part of the reason I'm able to do what I do now. So I think it's helpful for others to know why I am how I am and to understand my story.

Some of you might feel I'm being overly frank or sharing too much here. I respect that but I don't agree. I think it's my responsibility to talk about this stuff, unpleasant as it is to hear. Kids are being abused right now and they need to know they aren't alone and, more importantly, that there is a future for them. I've talked about my abuse throughout my year's running and countless individuals have told me how much it has meant to them, and how my story has given them hope. I want children and recovering adults to know they don't need to be ashamed. I'm not ashamed. And they don't need to be silent. I think we should talk about this stuff more and do more to stop it. I don't know what exactly, but getting things out in the open has to be a good start.

Thirteen days into my running and I'd done 17 Richmond Park marathons, including two double marathons. My feet were pretty blistered, my stomach was cut and the wound had become infected, and my muscles, tendons and bones were tired and probably a little shocked. But I was as determined as ever. All that time I had been spreading the word about what I was doing through social media, but I'm not sure anyone was taking me very seriously yet. I think I'd asked for that, calling myself Marathon Man after I'd run only a handful of marathons.

On the fundraising front, I'd had only a small trickle of money into my Just Giving account, so I knew I needed help. I needed someone with a big mouth who wasn't afraid to use it. Lucky for me, I knew just the guy.

Ali Parkes is an ex-England Colleges prop forward, 6 feet 4 inches tall, built like a barn door, and with a smile like a Cheshire cat's. I'd first come across him in April 2012, when Joanna told me about an event he was organising at the local school that summer (she was nannying for children at the school at the time). A few weeks shy of the London Olympics, Ali and Vivienne Alexander, two parents at Sheen Mount primary school, were planning a fundraising event. With a team of parents around them, and a whole lot of work and effort, they invited Olympians and top sports people to a day of sporting fun and games to inspire the kids and raise vital funds to build a new playground.

Raising money to help kids? Inspiring people to exercise? Count me in, twice over. So I arranged through Jo to meet Ali in late spring of 2012 to see how I could help with the event. Five minutes after meeting Ali, I got swept up by his infectious enthusiasm. He's a sentimental, massive-hearted gentle lion of a man who talks like it's a national sport and gets people around him fired up. He'd also do anything you asked him to, if he could, or he'd find someone to help you if he couldn't.

That year I helped Ali with the fundraiser by using some of my pro-cycling connections at the time. I drove a couple of road bikes, donated by a local cycling shop, up to the Manchester Velodrome, where I got them signed by Chris Hoy, Jason Kenny and other members of the GB cycling team. The bikes proved to be prized auction items at the fundraiser and they raised a pretty penny.

On the day of the fundraiser, I helped at the school running a competition. I had a stall in the playground with a static bike. People had to guess how far I would cycle in two minutes on it, with the one who came the closest winning the bike. It was a great day, with David Weir, James Cracknell and several other Olympic stars turning up to show their support and engage with the kids. The day ended up raising a staggering £50,000 for the school's new playground, which is some kind of record for a primary school fundraiser.

I felt I could do with some of that muscle in my corner.

Since that first meeting, Ali and I had become friends. We'd played junior rugby together, for the third team at the Bank of England Sports Club. Somehow, Ali had persuaded me to join in, even though I'd never played rugby before. It turned out I wasn't the luckiest player in the world. In the space of a year I ended up breaking my finger in one game and my collarbone in another (we had no substitutes that day so I played the remaining 60 minutes of the game with a broken collar bone. At least I got some kudos for that – Ali couldn't believe it). Something told me rugby wasn't for me. However, Ali and I had become friends, and he was someone I could trust to help me with my running goals.

So, two weeks into my challenge, I went down to the Bank of England Sports Ground to find him. I hadn't seen him in a couple of months and when I finally caught up with him he hadn't heard about my running at all. His chin almost hit the floor when I told him what I was up to in the park.

'A marathon a day?' he said incredulously. 'For a year?'

'At least one, sometimes two. It depends. I'm trying to beat the record, like I said.'

'But you hate running. You always said you were slow.'

'I like it a bit more now. It's growing on me.'

He was surprised and disbelieving, but also impressed by what I was taking on. I could tell he was interested in helping me; it was his kind of project. He said he'd try to help however he could. Like me, he was a big kid and loved the idea of doing something extraordinary. Something inspirational.

I think if he'd known then that his involvement would become an obsession that would take him away from his family for most of the year, he would have made a hasty retreat, told me it sounded great but he really didn't have the time, and wished me good luck. But he didn't know, of course. So Team MMUK had its first recruit after Buddy and Joanna. Now it was time to take on the next part of my challenge.

CHAPTER THREE
To Milton Keynes and Beyond

27 April–11 May 2014

Having run nothing but Richmond Park marathons for almost three weeks, I was looking forward to a change in surroundings. So I started looking at the UK marathon calendar and began booking myself onto official marathons at the weekends (with one eye on breaking Larry Macon's world record of 259 official marathons in a year). In the beginning I signed up to a couple and paid the race entry fee, but I couldn't afford to keep paying for marathons every weekend. So I started calling and emailing the race organisers, telling them what I was doing and asking if I could get any help with the fee. Thankfully, the majority of them were happy to help me out and I ended up saving about 20 per cent on entrance fees throughout the year.

The first official marathon I ran was the Milton Keynes marathon on the Bank Holiday Monday, 5 May. I stayed the night before in a hotel with Joanna and Buddy, which was really good fun. There wouldn't be too many more occasions when I'd get a good night's rest on a soft bed with my family by my side, but it was nice while it lasted. I couldn't have been happier or more excited, except for the pain in my right knee, which had become really sore. I realised I would probably have to get it looked at by someone.

Registering at the start, getting my race number and being around all the runners for my first *bona fide* marathon was amazing. This was like the park runs I'd been to, only bigger and better. I'd run 25 marathons in the three weeks since I'd started, and though people had come out to cycle and run with me, there'd been a lot of unaccompanied miles, too. I'm not a loner by nature, as I love being around people, chatting, hearing their stories, so this was a welcome change of atmosphere. I was in my element.

I love the moments before and after a race: the chat and the build-up, the story-sharing and the nerves, and finally the camaraderie, celebration and joy of the finish line. The running community is made up of some of the best people you could ever meet. Over the next few months, they'd come to feel like a second family to me, giving me lifts, advice and lots of help when I needed it. I'd meet up with so many of the same people again and again throughout my year, the hardcore fanatics, as well as occasional marathoners and first timers, all running for a variety of reasons but with a shared spirit of 'let's get through this together'.

That's what running is about for me, and it's very important. There's an unwritten code: you help each other to cross that line, sometimes sacrificing your best time to help another to finish in any way you can. And the more you help others, the more you become a part of the running community. Until eventually, over time, it feels almost like they are a part of your family.

That first race in Milton Keynes was fairly straightforward and, after a sluggish start, my knee started to behave and I felt pretty good. The arches in my feet, particularly my right foot, were starting to bother me in the second half of the race, though. It wasn't anything too serious, but it wasn't ideal. I got to the finish and hung around to share a few jokes with other runners. When I can and I don't have to dash off to another event, I like to stay around at the finish to cheer people in.

After completing the race in just over 3 hours 50 minutes, I stood at the top of the Stadium MK and watched the streams of people finishing their race. I was happy; the empty spot inside that's been there for as long as I can remember was filled. I have a beautiful family and great friends – all that I ever wanted really – but still it's always felt like something was missing. That feeling has lingered and I've never been able to shake it. I wondered if maybe this shared experience of marathon running could be what was missing.

That day in Milton Keynes is a good memory. The newness of the experience and having Joanna and Buddy with me to share the moment were special. But, as I said earlier, travelling to and from events with my family and staying in hotels was not going to be an option going forward, and most of my weekends away would be solo missions.

The money side of things would become a bit of an issue for us throughout the year. I made a decent income in my job, but all the running gear, the train journeys, the hotels, the registration fees and food began to take a big bite out my wallet, and pretty soon we were surviving off savings. Getting some sponsorship to help me out was going to be essential if I wanted to continue, and I was sure Ali would be able to help out on that front, as he's always happy to ask for things, but in the meantime I had to do what I could myself.

The next morning, after running a marathon in Richmond

Park and getting to work, I phoned Virgin Trains. I was going to Halstead in Essex the following weekend to run their marathon and I wanted to get some help with the journey. Eventually I got through to someone there and told her what I was doing and asked if Virgin Trains would help me get to and from races. To my surprise she issued me with two passes there and then for any Virgin route for the whole year. I couldn't believe it. They were my first sponsor and I was so glad for their support.

Although I'd use those passes several times in coming months, I ended up getting a series of coaches to the Halstead marathon in the end (it worked out quicker that way). I was beginning to find out that getting to and from marathons around the country would be almost as much of a challenge as running the races themselves. I've been late to a few, stranded at a few and run through the night to get to others, but I made it to the start of every marathon I set out for, which is something of a miracle. I always said from the start that I'd need a whole lot of luck for my challenge to be successful. And for the most part, I've had it.

On Saturday 10 May, I slept in. And I needed it. For the last 26 nights I'd been averaging about three or four hours of sleep and it was taking some getting used to. More than once I'd fallen asleep on the train to or from work and missed my stop. My body was taking a hammering, too, and in particular my knee was bothering me. But that wasn't all: the cuts on my midriff, caused by my kilt belt buckle digging in while running, had become infected and looked pretty bad, and my feet were pretty blistered by now, too.

Anyone who has done much running will know the problem of suffering from blisters. However, if you've got a blister, don't get down about it. Blisters, and blister management, are a normal part of the marathon runner's journey. When you discover you have a blister, you need to think about what might have caused the blister in the first place. Do your shoes fit properly? Is there a hole in your shoe letting in stones and other debris? What can you do to avoid this happening in that spot again?

You might find that lubricating your skin with Vaseline or skin cream will help you avoid blisters. Some people recommend wearing two pairs of socks, so the rubbing occurs between the socks rather than the sock and your skin. However, I've never bothered much with either of these methods. Blisters are more of a problem for the occasional runner – my feet are so used to running now that I rarely get any blisters and if I do, they're the least of my problems. If you do get a blister on the foot it can be tricky. Sometimes you get a blister under a blister, which is difficult to pop, but the most annoying ones are those you can get under your toenail. In my experience you'll usually lose your nail with those.

Once you have a blister, I have found the best thing to do is pop it. It's important you use a sterilised needle to do this and I usually lance the blister in up to three places. I then squeeze out as much fluid as possible and apply antiseptic cream to the area (I use a hydrogen peroxide based product). Then leave my foot to dry in the open air. It's important to do all that you can to make sure your popped blister doesn't get infected.

With all these various niggles building up, I started to think that I'd need some medical attention and advice on how to look after myself a bit better. Ali had told me he'd asked his friend and top physiotherapist Pippa Rollitt to have a look at me and I was set to meet her the following week. I had also spoken to Dominika Brooks, a sports masseuse I knew and a friend of Joanna's, about whether she could give me some massages to help keep me going.

I felt good in spirits, though. In my experience the body will adapt and find a way to get through most things. I like to think if the mind is strong the body will follow. But it is certainly worth getting yourself checked out if you are suffering from a persistent problem – I know that I respond to these sorts of problems in a different way to most people.

While everyone assumed my legs and feet would be my biggest problem areas, actually one of the most annoying things I had to contend with was my nipples. If you'd seen me finishing a marathon in those first few weeks, you'd have seen my shirt covered in blood. It all came from little cuts in my nipples, opened up by the constant movement of my shirt while running. They hurt pretty bad. It's a common runner's ailment and I tried putting Vaseline and tape on them, but still they bled. After a month or two, they hardened up and I didn't have too many problems with them after that.

On that Saturday, having slept in, I went to the Sheen Mount School 5K Fun Run. I love kids, as I've said already, and encouraging them to exercise and be healthy is part of what motivates me. So I decided to run with them before doing my marathon. The parents at the school knew me from the Olympic fundraiser, so it was a good chance to let them know about what I was doing and ask for their support.

At the end of the run, a friend of mine, Dustin, who Ali had roped in to help with copywriting for my website, got on the tannoy and told everyone what I was doing. I'm pretty uncomfortable with that kind of attention, but it was something I knew I'd have to get used to or at least put up with for the time being. I stood there like a lemon while everyone turned to look at me. I could feel them collectively wondering, 'How on earth are you going to run a marathon every day for a year?' I chatted to a few people who were all amazed at what I was trying to do. A few generous donations went into my Just Giving page that night, so those moments squirming under the spotlight were worth it.

After that, I ran a marathon in the park and then met up with Ali to chat with Nick, the manager of Sheen Sports, the local high-street sports shop. My shoes were getting ragged and Nick offered me a new pair and said he wanted to help however he could. This was going to be a huge benefit to me, as I was certainly going to need a few more pairs of trainers in the course of the year (I would end up getting through a pair of trainers every two or three weeks).

The next day was the Halstead marathon. This was probably the first time I discovered that the running community were starting to take notice of me, but getting there in the first place was a challenge, though that would become the norm for weekends that year. I woke up at 6am, after only two and a half hours' sleep, and stuffed my running gear, half of which was still wet from being washed the night before, into my rucksack. Then I cycled to the station, got a train, two coaches and a taxi all the way over to Halstead for the start of the race at 10am.

I decided not to wear my kilt as it was still wet and heavy from being washed the night before. At the start of the race a few people said hello, congratulating me on what I was doing and wishing me luck. Then, as we were gathering at the start line, the announcer came over on the tannoy: 'Someone just told me Marathon Man UK is planning to run in shorts today. We can't have that! Will someone go and find his kilt for him. It must be somewhere.'

So I had to go and get my wet kilt and put it on while they all waited for me. It was funny and embarrassing at the same time, but at least the kilt was working in terms of building my profile. Running in a wet kilt was a small price to pay if the funds started rolling in for my charities. The race itself was amazing – one of the best I've done to date. It was a challenging course, with lots of undulation and some amazing scenery. The organisation was spot-on and everyone seemed to be having a good time.

I've come to see that each marathon has its own inimitable spirit. It's a feeling that dominates the event and can vary from lively and magical to fairly dull and uninspiring. Usually the smaller the marathon the more spirit it has, though with certain big marathons events, like the epic London marathon, that logic doesn't hold true.

That day I met a great guy called Nick Kyritsis, who was running his 200th marathon in ten years. Isn't that something? I was so impressed. We got chatting in the race and ran the last half of the marathon together, chatting and sharing stories. We finished hand in hand in 3 hours 46 minutes, which is a good time for that course. It was an amazing moment and one of many high points in my year's running.

If that wasn't enough, I also met a guy there who was running his 600th marathon! To me that's astonishing and I was honoured to be in his presence. I would end up seeing him a few times at other races throughout the year and always went up to say hi and pay my respects.

Back in the 1980s, aged about six, it seemed I was always either getting beaten up or recovering from a beating. One time I remember, I found a leaflet by the door that had been dropped in by some Christian evangelists. I never had any books or comics to read so I took the leaflet to my bedroom, as if it were some kind of exciting blockbuster, and hid it. It turned out to be a bad move.

Soon after, my dad found the leaflet in my room and he was furious about it. He came after me, in a rage, about as angry as I can remember seeing him. He grabbed me by the wrist and dragged me to the floor. 'You like this, do you?' he shouted, brandishing the leaflet in my face. 'You want to be like Christ, do you?'

Then he went to the outhouse and came back with a hammer and a nail. He dragged me over to the bottom of the stairs and took my shoe and sock off. I had no idea what he was going to do. He held my foot down and placed a nail against the top of my foot. Then he lifted up his hammer and started banging a nail into it. I screamed out. The pain was excruciating. He kept banging until that nail went all the way through my foot and out the other side. Then he placed the nail against one of the uprights of the banister and started banging it in there. It was horrific. There was so much blood all over the stairs, his hands and my clothes.

All the while I begged and pleaded with him to stop. But he didn't. I tried to block out the pain by switching off, but the sharpness of it hit me full on. By then I was screaming and in agony. Even now it still makes me agitated to remember it. How dare he do that to me when I couldn't defend myself. The anger rises up in me, as I remember that day, but only briefly; I won't allow myself to stay angry and I have forgiven him for everything he ever did to me. He has no power over me now.

He stepped back from the stairs to look at his work, my blood all over his shirt sleeves. I was pinned to the stairs by my foot. 'That's what Christ feels like,' he said. 'What do you think now? Is that what you wanted?'

He pulled the nail out later on and gave me a rag to tie round it. My mum patched me up when she came in, as best she could. I never went to hospital for things like that, we just had to cover up and pretend everything was fine. It was a kind of grim survival and I never knew what he would do next.

My mum and sister weren't spared either. My dad used to abuse my sister sexually. I know this because he made me watch him doing it. He'd put me in a chair right by the bed while he raped her. I used to look away, or tried to. I was only young, but every cell in my body knew this wasn't right. He wanted me to watch, so he'd tie me to the chair with a belt so I couldn't look away. It was horrible and I think I was sick once, but shockingly it had become our kind of normal.

I don't know if my mum knew about his raping my sister; he did it only when she was out. I know Mum lived in terror of him and I don't think she felt she could ever leave him. She'd been bullied and goodness knows what else for years, so she didn't have much strength left. I do know my dad used to put cigarettes out on her, and there might have been other things that I don't know about. I certainly don't blame her for what went on.

I don't think my dad hated my sister and perhaps his abuse was some sick kind of affection. Instead, he saved all his hating for me. So when it came to sweets, presents and even food at times, my sister got the luxury treatment. It wasn't five-star exactly, but she did at least get sweets and gifts, unlike me. My mum used to try and bring me treats some-times, but if my dad found out she'd get told off and I'd get a beating, so she soon stopped doing that.

One time I remember sitting on the couch with my sister and she left a sweet packet next to me when she went to the toilet. I couldn't resist it and took one of her sweets and popped it in my mouth, just as she was coming back in, so she went and told my dad what I'd done. He stormed in and gave me a right telling off but he didn't hit me, which I thought was strange. Later on, my sister went into the kitchen and came back with a fork and, out of nowhere, stabbed me in the leg with it, below my right knee. I still have the scar there now. My father was laughing – he had told her to do it. My sister was laughing too, which really broke my heart. Then he started beating me up and my sister went up to her room to be away from it.

No matter the pain and the humiliation taking that sweet might have caused me, it was worth every bit. To experience the watering frenzy of that sweet on my tongue, the sweet/sour sensation was really something amazing. It was my moment of defiance. I felt I was telling him I deserved nice things too, and I wouldn't stop trying to get them.

After beating me up for a while, he went to get a suitcase – a prop in one of his favourite games (and in fact mine, too, although I didn't let on). It was one of those old-fashioned, hard suitcases, the kind rich kids used to take to boarding schools. The game essentially involved dragging me upstairs (which I didn't like), putting me inside the trunk, closing it up and pushing it down the stairs. It wasn't pleasant, but it was a rush. It was dark and cramped in there. Sometimes the metal clasps inside would dig into my head or into the back of my neck, which was pretty nasty. The only real danger was if the case opened up on its way down the stairs, when I could be thrown out. I had some nasty knocks playing that game and I've a few scars from it, too.

After that was all over I went to my room, glancing in at my sister on the way. The look on her face told me she was sorry. I could tell she knew the pain I went through at his hands, but this time she had joined in. She was too young to know what she was doing. Her mind was being twisted by being around my dad, I guess. I hope she doesn't blame herself for what went on that day, because I certainly don't.

When people ask me how I can possibly run all the miles I do, I wonder if those early days taught me how to deal with pain, taught my body how to recover from trauma. I think I learnt a trick to go beyond pain, out onto the other side of it, which meant that my suffering could become a distant irritation rather than a pressing and inescapable ordeal. It must be a survival reflex, a door you can only work out how to open when your life depends on it. It's not something I've ever been able to teach to another person, so that they can learn how to do it – and it's definitely not something I'd ever want another person to have to go through. But if there's one benefit to come out of the whole experience of abuse that I suffered, it was that it's prepared me to cope with the pain I experience during my long runs.

CHAPTER FOUR
Never Give Up

12–16 May 2014

After about three weeks of running marathons, I found that my body had adapted to the effort I was putting it through. It was as if it had started to accept the new regime and understood that this was how it was going to be from now on. After another week, my mind adapted too, and all the shock and trauma of daily marathons became almost normal – a very tired kind of normal, admittedly, but my body and mind had stopped fighting how things were and a kind of peace had settled in.

Now I was a month into my challenge and I felt adapted. There was still something going on with my knee, though, so I was looking forward to chatting with Pippa Rollitt about it. I met her for the first time at her clinic in Richmond on 12 May. She's a top physio, used to working with world-class rugby players and other top-level athletes. Those sorts of characters tend to rest properly, attend to their nutrition and get plenty of sleep, so she was a bit wide-eyed when she met me and heard what I was doing and the manner in which I was doing it.

'So what do you eat before runs?' she asked.

'Nothing usually,' I said. 'Just some coffee with sugar in it, to wake me up.'

'And afterwards?'

'Whatever I can get hold of, really. I like jam sandwiches, and chips, Doritos, sandwiches. Thai curry's my favourite,' I replied.

'And what do you drink?'

'Coke, Fanta, Red Bull, Lucozade, orange juice, water.'

'And what kind of vitamin supplements are you taking?'

'Vitamin supplements? Oh, I don't take anything like that . . .'

And so it went on – I think it's fair to say she was pretty horrified by what I told her – a look of incredulity turned up on her face and didn't go away. My slapdash approach to everything was clearly a million miles from what she was used to. She told me I needed to attend to my nutrition (what I ate and when) and get more sleep. I was already getting massages from Dominika, and she advised me to keep doing that to 'flush the muscles out'. She also said she'd email Dr Courtney Kipps, a consultant in sport and exercise medicine, involved with the marathon and elite performance. She said he'd be interested in what I was doing and might have time to help me and keep me from doing myself any harm. It all sounded a bit dramatic, but I was glad for the help.

'You've got to eat properly, though, Rob,' she added. 'The right foods and at the right times – not just when you're passing a chip shop.' She was like a lovely big sister. I had lost a good 15kg by then, but I thought I was now eating enough to make up for it.

To be honest, at that stage I simply thought I'd be fine; I don't need too much food or sleep. Later, I started listening more closely to the medical advice I was getting, but running at least a marathon a day, doing a full-time job and living on a budget, there was no way I could do everything I needed to do. I felt I could rely on my inner resources to get me through and had decided that would be enough – Bulldog British spirit. But over the course of the year I'd come to need plenty of devices, tricks and vitamins to help me through as the year went on. Science, in the hands of qualified medical professionals, was a useful friend to have, too. 'Never Give Up' may have been my mantra, but 'Get All The Help You Can' needed to be a close second.

At that time, however, I wasn't quite ready to embrace all the suggestions on offer. Whether I followed Pippa's advice or not, I appreciated her trying to help and being in my corner – and for free, too. I could never have done half of what I did without her help and the support of the rest of the medical team. Someday I hope I'll be able to show them just how grateful I am.

A couple of days after seeing Pippa, I got a chance to sit down with some of the key people from the Dreams Come True charity. While people in the running community and in my local area were getting to know me, I'd raised only a couple of thousand pounds to that point. I was pretty frustrated that I'd not been able to generate more, and wanted to find out how I could do a better job on that side of things, and felt I needed some help from people who did this for a living.

Of course, the way I'd gone about this whole thing was the reason the money wasn't rushing in in greater amounts. There'd been no fundraising plan, no preparation, no PR company, no strategy from the get-go. I'd just started running and had been trying to add all the other bits in as I went along. That's just how I am: spontaneous, I guess. Being like that certainly helps me get the hard yards done, but I recognised it hadn't helped in other ways.

When I heard some of the big success stories in marathon-running fundraising, it made me even more disappointed. In 2010, Irishman Gerry Duffy ran 32 marathons in 32 days, one in every county of Ireland, and raised over €500,000. Now that's more like it. The fact that I'd already run more marathons than Gerry and in fewer days (34 marathons in 29 days) but had raised less than 10 per cent of his donations was a bit depressing, if I'm honest. I needed to get my act together.

On 15 May I met Sue and Martin from the Dreams Come True team in the local pub, the Victoria, after an evening marathon. I turned up late, and they were already sitting down with Ali and Dustin chatting over a drink when I arrived.

I liked them both from the very first moment. They were really grateful that I was doing this challenge for them and couldn't have been more enthusiastic and positive about it. That's what I wanted: people who cared. They wanted to throw all their resources behind what I was doing to support me in any way possible. We spoke about their work and how they might be able to help, as well as the logistics, and how fundraising for multiple charities might work.

Martin mentioned that he'd run a marathon in a big hippo outfit once, when he was working in conjunction with Silentnight mattresses, who have a hippo on their logo. That sounded awesome! Now I wanted to run in a hippo outfit. Martin said he still had the outfit somewhere if I was interested. So while everyone else was talking about PR companies and media opportunities, I was picturing myself hobbling around Richmond Park in a hippo suit.

The hippo plan didn't go down well with my team, who were concerned how much harder it would be running in a heavy costume. That didn't worry me a bit – think of how much fun it would be. It's not like I was going to run every marathon in the suit. Not this year anyway. The others laughed off my harebrained plan, but I gave Martin a conspiratorial nod to let him know I was serious and wanted to hear back from him about that hippo suit.

The meeting went well and wheels were put in motion to get some PR going with their team so I could generate some coverage in the papers and even get the TV news teams interested. It all sounded very promising.

The next day I met up with the rapidly growing MMUK team that Ali was forming around him. At that point Angela Cluff, a senior charity consultant and a Sheen Mount parent, had offered her advice on the fundraising element. She was really helpful in many ways and gave us some great pointers. It was she who suggested that the NSPCC would be a good fit for me. She knew I was looking to support another charity, and she had worked for the NSPCC in the past for many years.

It was a good idea. I was motivated to help children who needed it, not specifically children who'd been abused like me. But I could see that supporting the NSPCC and the amazing work they were doing made perfect sense, so I added them to my roster. Now I had three charities to feed, so I knew I had better get some coins rolling in.

At that time, while Dreams Come True were giving me the personal treatment and throwing their resources behind me, Great Ormond Street Hospital had appeared to keep me more at arm's length. They'd sent a supportive email with lots of suggestions on how to raise funds, but I'm not sure how seriously they took what I was doing. It was understandable – I think a lot of people were expecting me to tire and fade away. After all, nobody knew me, and I had no track record in this field, and who else would have taken on this challenge, never having run a marathon in his life beforehand? I thought it was a shame, because the PR that a big charity could muster would have really helped to get my fundraising going. I knew what I was doing was at least as challenging as what other people had done in the past, if not more so.

I reasoned all I could do was to keep turning up and finishing marathons. With a good team forming around me and the press starting to become interested, I couldn't fail to gradually become a better-known story and with that the donations would surely come.

I'd been working for Ken at the car parts business ever since I'd quit professional cycling in 2008. I had a close relationship with him and I like to think we had a lot of mutual respect. I did things unconventionally – adverts in car magazines that nobody else would have thought of doing – but they got results and I'd helped make the business more profitable year on year. I also did things to improve the efficiency of the company overall and make it run smoother.

I'd decided to keep quiet about my running at work, until I felt the time was right to tell him (or I got discovered). Although I was physically spent and sleep deprived, I still managed to get my work done. I'll admit probably not with the same level of inventiveness or efficiency as before, but still enough for me to be comfortable in saying I was doing my job. I'm sure my appearance had changed and that was probably ringing alarm bells, but there wasn't much I could do about that.

Whereas before I had been clean-shaven and well turned-out, these days I was red-faced or pale, often unshaven and tired-looking. Marathon running has a well-documented effect on the body, altering breathing rates and depth, and causing trauma to the heart, muscles and major organs. Blood is rushing to the aid of exhausted muscles, so you end up looking pale as little blood is pushed to the skin. So each day at work I was essentially in a state of recovery, my body working hard to recover its natural balance. My new regime was leaving a mark on me and I don't think you needed to be a private detective to see it.

The reason I hadn't told Ken about my running was because I knew what he would say. He put work, profit and his business at the top of his agenda and the rest came a distant second. He might have cared about me as his hard-working assistant, and maybe a bit more than that, as a son almost, but I knew he wouldn't understand my dream. I barely did myself. I was certain he wouldn't like it when he found out. And I was right.

In the end, Ken cornered me and asked what was going on, so I told him everything. When I'd finished telling him about the marathons and the charities there was a long pause while he looked at me in disbelief. To break the silence I smiled and said, 'It's just a bit of running.'

'A bit of running! You're bloody mad, Rob. I've never heard of such a thing. Well, this explains a lot,' he said.

'What do you mean? I've still been getting everything done.'

'You don't look well, Rob. You're pale and you must be exhausted. How long do you plan to keep this up for?'

'A year. I'm trying to break the record. Haven't you been listening?'

'You can't run marathons for a year, Rob. Nobody does that. You'll bloody kill yourself.'

We didn't agree, but as long as I was punctual and getting things done we'd be all right. I knew to keep it to myself at work and Ken would be fine. I knew how to keep him happy, I thought. I didn't know what all the fuss was about, anyway. After all, it was only a bit of running.

When people asked me about the running and how I was, I'd always say I was fine. I'd let members of my medical team know about some of the things that were hurting, but there was no point airing that with other people. Truth be told, I even kept several things from the medical team, such as a broken toe later in the year. I like to deal with some things in my own way and it helped to keep me positive not having them fussing over me all the time.

This book is full of various bits of advice that I hope might help other runners, but my best advice remains: 'Do it your way.' Even if taking that route will certainly have its short-comings. If you try to do something as ridiculous as running a marathon every day for a year, the only way you'll have a chance of succeeding is by trusting your instincts. There is no path in a book. The path is under your feet.

Of course my legs felt like jelly and I had cramps and pains and various things that I didn't talk about. I had blisters on every toe and on my heel, as well as a few missing toenails. My heel arches were cut and scarred. The inside of my thighs and armpits were red and sore from chafing. I'd had several nose bleeds (though I'm not sure if that was related to the running) and my legs felt completely dead all day long. And of course my nipples were still bleeding during every race, despite putting zinc tape on them. That had certainly helped but, boy, when you took it off . . .!

The best thing for me was to put a brave face on it and laugh about it. Nobody likes a whinger. The mental aspect is the most important thing when you are taking on an extreme challenge, and you can't go around being negative, either in your thinking or your speech. You have to keep upbeat and light, put the troubles into the distance so they become little dots on the horizon, then they don't look so threatening.

Your mind can be your greatest ally or your greatest foe. It's up to you. With it you can do anything you desire. People spend their lives talking about 'I want' and 'I should', but this doesn't help; you just end up covered in wants and shoulds, barriers around you that become too big to break through. Don't let that happen. You must believe in the possibility for change. Then you must go and change the things you want to change. Only you can do it. You must be the source of the change; don't wait for it to happen – make it happen now. There'll never be a better moment for it.

While the running was tough in some ways, the truth was that in others it wasn't tough enough. A part of me didn't feel stretched yet and I wanted to do more. I had a marathon to squeeze in each day, but I knew I could do it. I never really believed it was in doubt and I was secretly getting bored of my marathon-a-day challenge. After a month or so, it didn't feel much like a challenge any more. And if I was bored then I was convinced all my followers would think the same thing. So, as time went on, I couldn't help but think about things that would make my quest more epic.

One of the things I always did back then was run further than a marathon. I'd often run an extra 5k lap at the end of the marathon, just to show anyone who might have doubted me that I was for real. I tried to drum up company for my runs on social media, asking people to join me on my mid-week Richmond Park marathons. That was as much for the company, which I always enjoyed, as for the corroboration. I was always thinking about the doubters who might say, 'I know he says he runs all these marathons, but how do I know he's really doing them?' I wanted to make sure there was no room for any doubt.

Most of my Richmond Park runs were at silly o'clock, either from 3.30am to 8am, or in the evening till late, but as word spread more people joined me and cycled or ran along-side me for part of the way. Near-strangers got up out of bed and made the effort to support me time and time again. I'd appear at a gate on a chilly morning in May and out of the darkness someone who'd heard about me and decided to come out and run with me for a few miles would introduce themselves. We'd chat and I felt so good that I was reaching people with what I was doing.

I experienced a thousand such kindnesses over the year, things that kept me going. One that I'll never forget is when Pip Wilson, a dear friend who became part of the MMUK team, left a piece of carrot cake and a can of coke out by my bag at Sheen Gate for me. I can't tell you how good that tasted. It was early morning and cars hadn't been allowed in the park yet. So I lay out on the floor in the middle of the road and ate that cake, washing it down with coke. All that sugar entered my bloodstream and, although I was freezing cold, all the pain disappeared for a minute. I was as high as a kite.

Everywhere I went, people rallied to do what they could for me. It was awesome! My running seemed to be bringing the best out of myself and others, too. I just had to keep it up so I didn't let anyone down.

Another thing I started doing to make things more interesting and to get people to take notice was to sign up to difficult races. I started looking at the calendar for more ultras. I didn't tell anyone because I knew what they'd say: 'Why jeopardise your world record by running further than a marathon in one day? How are you going to recover for the next day?' The truth is I needed to keep this interesting for me. If I was bored then I knew I'd be in trouble.

Running further and thinking of ways to test myself more kept me interested. How far could I go? How many marathons could I do in a weekend? Where are my limits? I was determined to find out, even if it meant risking serious injury. Pushing through my limits was exciting and I wanted to know just how far I could take things.

CHAPTER FIVE
The Bets Are Off

17–29 May 2014

Awful as they were, my childhood beatings have taught me how to do two important things that have served me well in life (and marathon running in particular). The first is how to distance myself from pain, to shut myself off from it. It's a little trick I learnt through those daily beatings – a survival response, I guess. I do it very consciously now, when things become too painful. It's like flicking a switch in my mind and I move away from the pain to a different space, separate from the pain. Then I can witness the pain from afar and it doesn't overwhelm me.

The second thing I learned to do was to control my emotions and fear. 'The Dangling' taught me that. 'The Dangling' was the most terrifying thing my dad used to do to me. At some point during a long beating, which usually took place in the living room, my dad would get bored, and then drag me upstairs. Picking me up by my ankles, he'd shuffle me over to the bottom of the stairs. When he did that I knew what was coming, so I started to prepare. I'd go deep inside myself and get really focused and quiet. Then all that was happening around me, the noise of my dad's shouting and the jolts and blows, would get turned down, softened.

We had a big wooden staircase that went up in a straight line before turning off to the right. Dad would drag me up the stairs, my head hitting most steps on the way up (I tried to lessen the impact with my arms but was never too successful). By then I was in the zone, prepared; I call this my 'locked-in' state.

All my concentration had gone into pushing my emotions and thoughts to the back of my head. It's as if my head is divided into two. The back half becomes full and locked, and the front half is empty. I have learnt to talk, understand and be half with my surroundings while still being focused on my locked-in state, keeping it intact, so my troubles can't break the lock and cause me pain. Like that, I was ready for anything.

When we reached the top of the stairs, my dad would dangle me over the stairway. 'Don't move, boy!' he screamed at me. 'Don't you dare move or I'll drop you like a stone.'

He told me if I flinched or made a noise or cried then that was it, he'd drop me head first down the stairs. Before I'd learned to control myself, he would drop me and I'd crash down the stairs. The wrong fall could have broken my neck and I was lucky to have avoided that, but young bodies are supple, so that was in my favour. In the beginning, I'd panic and struggle or whimper, and of course he'd drop me. But over time I learned to be completely still while he dangled me, like a little Buddhist monk hanging by his ankles.

'Look down at the stairs, boy,' he'd shout at me. 'Don't you dare close your eyes or I'm gonna drop you like a stone.'

So I'd have to look down at the stairs beneath me. It was very daunting, but I learned to face it calmly and not to cry out or panic. If I broke from my locked-in state, I'd have to quickly refocus my gaze on the tip of my nose, in an attempt to re-establish the 'lock'. If that failed, then biting my lip was the next ploy, a distraction technique to attempt to deflect the pain I was feeling elsewhere. By creating pain in another area of your body, it takes the attention away from the source of your greater pain.

While he was dangling me there, my father would sometimes hold me by just one leg and drop me, catching me quickly by the same leg with his other hand. He'd move me about trying to terrify me, trying to distress me as much as possible. I probably looked terrified but I didn't make a sound. I was waiting the whole time. Waiting to be dropped and thinking about how I would protect myself when I landed. I was relaxed and locked in, knowing that if I made a sound or closed my eyes he'd drop me.

Sometimes he'd drop me even though I didn't flinch, just to let me know nothing could save me, I suppose, but I don't think I ever cried or begged for him to stop. I hope my quiet acceptance bothered the hell out of him. I like to think he knows he didn't crush me. In the end he only made me a stronger person, and by giving me reason to learn my coping techniques, I also eventually became a softer, calmer person.

Over the years I have learned some great pain-relief tools that I know from experience really work for me – but then I have had plenty of practice. The important thing to remember is that the mind works like a muscle – it just needs to be exercised in order to become useful to you. Relaxation is the key, always. If you can stay relaxed, even under great duress, the pain will be less and the healing power of the body maximised. This is the method that works for me:

1. Put yourself in a relaxed, reclining position in a dark room. Either shut your eyes and try to picture

something pleasant or focus on a single point in the room.

2. Breathe deeply and allow your breathing to slow down. Use your chest to pull the breath into your stomach.

3. When you feel you are nicely relaxed, you are ready to use some of the mind-control techniques detailed below.

The imagination technique: Think about a place from your past when you were pain-free. For me this is the Grober Alpsee, a lake in Germany I visited one summer for a cycling race. It is beautiful and peaceful beyond description. Close your eyes and imagine yourself in that place. Notice your surroundings, observe all the aspects you remember from that location. Enjoy the memory in its fullness. Transport yourself there.

(If you don't have a place that works for you, you could focus on something that you love, such as your favourite chocolate bar.)

Doing this repeatedly will become more and more powerful (although even on the first attempt I predict you will notice some benefits). By taking your mind off your pain, you will allow your body to relax, including the tensed muscles surrounding the site of your pain.

The diversion technique: With your eyes closed, switch your attention to a part of your body that is not in pain. At first you might think there is no such place, but with persistence you can find it. It could be your toes, your ears or the back of your head. Focus on that part of your body and relax into the pain-free sensation there, allowing it to become the predominant sensation if you can, even if for only a few moments. This shows you that you are not totally engulfed in pain, but there are places where your body is at peace. Dwell there and those spaces will increase.

When I had been beaten as a child, I would lie in bed and move my feet in a circular motion before scrunching them up. My feet were pain-free and by focusing on them it helped the rest of my body to share that feeling of ease and comfort. It's miraculous really when you think about it! It is the physical equivalent of positive thinking. When all seems to be going badly, try to focus on the things you are glad for. We all have them. The more you look for them and focus on them, the quicker the other areas of our lives improve.

Be patient with yourself when trying these techniques. If they don't seem to help right away, take a deep breath and send good vibes/thoughts to yourself. These techniques take practice to become effective for managing serious pain, so work at it. Practise them for about 20 to 30 minutes four times per week. With time you will find that your power over pain will increase and it will take less mental energy to achieve more pain relief.

By the way, I should stress that these techniques are there for pain relief only. They won't cure any underlying problems, and it's important you don't rely on them instead of going to a doctor for proper treatment.

Halfway through May, the weather was starting to get better, and that helped ensure more and more people were joining me in the park for my weekday runs. It seemed like things were gathering momentum. I was seeing Dominika Brooks for regular massages. She and her husband, Dustin, lived near the park and I used to pop in after a run in the evening and Dominika would work on my legs and give me some food. If she wasn't around, I'd play football games on the Playstation with their nine-year-old son, William. He used to thrash me, but it was a nice break from everything and we'd have lots of laughs. As I've mentioned, I love hanging out with children – they're naturally positive and a bit silly, like me.

We'd get Dominos pizzas in, which William would get very excited about, like it was Christmas, and when Dominika returned she'd have to start working again, this time on me. Sometimes her massages became very painful and then I went into that place where pain is distant so I could handle it. She used to say my eyes glazed over at those times and she knew when I was locking myself in. Anyway, I always felt much better after her massages, a lot of the tightness was eased and my legs felt flushed out and released.

As far as massages go, I learned one important thing throughout the year: to have the shoulders massaged first, before anywhere else. While my legs were tight, my shoulders and lower back were too, and that tightness was more difficult to shift. In the beginning, I tried to stretch my arms and upper body myself, but it didn't help. So I asked Dominika to work on my shoulders and upper back before my legs and, incredibly, the next day's marathon was much easier – my legs, back and shoulders were all released of tension. If you are planning on doing something similar to what I've attempted, you're going to need plenty of massages. If you do, I'd recommend getting your shoulders worked on first, followed by the legs and then finish with the back, if there's time.

I put Dominika's business logo up on my Facebook page that evening, along with Virgin Trains and Sheen Sports, who had given me some shoes to wear. I was still trying to find the perfect shoes for me, as my arches still hurt quite a bit. It's always going to be a case of trial and error before you find the right shoes for you, but don't carry on with trainers that cause you discomfort. Keep looking for the right pair – your feet have enough to put up with without being in the wrong shoes.

It was around this time that I got introduced to Ben Thornton, who'd become a constant companion on my weekday marathons. Ben's a local dad and decent marathon runner himself, who joined me on one or two marathons a week during that summer. Apart from the competitors in the Race Across America (RAUSA) series the following year, nobody else ran as many miles with me during that year. He was moved by my fundraising efforts for Great Ormond Street, especially as a close friend of his had a little girl, Emma, in the hospital at the time. She'd recently had a heart transplant and the hospital staff were doing all that they could to get her back to a normal life.

On Saturday 17 May I ran the Orpington Marafun, which was well organised and run in a great spirit by a good crowd of runners. That evening I went on Facebook and dedicated the race to Emma and to the staff at Great Ormond Street Hospital. I hoped she would manage to keep fighting and defeat the odds that seemed stacked against her.

The next day was the official Richmond Park marathon. I was getting known in my own back yard, so I was well backed by friends and supporters for this one. Plenty of friends as well as complete strangers cheered me on and told me they thought what I was doing was amazing. This was the 36th time I'd run the Richmond Park marathon course in the last 35 days, so at least there was also no chance of my getting lost. That's not something I can say for every marathon I've ever run, as you'll soon discover.

It was good to run in the park with so many people and in the middle of the day, too. The conditions were very warm, but I got some relief on the third lap when I started a water fight with some kids I knew – they gave me a good soaking which helped cool me down. I ended up finishing in a decent time and got to play with Alexander at the finish as well.

The fact that I can remember that moment after the race highlighted a major problem with my challenge. It had become very clear that the year was going to be pretty full-on and the thing that would have to be sacrificed most was time with my family. Joanna was already complaining that we weren't spending enough time together, and of course she was right. I was averaging three hours of sleep a night just to fit it all in, so finding more time to hang out with her and Alexander was next to impossible.

I'd see her in the evenings when she'd order me a curry or cook for me, but I can't say I was giving her quality time, though. We'd regularly have a discussion where Joanna would point out that I was not spending enough time with our family, which she rightly believed should be my first priority. I tended to respond by explaining that I was running a marathon every day, doing a job, meeting charities, giving interviews and having massages to hold me together. I felt I needed her support in all of this, and that I didn't have the time to be worrying about her and Alexander. Sometimes this conversation was light-hearted; at other times less so. I understood her frustration. Things weren't the same as before, in any way, and I missed her, too.

The importance of family was brought home to me even more that week when I learned the sad news that Emma, the girl who I had dedicated a marathon to only days before, had died in hospital. My heart went out to her family and I couldn't think of much else for a few days. It made me think even more about the missing part of my own family, my daughter Olivia from another relationship.

Six years before, I had been living with someone else and we'd had a beautiful daughter, Olivia. The relationship hadn't worked out and I'd moved out. Seeing my daughter had been very difficult since then, for various reasons, but although I don't get to see her right now, she is in my thoughts every single day. I love her with all my heart and soon I'm sure she'll be back in my life again. As much as Alexander and Joanna, Olivia is what keeps me going and without her in my heart I'd be weaker.

Family is everything to me. Joanna, Olivia and Alexander gave me strength and were the reason I could do what I was doing, but at that time they had to be patient and wait for me. Until I was finished there just was no way we'd be able to have the kind of family time that we'd all have liked. On a few weekends, Joanna and Alexander joined me at the marathons, and they were the best times. Our trip to Flete, Devon, was a perfect example.

On Saturday 24 May, I ran a marathon in Richmond Park in the morning and then Joanna, Alexander and I got on a train to Devon. The Endurancelife Flete CTS marathon was being held the following day. Running along the coast in Devon on a summer day sounded about as good as a marathon could get.

When we got to Devon and down to the race HQ in Flete on the Saturday evening, we started looking for a hotel or a B&B. I thought it would be pretty easy to find somewhere to stay, but we turned out to be in the middle of nowhere. After walking for a while we saw a big stately house, which I thought must be a hotel. So I marched up the drive, opened the front door and stepped into the reception. No one was around, so I just waited and looked at some of the pictures on the wall. I wasn't standing there long before a man appeared, who looked at me rather suspiciously.

'Hello. Do you have a room for the night, please? There are three of us.'

'This isn't a hotel,' he said.

'Oh, I'm sorry. I'd assumed that it was.'

'It's my home,' he added.

It turned out I was standing, uninvited, in this gentleman's front room. Nice one, Rob! Anyway, we got chatting and one by one his friends and family joined us in the front room. It seemed he was having a party. Pretty soon I was telling them all about my running and they were fascinated. They asked me to bring Joanna and Alexander in to meet them, we had a drink and were talking and laughing like old friends.

John Morgan was the man's name and he was a real gentleman. He told us he knew somewhere we could stay and walked us down to a guest house that was part of the property. It was a five-bedroom guest house right on the beach – what a result! John got me out of the doghouse with Joanna, who was a bit annoyed I hadn't even sorted out a hotel. Goodness knows where we would have stayed if John hadn't been kind enough to let us stay.

The family (including John's children, William, Sophie, Sonia and Hannah) brought us some food for dinner and milk for Alexander. After we'd eaten, we walked the Morgans' dog on the beach as the sun was going down and it was one of those beautiful moments where you feel the world is on your side and there's no stopping you.

The next morning I felt refreshed and ready for anything. The view outside our bedroom was superb, the sea and the south Devon coast stretching for miles. I got myself together and walked the few hundred metres to the start, looking forward to the day's race. I'm so grateful to John and his family for their generosity that night, which typifies the kindness my family and I were shown by strangers through-out my crazy year of running.

It was a beautiful, sunny day and the race was amazing. Tough, but amazing. The countryside in Devon is stunning and the course was well organised with lots of brutal hills. The terrain was varied; we covered every surface imaginable, roads, grass, mud, stones, river crossings (my sopping wet kilt must have weighed a couple of stone!). We went through fields of sheep, cows (and bulls too), over gates, through gates, under gates. It was exhausting but a great challenge and I liked the adventure aspect. Some of the hills were slippery under foot and so steep they felt dangerous. It was a nice change of pace from the Richmond Park marathons that offered no threat to life and limb.

If you're a UK marathon runner looking for an exceptional, if tough, marathon, with amazing views that's really well organised, then make the trip down to Devon for this one – but do remember to book some accommodation before you set off!

The Flete ultra marathon was my 46th in 42 days. Four more marathons and Joanna would have to hand over her 20p – after that the bets were off. Literally. Running was becoming very tough by now as my knee was hurting so much that I had my doubts, at times, about how long I could go on for. Sometimes it felt like I was hanging on to a runaway train, just trying not to get thrown off.

Having said that, it's also true that there were other times when I felt unstoppable. I seemed to alternate from feeling like I wouldn't be able to continue, to thinking it was all too easy. And when a friend lent me Dean Karnazes' bestselling book, *Ultramarathon Man: Confessions of an All-night Runner*, I had fuel for my biggest dreams. Here was a guy who pushed the limits, running 100-milers repeatedly and, in the end, just for fun. He made me believe it was all manageable and helped dispel any lingering doubts about how far I could actually go.

I spent a fair amount of time wondering what that would be like, running a 100-mile race. The best runners were able to complete them in under 24 hours, which meant theoretically I could do one during this challenge of mine. The thought wouldn't leave me alone, so I started looking online at ultras, 100km races and even 100-mile races in the UK.

I couldn't tell Ali or Joanna. I knew they'd think I was crazy and that it was jeopardising my challenge, but the thing was I had to keep myself interested. I knew if I got bored on this challenge that would be the end of it. I could only keep up the feats of endurance if I felt pitted against a challenge that threatened to engulf me. That was exciting. Looking for the frontiers and going over them was what got my juices flowing. For some that was completely understandable, but those who didn't get it thought I was taking unnecessary risks.

At about this time Ricky, the manager at Up & Running, a specialist running shop in Sheen, got me on the treadmill to assess my running gait. He noticed I overpronate (which means that my foot tends to continue to roll inwards when it lands, causing additional strain on my ankles and shins as I push off again) slightly, so I tried on a few trainers he thought were a good match for me. They all felt good, so I ended up choosing the Brooks Ravenna because I liked the way they looked. A lot of my leg problems, and my sore arches, cleared up after I started running with these shoes and things got easier. It was lucky they did, because my knee was getting really sore by that point. I can't over-emphasise how important it is to get the right shoes for you. Keep looking until you find a pair that you know are right. You'll know them when you find them.

On 26 May I got a message on Facebook that I'll never forget. A week or so earlier, a woman had approached me in Sheen to ask me about what I was doing. We had chatted for a bit and she had started telling me about the sexual abuse she had suffered as a child at the hands of her father. She was very nervous and it was clear to me that this was something she'd kept to herself for a very long time. I came away thinking that it must have done her some good to share all that with me, and to realise that she didn't have to suffer in silence.

That day she messaged me to tell me our conversation had given her the courage to tell her partner about her past. She said she felt like a weight had been lifted, now she no longer had to hide it away or feel ashamed. Such connections re-affirmed my belief that it was important to keep talking about these things.

At that time, Ali was trying to set me up with a sports agent and some people were telling me to drop the 'abuse story', that it would hurt my chances of getting an agent. I didn't like that; to me that's just hiding in the shadows. I didn't think that would be helpful to anyone, so I've kept up my outspoken position on my abuse. It happened to me, it happened to others and it's still happening right now to thousands of children. We need to do much more to stop it. If I reach only a couple of people and help them, then that's worth all the lost sponsorship deals in the world.

But I know I've already reached hundreds of such people. Adults and children have confided in me their stories of abuse at talks during school visits and elsewhere. People have been given the confidence to stand up and face their abusers, in some cases. It might make other people uncomfortable, but it's really making a difference to those who need it most. If I can help them by telling my story, then I will.

A few days later, at around 10.30pm on Thursday 29 May, just 46 days after making that infamous 20p bet with Joanna, I completed my 50th marathon. And boy did it feel good! A group of local supporters showed up to run and cycle with me and it made all the difference. It really felt like I was at the centre of something significant that the whole local community could celebrate. It was always really important to me that what I was doing was embraced locally, and I started to get a sense that I was being more and more appreciated by local people and businesses, too.

Sadly, to this day Joanna hasn't handed me that 20p for winning the bet. I think I earned that money, so I'm still working on getting it back. I haven't hired a lawyer as yet, but I'm starting to give it some serious consideration.

Fifty marathons done! I was delighted to reach the first significant milestone on my agenda. I think it's important, when doing something epic over a long period of time, that you celebrate the little victories on the way to that final moment. You never know when the wheels are going to come off, so enjoy it while it lasts.

That night I went onto Facebook and dedicated my 50th marathon to my daughter, Olivia. She had been on my mind through many of the countless hours of running for the last month or so, keeping me company and giving me strength. I was exhausted and emotional that night; I missed her more than ever. She was the one piece missing on my night of celebration and I knew I wouldn't be able to fully enjoy any such successes until she was back in my life again.

CHAPTER SIX
Climb Every Mountain

30 May–15 June 2014

The day after I'd run my 50th marathon was a Friday and my first meeting with Dr Courtney Kipps. Pippa Rollitt, my physio, had told him about me and asked if he would see me. I'd learned he was the director of the ISEH (Institute of Sports, Exercise and Health) in London, a legacy project from the 2012 Olympics, set up to study elite sportsmen and women in order to help improve performance as well as to prevent or manage injuries. Dr Kipps is also the assistant medical director of the London Marathon, so I was pleased that someone of his stature, on Pippa's recommendation, had agreed to see me.

We met in his clinic in Putney and I liked him right off the bat. We chatted for a while about the issues I'd been having with my nipples, waist, knees and arches. He listened very carefully and was quite surprised that I had managed so much already, with so little sleep and with a very casual attitude to food and nutrition. I remember him telling me that I needed to eat 'a bit more than jam sandwiches' if I was to keep myself in one piece and achieve my target of 367 marathons in a year, which made me laugh. I don't think I told him about all the Doritos and curries and coke that I had used to fuel me throughout my runs. I didn't want to get into more trouble than I was already in.

After analysing my running style on a treadmill and hearing my stories of sore heels in the second half of races, Dr Kipps had an interesting theory. He said that my tactic of running a quickish first half-marathon followed by a slower second half was what was hurting my feet. He noticed that at the quicker pace I was landing on my front to mid foot, where I should be, but when I slowed it down a bit, I started to heel-strike. So, in effect, by putting the brakes on, slowing down to conserve energy for the next day's exertions, I was doing myself a disservice. I needed to run faster, and that way my feet would be fine. 'That's easier said than done,' I told him.

While I liked Dr Kipps very much, and really valued his input and time, there was always this tension between us. He wanted me to think like an elite athlete, which meant getting adequate rest and recovery (which I couldn't do), as well as to observe a very careful diet (which I wasn't very interested in doing). He wanted me to listen to the data and to play it safe. And of course I understand that. He's a doctor, focused on my best interests. I, on the other hand, am a plodder who will plod through the pain barrier when nobody else will plod any more. I don't consider myself an elite athlete – just a stubborn one.

Really, what I wanted was for him to patch me up and send me on my way, but he wanted me to rest and recover, and to avoid at all costs the risk of an injury. I knew the risk of injury was just something I had to live with and that there was no 'safe' way to do what I was doing. That's the nature of extreme endurance. And the fact is I had to work and I did have a family, so I couldn't spend all my downtime in an ice bath, sleeping or recuperating. But all credit to him, Dr Kipps agreed to help me, even though I was making plenty of choices he couldn't condone, because he knew I'd be better off with him than without him.

Dr Kipps recommended I visited my local GP to get them onside with my activities so they could keep an eye on me and help with the abrasions on my midriff and my sore nipples (Dr Kipps thought, possibly rightly, that using zinc tape was doing more harm than good), as well as to be there for other potential issues throughout the year. He recommended they have my blood analysed too, looking for vitamin deficiencies among other things. Going forward he recommended more sleep, better nutrition, ice baths, strengthening exercises and ongoing physio and massage, some of which I was able to do.

Over the course of the year, Dr Kipps, Pippa and sports masseuse Dominika Brooks would be my medical team. They'd all be at the end of the phone to advise, massage or work on me, often at the drop of a hat. I never thought I'd need all that support when I started running, but it turned out they'd be absolutely essential. After that first meeting, Dr Kipps took me on as a 'person of scientific interest' and I'm indebted to him for his involvement throughout my year.

The next day was a Saturday, but having failed to get any official marathons, I was left to run the Richmond Park marathon course again. I've often said that the logistics, the travelling to and from events at the weekend, has been the hardest part of the challenge, so a quiet weekend gave me some time to rest and spend time with my family, which I appreciated. But I have to say, running those official marathons on different courses, meeting new people and even the craziness of getting between marathons was something I looked forward to during the week. I could see I was becoming a marathon addict, which is hilarious when you consider just how much I used to hate running.

Growing up in Yorkshire, we had a beautiful mixed breed dog, his fur was mainly black but with little white patches. I don't remember his name, but I loved him. As I've mentioned, I didn't have toys back then, so for me that dog was entertainment enough to last for hours. One weekend my father said he was taking us camping. We were all a bit surprised to hear that, as we never went anywhere. But we got in the car and off we went, hoping it might actually be a holiday. Eventually, we arrived at the campsite and got set up for the night.

The following day we went for a walk and ended up alongside a race course. Then, suddenly, and for no apparent reason, my dad became irritated. I had the dog on his lead, but he snatched it off me. 'I think we've had this dog long enough now,' he said.

Then he picked the dog up by its lead, so it was hanging by its neck, and carried it over to some trees. My mum freaked out; she seemed to know what was coming and told my sister to look away. They both walked off, leaving me with my dad and the dog.

'That's right, get lost!' he shouted after them.

I was frozen to the spot. My dad told me to stay where I was and to watch what he was about to do, so I stood and watched as he tied the dog to a branch of a tree and left him hanging there. Then I watched him struggle until he died, too scared to do anything to help him. I remember being frightened but also angry. I wanted to shout at him: 'What did you go and do that for?' I wanted to tell him he was a cruel, nasty man, but I just stood there in the end, too scared to say a thing. Inside I was full of anger and sadness. If I'd

66

had the power to do the same thing to him, right then, honestly I think I would have.

Eventually, my dad cut the dog down and took it into the woods, put it in a bush and threw some leaves over it. Then we started to walk back to the campsite. I kept my eyes down. We walked in silence for a bit, but then he stopped in his tracks and started giving me a hiding, telling me it was my fault the dog was dead, which confused me. I was experiencing so many emotions, but all I knew was to keep quiet. I just wanted to get to the car and go home without anyone else getting hurt. To this day I get really upset if I see any animal suffering, and I'm sure that awful day had a very big effect on me.

So that was our weekend's camping. I knew when we set off in the car it was too good to be true. After that, we were all sad, but things just carried on as usual. We got on with the business of surviving each day and we never again spoke about the dog, even in private. My mum was pretty shaken up by that day, too, more than the rest of us. I think my dad killing our dog had frightened her. She was already a woman on the edge, facing more in my dad than she could possible handle. What it must have been like for her, watching her family suffer like that and being powerless to help, I'll never know.

Eventually something happened to change everything. It almost killed me, but it turned out to be just what was needed to get us out of there.

It was June now and starting to warm up. Not that I was seeing too much sunshine, as I was running mainly in the early morning, with the occasional evening run, so sunrise and sunset were often my running companions (though I continued to be joined by more and more friends and supporters, at least for the later laps of the marathon and sometimes for the entire run).

That first weekend in June I was registered to run in the Viking Coastal marathons on the Kent coast, one on the Saturday and another on the Sunday. I got the train down there late on the Friday evening, and by the time I arrived I was starving and went looking for a hot meal but couldn't find anywhere open. Eventually, I found a restaurant that was closing, but they agreed to give me a meal.

After dinner, I went to the race HQ on the seafront in Birchington to set up my tent. The best place I could find was on a bit of concrete between two beach huts. Strictly speaking, I shouldn't have been camping there and when a patrol man found me I thought I'd get moved on, but after he'd heard my story he said he'd turn a blind eye.

I didn't sleep great that night and woke at 5.30am and crawled out of my droopy looking tent. I put on loads of clothes to keep warm before watching an amazing sunrise while eating jam sandwiches and drinking Lucozade. Now I was ready for anything.

The course consisted of a flat, coastal path which we had to run along and back, four times. There were no special features or challenges to it, just flat running on firm ground with the wind in your hair and the ocean always at your shoulder. The sky was blue and the sun shone a steady 70 degrees. The simplicity of the course, the pleasant conditions and the small field of about 60 runners made for a good race. What it lacked in drama it made up for in friendliness and scenery.

This was an event put on by marathon legend Traviss Willcox. He is possibly the most respected multiple marathoner in Britain, and his was an even more unlikely story than my own. In 2009, he was a fairly unfit 42-year-old who got the running bug after struggling around his first 5k course. Since that time he has achieved, among other things, the world record for being the fastest in history to run 100 official marathons, completing them in just 688 days.

I got to chat with Traviss at the event, though we had already been in communication by email. He's a very likeable and modest guy who was one of the few people who had an idea what I was going through. He was full of good advice on both the physical and mental aspects of multiple marathon running, much of which has been very helpful.

I had already taken to heart Traviss's most enduring advice: never ever give up. The difference between those who can and those who can't is often a question of resolve. How much do you want it? How much are you prepared to endure? It was inspiring talking to him. Here was another guy as ordinary as me but willing to achieve something extraordinary at almost any cost.

With nowhere to rush off to after the race, I was able to fully give myself to the occasion, encouraging other runners, taking them gels and drinks during the race. I have learned that the best way to enjoy a race, and to be energised by it rather than worn down, is to focus on helping those around you. I often take extra food bars to share with other runners and if I see someone struggling, I'll always stop to see if I can help. Sometimes it's a question of a few words – 'Don't give up!', 'Well done, you're doing a great job!', 'You're doing really well.' Or sometimes a bit of silliness can relieve the tension and if you can make someone laugh or be distracted from their pain it can help them get past a difficult moment.

Many a time I've done a silly fairy dance on a course or airplaned past someone singing a song to take the heat out of the moment ('I love you, baby', the refrain from Frankie Valli's 'Can't Take My Eyes Off You' being my favourite). Sometimes I'll lie down in someone's path so they have to jump over me – anything to make light of a situation that is becoming heavy. Heaviness is not good for marathon running. You need to keep mind and body light out there. So have fun and spread good vibes where they are needed, that's my advice to anyone looking to do any endurance event. Focus on helping other people and your own problems seem smaller. I call it the double-reverse psychology: do or say something to another to take both of your minds away from the suffering of the moment. It really works – try it yourself and see.

At the end of the race, I tend to stay at the finish line to congratulate runners as they arrive. I met some great people that day and swapped stories with them during and after the race. As always, they were incredibly supportive and prom-ised to pledge money to my charities and keep an eye on my progress online, throughout the year.

Eventually, everyone went their own separate ways and I got a coffee at the start/finish line and settled down with my Dean Karnazes book. That day I read his account of his world record 350-mile non-stop run without sleep. He only stopped running when he lost consciousness mid-stride. Running until you could run no more – wow! That sounded like my kind of challenge.

Just as I was turning a page on my book, Dustin and Dominika turned up with their son William. They'd driven down to have dinner and camp with me for the night. They were a welcome sight. We played football on the beach and larked about. This helped take my mind off things. It was warm and soon we'd stripped off and were wading out into the Channel – well, the three boys at least. The sea was a welcome tonic for my legs. I challenged Dustin to a swim out to a distant buoy, but he wasn't up for it so after a bit more splashing about and dunking William, we came back in.

It was evening now and we drove into the nearby town to get a takeaway dinner. We ate our food and watched the sun set before putting up our tents, this time on a patch of grass at the race finish, just 30 yards from the beach. Weekends like this, away at marathon events with friends, are what it was all about. Being outdoors, exercising, camping – the simple pleasures are what make me happy. I wished Joanna and Alexander could have been there, too. That would have been perfect.

The next day was more of the same, running the identical course, my 60th marathon. Dustin tried to run his first marathon that day but ended up stopping after 13 miles. He was just one of many friends and acquaintances who were inspired by my running to take on their first marathon. He'd get there in the end and run the full distance later that year with me. That day I ran the exact same time, 3 hours 42 minutes, as the day before (spooky!) and came third overall. I met more great people and the sun shone.

Since wearing the Brooks Ravennas for a while now, my feet were much less sore and my arches didn't ache in the latter half of the race, which was a great relief. Maybe there are a few more marathons in me yet, I thought.

The week that followed involved five more early-morning marathons in Richmond Park. I was so busy with work and running and family life that the week pretty much flew by, but one of those mornings was different, though. As I came around to Sheen Gate after the first loop of the marathon, I found a woman waiting there who had come out to meet me. We got talking and she began to tell me why she had done so.

'I know about what you went through as a child,' she said.

'Because I went through what your mum went through and my son lived through what you had to. But you are really strong and my son wasn't ...,' she paused. 'So he took his own life when he was seven years old ...' Her eyes filled with pain and tears, and I took her hands in mine.

'You have to understand,' she continued. 'You are a blessing to all of us who have suffered. You don't know what you really mean to us. Please continue what you are doing and share your story, our story, with the world.'

Wow! I was completely blown away. We embraced. It was a very emotional moment for us both. 'You're a really brave lady for coming down and sharing that with me,' I said. 'I feel your pain and I promise to finish my year one way or another and to keep telling my story.'

It amazed me that my story seemed to be making such a difference to people like that, people I'd never even met before. If ever I felt like quitting, I would remember her words and they would give me added resolve to keep going.

Soon enough the weekend had come around again and I had my biggest test to date ahead of me: the Scafell Pike Trail marathon. Officially an ultra marathon at 44km long, it takes place in the Lake District, in the North of England. (I should add that currently the definition of an ultra marathon, or ultra distance, is any foot race longer than the traditional marathon length of 42.195km (26.219 miles). But I think an ultra race is more difficult to define than that and depends on the person. For me, an ultra is any race which takes you beyond your physical capability to the point where you need to rely on your mind and whatever else you can find within to get through it. For trained athletes, an ultra might need to be at least 100 miles, but for others it could be as little as 3 miles.) It's a serious race for serious runners, and they didn't just let anyone turn up and race.

And for good reason – the Scafell Pike Trail marathon was part of the European Mountain Marathon series and some of the best trail runners in the world would be racing. The current World Trail Running champion, Ricky Lightfoot, a legend of the running world, would be there. The course had over 4000 feet of overall elevation, taking us to the peak of the highest mountain in England, Scafell Pike, and over some very challenging terrain. It was, by all accounts, a bit on the tough side.

Ordinarily, a plodder like me wouldn't have been allowed entry to a race this tough, and the organisers had initially turned down my request to race. My lack of trail running experience made me a liability, they said, but after a bit of persuasion they changed their mind and let me run. Ali thought I was crazy for doing it. He said I was jeopardising my challenge by taking it on. What if I couldn't finish it? What then? My challenge would be over if I couldn't finish 26.2 miles in a day. There'd be no time to get back to Richmond Park to trot out one more of the old faithful. I thought I'd be fine, though I was a little nervous, I'll admit. The way everyone spoke about it, like it was a monster that could swallow you up, made me a little uneasy. Surely it was only a bit of running? I'd done plenty of that by that stage.

This was one of those occasions where I had Joanna and Alexander with me, so I was in a good mood. I think Joanna was a little nervous for me, but Alexander looked unworried so I took confidence from that. That Friday night, the three of us camped by Derwent Water, in the Borrowdale valley right in the heart of the Lake District. Borrowdale has a reputation as the most beautiful valley in England and it is breathtaking. Camping by the lake in this place, surrounded by craggy fells and lush green, was a serene experience, something to really savour.

At the race briefing on the morning of the race, I nodded confidently when the race director spoke of the essentials we all of course, by requirement, had in our bags: compass, mobile phone fully charged, waterproof top and bottoms, first-aid kit. I did have a mobile phone, but it had no charge. The other items were sadly absent. I'd have to get myself more together, I thought.

Ricky Lightfoot was there and I said hello. 'Marathon Man!' he said when he saw me. Wow, Ricky Lightfoot knows who I am! 'We'll find out what you're made of today, hey?' he joked, a big smile on his face. He was warning me this wasn't going to be like the Richmond Park marathon today. Was it too late to change my name to 'Half-marathon Man'? They did have the shorter distance here. It was good to talk to Ricky and I liked his attitude. He was relaxed but confident. We'd stay in touch on social media after the race and I'd rate him among the most impressive and helpful guys I came across in my year's running.

At the race start, I reminded myself that an elite world champion was expected to win the race in a time close to four hours, so this was going to be a long day for someone like me. Best to just take my time, feel my way around the course and, as the day went on, pick up the pace if I felt it was in me.

I kissed Joanna goodbye at the start and Alexander slapped a dirty hand in my face as I tried to kiss him. I think it was his way of saying, 'There'll be time for that later, Daddy, right now go race!'

The gun went off at the start and we were away. The majority of the 200-strong field went off like it was the start of a 400m race. I was baffled: this is a marathon, right? One of the toughest trail marathons in Europe, too. Do these guys know something I don't? Typically, my plans went out the window as I tried to keep up with the field. We ran along the flat for a bit, around the lake and then onto woodland trails. I was in the leading pack for a while, but then we started to ascend – steeply. My super-fit companions skipped up the rocky slopes like they were mountain goats and I was left struggling to stay in touch. Then they pulled away and other runners started to overtake me. You're not one of them, Rob, I reminded myself, but nobody likes being passed in a race, even if it's by world champions.

I made my way up the steep incline as best I could. The scenery was stunning, though I was struggling to appreciate it. We climbed up to the right of Castle Crag, a small, 300m hill, but a tough ascent. At the top we started to come down the other side. Many of the quicker runners who'd gone by me earlier were picking their way very gingerly down the other side. Too much caution, I thought. I can run this.

So I almost sprinted down; I was in my element. I flew past the more cautious runners, focusing intently on my feet placement over the rough terrain. I went past two guys and heard one say, 'Jeez, that guy's going to kill himself!' I think that put some doubt into my head, because the next thing I knew I slipped and wiped out in spectacular fashion.

It felt like I tumbled head over heels a few times before coming to rest. It was pretty bad; I had cut my legs up a bit and managed to wind myself. A couple of guys stopped to check I was OK. I waved them on, 'I'm fine,' I said, holding my thumb up. Then the rest of the field ran past as I dusted myself off and gasped for air. Ouch! Nice one, Rob. The new boy was clearly out of his depth.

I'm sure that wouldn't have happened if that guy hadn't mentioned the idea of falling. It goes to show how important the words in your head can be – that's why I always try to give people some encouragement. Most of the words are your own, the thoughts which you can keep an eye on, to make sure they're on your side, but there's not much you can do about what other people have to say.

Running downhill in races is something of an art. Ricky Lightfoot showed me a method for descending later that evening, which really helped in future races. He said you need to raise your arms in the air, to roughly ear height, when coming downhill. Then you can let yourself kind of fall down the hill, descending at speed. Holding your arms in the air helps reduce any tension as well as making it easier to steer to avoid obstacles (drop your left arm down hard to turn left, etc). With your arms down by your side, it is too easy to resist the slope, adding tension to your body and slowing you down. I practised this repeatedly on downhills over the course of the year and it really does work. You have to overcome that fear of falling we instinctively have, which makes us put the brakes on.

I wasn't too badly hurt so I soon got moving again. It wasn't far to Seathwaite and the first feed station. I wolfed down some treats there and got some liquid on board. I was sweating more than I'd expected, the effect of all the climbing and the considerable heat, too. Getting going again, the real ascent started, up to Styhead Tarn and beyond to the Corridor, up Scafell Pike itself. It was tough going and I made slow but steady progress. Some bits were so steep I was using my hands to scramble my way up.

The path was hard to make out at times and it was only following other runners that kept me going in the right direction. I'd later learn Ricky got lost way ahead of me, so it was clearly hard for us all to stay on route. Picking my way through vast swathes of boulders along the edge of Styhead Gill was a real challenge.

At the first mountain checkpoint, I was surprised to see no water or supplies, just a check. Of course they couldn't get hundreds of litres of water and food up there. Fortunately, I thought I had enough food and drink in my pack to keep me going, so I stopped to eat an energy bar. Other runners did the same, their faces grimacing with pain. This wasn't easy for anyone.

I got going again and felt recovered after the pit stop. There was fog on the mountain now, so keeping to the trail was a challenge. At Skew Gill a slab of rock lay ahead of me. Am I expected to run up that? Using my hands as much as my feet, I scrambled my way up. I stopped for a break at this point when a guy I'd met on the bus the previous day came past. 'Come on, Rob. Let's finish this together,' he said, but he was in better shape than me and I couldn't match his pace, so he went on alone.

There were sheer drops on the course that I'll admit were a bit unnerving. If you don't like heights then this will test you. I made slow progress up the Corridor and eventually came to the boulder fields. Scafell Pike is made up of volcanic rock that dates back 450 million years. The rocks at the summit had shattered into countless pieces turning it into a boulder field. Picking my way through them for the final half a mile to the top was slow going. I was cold now and visibility was very poor in the thick fog. What I would have given for a nice cup of tea!

Just shy of three hours after setting off, I reached the summit of the mountain and England's highest peak. I was battered and bruised but on top of the world (well, England, at least). I noticed I was running out of water, which was a bit of a worry. I didn't pause for long as I needed to keep in touch with the guy ahead who I could still see starting his descent. I really didn't want to get lost out there on top of everything else.

Coming down was a relief after so much ascending and my muscles were glad for the change. I was more careful on my way down, after my earlier fall, as I just wanted to finish safely now. The last 13 miles were slow going as I picked my way down the mountain in a state of exhaustion. I got there in the end, though, and 6 hours 13 minutes after setting off, I crossed the finish line and collapsed on the grass with a big smile on my face. I'd come 95th in a field of over 200 top runners, which shows I belonged in the race. I think a lot of people in the marathon community saw I was for real after clocking that run. At the time that was important to me.

Later, at the awards ceremony, I caught up with Ricky Lightfoot, who'd been narrowly beaten into second place that day by Cristofer Clemente, the leader of the European Mountain Marathon Series at the time. I'm not usually one who celebrates runs much. Once something's done I'm immediately thinking about the next challenge, but this felt like an achievement. I shared a beer with the runners (or it might have been a coke) and before long Joanna, Alexander and I started our journey back to London. Apart from a few cuts and a big old chunk of skin that somehow went missing off my heel, I had survived the Scafell Pike marathon.

Now I wondered what else I was capable of including in my year of running marathons.

CHAPTER SEVEN
Out of Breath

16–27 June 2014

Things sometimes have to get worse before they get better. That's been my experience anyway.

When I was about six years old I got the beating of my life. My dad came in from work one night and he was drunk. I was in my bedroom and I could hear lots of noise downstairs, doors slamming, plates being broken and my mum screaming and crying, so I knew something was coming my way sometime soon – it was just a matter of when.

Soon enough, my dad yelled out my name and I came running downstairs fast as I could. I remember seeing the look of terror on my sister's face as I ran past her room and down into the living room. My father didn't say a word. Instead, he grabbed me and threw me onto the floor. Then he started telling me he was going to really hurt me this time.

'You'd better be ready, boy,' he screamed. 'Because tonight's the night.'

My mum was hysterical, crying and telling him to stop. She seemed to sense something wasn't quite right with him.

Every now and then, he'd turn and hit her, telling her to quit yelling, that he would do whatever he wanted.

'Tonight's the night!' he kept yelling. 'Tonight's the night!'

Tonight's the night for what though, I had no idea. All I knew is he seemed possessed with a manic urgency I'd never seen in him before. He threw me onto the settee and then stopped for a minute, getting his breath. Next he disappeared through the kitchen and out into the back yard. A minute later he came back with some planks of wood and some rope. He started hitting me with the planks. Boy, they hurt! One of them clipped my ear and I started bleeding.

After a while doing that, he picked me up and dragged me up to the top of the stairs and 'the Dangling' got underway. He held me over the bannister and I stayed still and calm, giving him no cause to drop me, but he did it anyway. I managed to avoid falling head first onto the stairs and broke my fall with my hands, hurting my wrists.

Then he started putting the rope around my neck. I looked at his face as he tied a knot in it; I could see he was lost in the moment. He lifted me onto the old metal coat hooks we had by the front door and left me hanging there by my neck, then he stepped back to look at me. I dangled helplessly, showing no emotion, for a few seconds before he stepped in and punched me in the stomach. That really knocked the wind out of me. My mum was going crazy by this stage and I could hear my sister crying upstairs, though I couldn't see her. I lost my locked-in state and tried to regain it, but I couldn't. I was becoming overwhelmed by the moment.

Hanging there, I began to feel the pressure building up on my neck; as I started to run out of air, I panicked. I could see my mum's anguished face over my dad's shoulder.

'Stop!' she kept screaming hysterically. 'Stop! I'll do whatever you want. Just stop!'

I remember my emotions getting the better of me and a tear falling from my eye. How I wished that hadn't happened. Then, just as I thought my neck couldn't take any more, my dad came in to hold my legs to stop me from struggling. I remember looking him straight in the face and smelling the alcohol on him. I thought of my dog and how I watched him struggle and then go limp. I knew I was going to die the same way, and I was happy about it, to be honest. I thought finally all this is going to end and I'll have some peace. But still it was terrifying. Let's just get it over with quickly, I thought.

Then, as suddenly as it started, it was all over. My dad unhooked me and I dropped to the ground. I just lay there, shaking with fear and pain and spitting up phlegm. I wanted to be still for a while. Mum rushed to help me and I started to cry, silently. I could see she was feeling my pain, too. Eventually she carried me upstairs. On the way past my sister's room, I turned my head to see her. She had tears in her eyes and knew I'd been beaten within an inch of my life that night.

Mum cleaned my wounds and put me to bed. Then she left me there, staring blankly at the wall. I was hurting everywhere. All night I couldn't find a position to lie in which didn't cause me pain. I spent what seemed like two weeks up there in bed; all the time I was planning how to get away. When I was strong enough to get up, I decided I would do something about this once and for all.

Then, one night I stayed awake until it was gone midnight and everyone was asleep and crept downstairs, carefully avoiding the creaky parts of the stairs. I went through the hallway and into the kitchen, took the keys off the hook, unlocked the back door and opened it slowly. Outside, it was cold and dark. I went out to the outhouse in the garden, opened the door and went inside. I looked around and saw the plank of wood which my dad had used so often to beat me with, but I didn't want that. I kept looking and eventually found it: my dad's axe that he used to chop wood. It was really heavy, but I managed to get it up and over my shoulder before heading back into the house.

I left the back door open on purpose, so I could escape if my plan went wrong. I was really nervous. I'd rehearsed this in my mind a hundred times up in that bedroom, but I knew there'd be no going back after this. I'd have just one swing and if I missed I'd have to run for my life. I slowly climbed the stairs, but accidentally stood on a creaky step. It seemed to make a hell of a noise, and I hoped it wasn't enough to wake anyone.

I got to the top of the stairs in time to see my parents' bedroom door opening. I froze in terror. Out of the shadows I came face to face with my mum. Thank goodness for that! She instantly knew what I was up to and tried to grab the axe from me, but I fought her to get it back.

'I'm going to get him,' I told her. 'I'm going to hit him so he'll never hurt any of us again.'

'You mustn't!' she said. 'You don't have to do this because we're going away.'

'You always say that,' I said. 'But it's never true.'

She told me that she really meant it this time. I didn't believe her, but I gave her the axe anyway. If she hadn't been there to stop me, who knows what I would have done? I'm sure I would have tried to kill my father. It doesn't bear thinking about. I went back to bed and lay there all night, crying and awake. I wanted to die, to fade away. I was tired and weak and so sad. I wished I had died hanging on the railings downstairs. Why did he take me down?

A couple of days later, Mum kept her word and took my sister and me to the local school and told them everything. They called up the social services and we were taken off to a 'safe place'. It was the end of my father's reign of terror and I have never seen him since.

After falling at the Scafell Pike marathon, I had quite a few cuts to look after and make sure didn't get infected. I had once heard of a quick way to deal with cuts to seal them up and avoid the risk of infection: using acid. I searched online and found what looked like the stuff and bought a sachet to try.

The next time I got a cut, which was after a fall in Richmond Park a few days later, I scraped all the dirt out of the wound with the edge of a plastic cup and then poured a little of this acid onto it. It fizzed up immediately, forming a white foam, like a chemistry experiment in school. I dried it quickly and it seemed to have done the trick, sealing up the cut and saving it from the risk of infection. It turned out the scarring from this little trick was minimal, too. Now that was one less thing I had to worry about.

But all throughout my year's running there was always some part of my body that was troubling me. I don't have perfect gait, with slightly flat feet and dropped arches, which I think causes some of my issues when I run. Finally getting a pair of Brooks Ravenna shoes helped me loads, especially with the pain in my arches, but still something was always hurting – and most of the time it was my knee.

When I wasn't running there were other plates to keep

spinning, almost as challenging as the daily marathon. My boss Ken was not happy with what I was doing, and it was clear I didn't have quite the bounce and energy he was used to seeing. I was getting my work done OK, but I was not pushing for improvement all the time and being quite as dynamic as I used to be. I could see he didn't like sharing me with the running and I sensed that at some point we were heading for a showdown.

Then there was the fundraising. I was really disappointed by the figure I'd raised so far, which was still just a few thousand pounds. Ali was helping, doing all he could, trying to spread awareness on Twitter and Facebook, but it didn't seem to be working. We needed some national exposure – a piece in the paper or a TV slot might help, I thought. I chatted with Ali about this and he went to work trying to rustle up some media attention. I felt I could do with a big PR agency taking me on board, so he said he'd see what he could do.

On the plus side, I seemed to be inspiring plenty of people around me to take up exercise. I think when people see someone doing something extreme it makes them think, well if he can do 26-plus miles a day then I can do at least a couple of miles. Most of the members of team MMUK started running more and signing up for marathons. Followers on Facebook got in touch to tell me they were encouraged to get off the couch and back into training. I was determined to get Ali around the marathon distance by the end of the year. He was a big man and in pretty good shape, thanks to his cycling and rugby, but a marathon would be a test for him.

People would often ask me for advice on running, and what they should do to prepare. My simple answer is always to pull on some shoes and just run. I don't stretch before running – the first few miles are always a bit tough, but I just fight through that and soon my legs wake up. I believe that the less you think about it and plan the better. What do Nike say? Just do it. That's my philosophy in a nutshell.

Once you start thinking too much, you'll find reasons not to do something, so bypass that by being impulsive and just doing it. Experts will frown on this simplistic advice, I know, but that's what works for me and what got me this far. Nothing will teach you more about running than running itself. Grab your shoes and go for a run. After a couple of miles, you'll be glad you did.

Things at home were pretty good at this stage. It was a given that I wasn't seeing Alexander and Joanna as much as I used to, and she got exasperated sometimes, particularly at my reluctance to answer my mobile phone when I was out. I know I wasn't very good at that, because I didn't have the energy for a conversation half the time and my phone seemed to have a very short battery life. But maybe I just wanted my own space sometimes, I don't know. Despite this, she was still behind me. So when I did get to spend time with Joanna, we had a lot of fun and it made up, somewhat at least, for all the time we had to spend apart.

I had one of my mega weekends booked – three official marathons in a weekend, with a fair bit of travelling between each race – which meant I'd be on a very tight schedule. I could tell sleep would have to take a back seat (quite literally, as the only chance I'd get was in the back of someone's car).

The weekend began on 21 June with the South Downs Trail marathon. It was to be my 73rd marathon/ultra in 69 days of running. Held together by a combination of zinc tape and positive thinking, I arrived at the race HQ feeling tired but ready. One of the privileges of the year's running was the amount of amazing scenery I got to take in. Travelling up and down the UK, and eventually across the United States, I saw the full variety of countryside, at all times of the day and in all weathers. And all I can say is: get out there. We're wildlife too and at our best outdoors, in fair weather or foul, moving forward, stretching ourselves and breathing in fresh air and fresh sights.

For some reason, I thought this race was going to be easy. I don't know why because I never look at a course before I turn up to run, but nobody had warned me about it, or told me I needed to be on my game. Ali, who always tended to be the one to worry most, hadn't suggested I was in any danger. So I thought it would be a leisurely one, with lovely views and no great elevation involved. How wrong could I be.

A couple of miles into the race, I followed a signpost left up a steep hill. About 250 metres up, I heard calls to stop and turn back. I looked behind me and could see the rest of the runners at the bottom of the hill heading in a completely different direction. I realised we'd gone wrong and shouted up to the runners ahead of me to turn back. Fortunately, they heard me and started heading back down, cursing and asking what the heck was going on. We made our way down the hill and got on the right route again. It seemed some smart ass had turned the signpost the wrong way. That's all I can think, anyway.

I was pretty demoralised by the wrong turn, after having made what I thought was a decent start. Sometimes, if you're not careful, something small like that can send your race into a tailspin. You have to make sure you don't spiral down with the annoyance and frustration. When you've climbed up a hill for no good reason and you're now at the back of a pack you were once leading, it's easy to feel hard done by. Instead, you need to be philosophical and accepting. Things go that way sometimes. It's just a few extra steps. Who was I racing against anyway, really?

I struggled on for the next five miles. My heart wasn't in it and I needed to get a grip. If you start looking for the finish line at that stage, then it's going to be a long day. And from my experience it's when you're in that frame of mind that injuries happen, too. I got some food at the first-aid station and a few jelly babies. Another runner noticed I was a bit down and gave me a pep talk as we ran along. I don't know his name, but I really appreciated it and I got my mojo back a bit. Running for me is all about such moments: everyone helping each other to get around. Sometimes you're the one helping, sometimes you're getting the help, but nobody runs a race entirely on their own.

I got back into my rhythm and made decent work of the rest of the race. With incredible views, I'd rate the South Downs Trail marathon as right up there, a real challenge but worth it. It has just the right amount of hills to make it a handful, but it's not impossible for the average marathoner. It's well organised, and with very tasty snacks at the food stations, you can't go wrong with this one (unless someone flips the race signs around!).

I finished in 4 hours 56 minutes and spent some time at the finish with the other runners, chatting and clapping them in as they crossed the line. As usual I had a fair number of conversations about what I was doing and why, and came away feeling like the marathon community, while initially hesitant about me, was warming to me (I think it helped having Ricky Lightfoot tweeting positively about me the week earlier). Finally, I felt I was being treated like a legitimate figure in the world of UK marathoning.

Then I was off to the Brutal Enduro 12-Hour race, which started in Bordon, Hampshire, later that evening. This was one of those races against the clock, where you run as far as possible in the time period. It was a 10km off-road lap and you had 12 hours to do as many loops as possible. I arrived at the event HQ at about 7.30pm under the impression it started at 8pm, and was disappointed find out it didn't get underway till an hour later. I had to get up to Cheltenham for an early start the next morning so I was keen to get going.

I registered and got chatting to a couple of guys, Darren and Mark, soldiers from the local Army base. We ended up starting running the course early that night, at about 8.30, which was a bit naughty, but I didn't have a lot of time. The race was officially underway by the time we finished our first lap and I continued for a further four laps, which was over 29 miles in total. It was about midnight by then and I needed to get going to reach the next race, so I said my goodbyes and off I went.

Taking trains and buses to arrive in Cheltenham took a while at that time of night, and I got to the race HQ at about 5am. I put my sheet down in a nearby park for a couple of hours' sleep, then I was up to register and run again. It was a very warm weekend, which was great for most people in the country, but not so great for those doing multiple marathons. All things considered, I was feeling pretty good physically, though the lack of sleep and the unrelenting heat were proving a challenge.

The race began in the morning and we ran a route that took in some of the Cotswolds, climbing at one point to the highest point in the area. It's a beautiful part of the world, with pretty cottages in little villages and narrow winding lanes. The route went right past the Cheltenham race course at one point – home of the famous Cheltenham Festival each March. There were no thoroughbreds in action that day though – just one tired old pony covering the ground as best he could.

I don't know if it was the heat and humidity or the proximity of the racecourse, but I managed to attract a swarm of flies who were dead set on joining me for the run. Buzz, swirl, buzz – hundreds of them swirling around me. I was endlessly swatting them off as they circled my face and arms. They were a constant irritation, but I couldn't find a way to shake them off. At one point I picked up a massive branch and shook it vigorously over my head, but even this didn't discourage them. Eventually I gave up and accepted them as my company for the race.

Towards the end of the marathon I started feeling a bit weird. My airways had narrowed and I couldn't breathe very easily. I was hot and flushed too, unnaturally so. I knew something was wrong. I finished the race and just wanted to get back home, so I didn't hang around at the finish line too long. I'd run 83 miles in the last 27 hours and had a fair few miles travelling, too.

On the bus back, things got worse and my throat closed up even more. Eventually, just a mile or two from home, I had to get off and ask for help. It was becoming really difficult to breathe and I made a decision I needed an ambulance. I couldn't speak at this point, so I signalled to a passer-by to call me an ambulance and I just sat down by the side of the road. I knew I had to stay calm. If I got into a panic then things would likely get worse, so I just focused on keeping calm and breathing what air I could.

To their great credit, the ambulance arrived quickly and they assessed me and gave me an injection. They said it looked like I'd had an allergic reaction to something – anaphylaxis, they called it. They got me in the back of the ambulance and we sped off to the hospital. The injection did the trick right away and by the time we reached the hospital my breathing was easier. At the hospital, a doctor examined me and confirmed I'd had a severe allergic reaction, maybe to a fly bite on the course, but he couldn't be sure. They gave me two more injections and finally my throat opened up again and I could breathe freely.

It was a scary end to a tough weekend and I was very glad for those injections. That hospital visit was a bit of a wake-up call and I started taking some of my medical team's advice more seriously after this, adding vitamins to my diet and trying to look after myself a bit better. Boring as I thought all that stuff was, it might just keep me alive.

I got home to Joanna and Buddy, who were concerned about me, as were the rest of the MMUK team, especially Ali. But I was all right, it was just a bad reaction I'd had, not something anyone needed to worry about. I just wanted some food, a cuddle and a few good hours' sleep and, lucky for me, I got all three. Well, until the alarm went off just a couple of hours later, then I was up and off to run another marathon.

In the week that followed, I required some attention to my legs, which were very sore after the weekend's marathon running. My left knee didn't feel great at all and behind it felt a strange numb sensation. I saw Dominika who massaged it with ice and got me on the dreaded foam roller again (anything but that, please!). I needed to do whatever it took to keep me going as I had quite a weekend coming up, too – one even more extreme than the one I'd just barely survived.

The weekend ahead would begin with the Giant's Head marathon in Dorset, one of the toughest trail marathons in the calendar, with over 3000 feet of elevation. After that I'd have to get myself 150 miles away over to the Brecon Beacons in Wales, for the Brutal Midnight marathon (I think its name lets you know what kind of a run that one is) starting that evening. Then I could get some sleep before an early start and a car journey of another 150 miles to Rhyl in North Wales for the Runfest Wales marathon on the Sunday morning.

But before all that, I had a week of daily marathons to do and a living to earn. The days were becoming a bit of a blur now and a constant challenge to get through. I think the lack of sleep was the most difficult thing. I'd be in conversations at work and just drift off in the middle of them, then I'd have to try to work out what on earth we were talking about.

I had a boss, a wife and my manager (though Ali never liked that title, 'I'm just a mate helping a mate,' he always said). All three were constantly looking to engage me about something 'really important', but I wanted to hide. I found dealing with a lot of the non-running stuff really difficult, so they probably thought I was being awkward or uncommunicative. The simple truth was I was trying to get through the day. Most of the time, it was all I could do just to keep running, without all the other stuff that came with it. Give me fields and rocky hills and miles to run, in all weathers, over the meetings and conversations and faff of everyday life.

CHAPTER EIGHT
In the Brutal Midnight . . .

27–29 June 2014

Getting away from my dad and into a safe house was a new beginning for us all. It was strange knowing he wasn't going to be coming through the door at any moment, angry, throwing things, shouting my name and demanding I come down to receive a beating. It took some getting used to. That said, I remember he did find us at some point. Fortunately, we were tipped off that he was on his way and were able to get into a car, and be driven off to another safe house. I never saw him that day, but it was a reminder that our safety was never going to be guaranteed, as long as he was walking around a free man.

At some point, I don't remember why, we left that safe house one day and headed off towards my grandfather's house in Hampshire. It was over 200 miles away, so I don't know how my mum thought we would ever get there, as we started walking in that direction – I can only assume she must have hoped someone would give us a lift. The three of us ended up walking along a major road – it all seemed about as well thought-out as many of my runs. I remember my sister and I falling into lots of pot holes in the grass and thinking it was hysterical.

Eventually it got dark and we were very tired from all the walking. As we had no money and nowhere to sleep, we just slept that night huddled up in a ditch together. It was freezing and the noise from the cars rushing by stopped any of us from getting much sleep. The next day we continued walking. My sister became really tired and kept stopping to rest. I ended up carrying her at times, as long as I could anyway.

Finally, that afternoon a car pulled over and an elderly man got out. He approached us and, though he didn't look threatening, we were all scared of what it might mean. I stood in front of my mother and sister to protect them, ready to fight, anything not to have to go back, so he retreated back into his car. Then an elderly woman got out, presumably his wife, and came to speak with us. She said they had noticed us walking along the road earlier in the day and they were now heading back home. They were surprised to see us again and wanted to know where we were going and whether they could offer us some help, food, shelter or whatever we needed.

They were just good people who wanted to help, so my mum ended up letting them give us a lift the rest of the way to my granddad's. On the way, we stopped at a café, probably a Little Chef or something similar, to get something to eat. After much persuading that it was OK to take their charity, I had a burger and chips. And I remember the taste of that burger to this day. I had never had good food at home, it had always been cheap stews – nothing that ever tasted great – so that burger was the most amazing thing I had ever eaten. It's still the most delicious meal I've ever had to this day, or seems like that in my memory.

You might think that was a happy moment, but it makes me sad to think of it now. It's probably the only memory that can bring a tear to my eye. The kindness of those people and the relief I felt that day was like the world had stopped for a minute, just so I could have that moment all for myself. I feel sad for that boy who was blown away by the taste of a cheap burger. Why should anyone have to feel that grateful for a simple meal? More than all the beatings and abuse I went through, that memory reminds me how bad my upbringing was. My heart goes out to that boy and his sister by the road-side, and more importantly, to all the other little boys and girls just like them out there today.

They're the reason I run all these races.

I never got chance to thank that couple properly, but I hope they knew what it meant to us, certainly to me, back then. Their help was the promise of a better life, a normal life, sometime in the near future.

They drove us all the way to my granddad's where we stayed for a little bit. I remember my dad contacted us there once and I spoke to him on the phone. For the first time in my life, I felt brave enough to tell him how much I hated him. I remember swearing at him, really letting him have it. It was probably worth a few years in therapy, getting that chance to express my feelings. And I didn't waste it. After years of being terrified to show him any emotion, especially anger, I finally felt far enough away to let him know what I thought about him. I bet he was pissed off that day. He prob-ably smashed up a chair or two and swore he'd find me and make me pay for talking to him like that, but he never did. I got the last word.

After that, I remember we stayed in a succession of homes in the London area. I can't remember why we couldn't stay at my granddad's house. It was then that I started acting up, being naughty and getting into fights with other boys, usually older than me. I obviously had a lot of anger and frustration in me and I needed to get it out. I remember enjoying hitting other boys, but I also relished getting hit by them, which is obviously a bit screwed up. Was I so used to daily beatings that I needed to be hit in order to feel normal? It's a worrying thought. Could someone confuse a beating with the idea of being loved? It was some form of attention at least. I guess these experiences leave a shadow, which needs a little working through.

I remember one time, still very young, going into someone's garage on our estate with some other kids and starting a fire in there. The plan was just to bake some potatoes, but it got out of hand and we ended up setting the whole garage on fire. Another memory from those days was climbing up a big tree, all the way to the top, and not being able to get down again so I had to be rescued by a fire engine. That's pretty embarrassing – I thought I was this tough kid, but I was too scared to climb down a tree!

So it wasn't a fairy tale, even though we were finally away from my dad. It was a difficult time, but at least we were safe. I started to go to school a little around then, which was something of a novelty for me. Soon, however, this new life came to an abrupt end. It turned out my mum was struggling. All those years under my dad's thumb had taken a toll on her and she felt she couldn't cope. I think she had a breakdown or something similar. Looking back, it must have been very hard for her.

In the end, it was decided that my sister would go to live with an auntie and I was put into care. I remember going berserk when I heard the news, but that didn't help. Aged almost eight, I was on my way to a children's home, the first of many. So it was another new beginning for me, and one with a whole new set of challenges. I would never live with my mum or sister again.

On Friday 27 June I completed my 80th marathon/ultra, through the wild bracken, grass and woods of Richmond Park. It was a regular four-and-a-half-hour marathon in the early morning, something I could almost do in my sleep by now (how I wished I could actually do that).

It's a funny thing as it's absolutely dead in the park in the very early morning – you almost never see a soul. Then at about 6.30am everyone just drops in like they were being parachuted in. One minute you have it all to yourself, the next there are a hundred runners, dog walkers and cyclists chasing each other around the Tamsin trail and the road inside the park. It happens like a switch has been flicked, not gradually as you might expect.

There was one old guy, though, in his seventies, who was just about the only other person I'd see there in the wee hours, before 5am. We spoke a little after seeing each other a few times, though your natural inclination is not to strike up conversations at that hour. I don't remember the man's name, but he was an interesting chap. He never said why he went running in the middle of the night, wearing just shorts and trainers, his chest bare as though it were a hot summer's day. It was just normal for him apparently, not something he needed to explain.

One day I saw him and he told me he was going in to have an operation the next day, to have a pacemaker put in. I wished him luck and didn't expect to see him for a while after that, but just two weeks later he was back, shuffling along on his runs, as though nothing had happened. I don't know much about heart surgery, but I'm sure his doctor would have recommended a bit more recovery time than that. I found it funny and reassuring to see another eccentric doing it his own way and ignoring medical advice. At least there were two of us.

That evening after work, I was picked up by Dustin and William and we headed off for the weekend's running – the Giants Head marathon, followed by the Brutal Midnight Mountain marathon on the Saturday and the Runfest Wales marathon on the Sunday.

After a three-and-a-half-hour drive, we parked up in a Dorset field in Sydling St Nicholas, along with rows of other runners' cars and their tents, just a stone's throw from the Giants Head marathon race HQ. We set up our tents before getting down to the HQ hut and helping ourselves to some chicken, potato and beans in the pre-race dinner that had been put on for the runners. It was quite a spread, put on by the local Women's Institute, who'd gone to every effort to make sure we'd all turn up to the start of the race with plenty of fuel in the tank.

That night I got to chat with a bunch of runners I'd seen at previous events, as well as meeting a few new people. There were quite a few 100 marathon club members there, serial marathoners who couldn't get enough of these things. I ended up taking some beers to the race organisers' tent that night after William and Dustin had turned in for the night. We drank until the early hours before I got back to my tent to crash out for the night. I didn't drink much of the beer by the way – I don't usually drink alcohol, especially before and after races.

The next morning I woke early and crawled out of my

tent into the field. I got dressed and made my way up the path to the race HQ half a mile away. Breakfast was starting and I got myself a plate of sausage and beans and pulled up a bench. Another marathoner, Paul, who I had met at a previous event, joined me. He and I chatted about the day's race and he assured me it was one of the toughest races in the UK calendar. I told him about my three marathons that weekend and he got very excited.

'Someone tried to do that last year,' he said. 'Well, he didn't run all three, but the Giants Head and the Brutal Midnight marathon. Yeah, I remember him. A short guy. Pretty quick too.'

'How'd he get on?' I asked.

'Well, he ran here and made it to the start of the Brutal, but he didn't finish,' he said. 'They pulled him off the hill at some point, suffering from exhaustion.'

That's encouraging, I thought. Then Dustin and Will turned up. Dustin had heard the same story, of the guy who tried to run these two races the year before. He looked a bit concerned but also amused at the preposterousness of it all.

'Apparently he trained for just those two races for ages. And he still couldn't do it. Makes you think, doesn't it . . .'

I was smiling. I admit I quite liked these moments when people doubt me and look at me as if to say, 'You've bitten off a bit more than you can chew here.' Of course I knew it was going to be tough going. I didn't think it would be straightforward, but I was beginning to be confident in my body's ability to get through this amount of miles. Two marathons in a day, I'd done that. Lots of elevation, scrambling up and down hills, I'd done that. There was no reason to think it would be more than I'd already taken on and managed.

It was just a bit of running, after all.

As more and more runners arrived and started to mill about at the start line, I could tell this was going to be a good marathon, and a tough one. A lot of the hardcore marathon set, the ones I'd see throughout the year, were here, as were plenty of guys in Iron Man vests. They had almost all run this race the previous year and they were back for more. That tells you something.

There was one guy there, Brian Mills, who I'd see many times throughout the year. He must be in his fifties, is covered in tattoos and barely says a word to anyone. He'd done over a thousand marathons and is a well-known figure in the running world, but still seems to find it hard to communicate, even with other runners. He cuts a silent figure at the race start with everyone around him chatting and socialising, but I guess that's just how he is.

The race eventually got underway in unique style, with a lady in full country regalia shooting her rifle into the air. I was still pinning my number onto my shirt, and I think eating a piece of pizza at the time. After arriving there some 16 hours before the race started, somehow I still managed to be completely unprepared.

It was OK, though, as almost 300 runners plodded and chatted their way along a path for about half a mile. It already seemed more like a gathering of friends, intent on catching up with each other, than an athletic competition. Soon we had turned sharply left and were making our way up the first, rather steep hill. There would be plenty more ups and downs to come in the race, with 3000 feet of elevation in total to face.

At the top, we continued onto some Land Rover tracks and soon I could hear cheering up ahead. Were women mud wrestling? Was there a shot-drinking competition in full swing?

Not quite. There were a couple of old dames and an elderly gentleman, each sitting in their own metal bath, drinking cider. The ladies weren't naked but the gentleman, who everyone told me later was a farmer, certainly was. Not something you see every day, I thought, and definitely worth a cheer.

At about mile 8, a marshal kindly pointed out the Cerne Abbas Giant himself – a huge chalk figure, 55m high and almost the same size across, etched into a grassy field. He's been there since the 17th century, apparently, though no one knows quite how or why he got there. He's most famous for his giant erection. At 10m long and pointing straight up it's the kind of thing that sticks in the memory – naked farmers in bath tubs and giant pornographic art. This was my kind of marathon!

The race continued with amazing aid stations serving up home-made cakes and snacks, and super-friendly marshals, too. This event was clearly a labour of love and White Star Running, the organisers, need to be given all the credit, as well as the Women's Institute they'd roped in to feed us so well.

The race continued with uphills and downhills, about nine in total. It was tough going. At mile 20 there was an aid station they had dubbed the 'Love Station'. They were offering cider, cakes, fruit vodka and big slabs of melon – as well as hugs for all runners. I love a good hug, but someone got a bit carried away and gave me a big smacker on the lips. Sorry about that, Joanna. I blame the Cerne Abbas Giant, who had clearly got everyone's juices flowing.

Soon I was coming along the final stretch, a steep downhill to the finish. It had been very tough, but I finished in 4 hours 34 minutes and felt good for it. There was an ice-cream van at the finish line and everyone was standing around in the sunshine eating enormous cones of ice cream and swapping stories. It was a good moment and a nice memory from the year.

Dustin and William turned up in the car and they were keen to get going. It was a shame to be missing the barn dance they had on for that evening, and I was sure that some-day I would come back and take my time down here. But today we had to be up in the Brecon Beacons for a 5.30pm start, so we had motorway time ahead of us. Everyone wished me luck as I climbed into the car and we headed off.

I snacked on a bag of Tesco's chicken and bits that I'd bought the day before. I drank a coke and tried to get com-fortable in the back of Dustin's estate car. Resting or sleeping in cars is not my favourite thing, and I'd have plenty of opportunities to get better at it throughout the year but never did. We played I-Spy and ate plenty of chicken and a giant bag of Doritos. I think we might have stopped for pizza by the side of the road at some point, too.

You need to get calories on board when you're doing more than one marathon. Healthy, nutritious food won't replace the amount of calories you're burning up, so chocolate energy drinks or thick fast-food milkshakes are good, as are burgers and pizzas. I've learnt to mix this with nutritious food before and after, but during weekends like this I eat what I want and as much as I want. For some reason I tend to lose my appetite at times, so I have to force myself to eat enough.

We entered the Brecon Beacons where everything turns deep green and the hills are spectacular. There aren't many places in the UK you could get lost and it be a problem, but this is one of them. It's where the British Army and the SAS do their training, pushing would-be soldiers beyond their limits to find out if they're made of the right stuff.

We arrived on time for the race briefing, in Talybont-on-Usk, a tiny little village which seemed to consist of a few houses and two pubs. Plenty of tough-looking guys milled around the village hall, which functioned as the race HQ. They were military types, I was convinced of it. I'd heard a lot of SAS guys did this run, and I'd later learn the course covered much of the same ground as the infamous Fan Dance, an SAS training run over Pen y Fan, the highest mountain in the Brecon Beacons.

The atmosphere even in the car park was unnaturally serious, tense. It felt like a pre-battle gathering (not that I've ever actually been to one, but I've seen a few movies). This was just a marathon wasn't it? Or had they dotted the route with Taliban soldiers? I didn't like it already. Give me naked farmers in bath tubs over this any day of the week.

Dustin lent me his mobile phone for the race briefing in case they wanted to check my kit list; I had the head torch but most of the other items were missing. The organisers were fantastic and were good enough to lend me the items I didn't have. The race briefing got underway. It was the most intense of my entire year. I felt like I had to spend a good deal of time that year overcoming other people's nerves, but this was too much. The race director, who was also wearing a kilt, seemed convinced many of us wouldn't make it around and would die on the mountain that night. I only listened to part of it, but at the first chance I got I slipped out the back into the car park.

It's just a bit of running, I reminded myself. I spent the next ten minutes before the race playing football with William in the car park. Messing around, playing games, and being around children really helps keep me relaxed and light. People are always making the mistake of being too serious for races. I've been at countless events and seen runners doing all the right stretches with a look of grim determination on their faces. They're usually the ones unable to finish the race.

You really need to let your mind know 'it's just a bit of running'. Once you become convinced you are entering the toughest thing you will ever do, you're almost finished before you've started. Don't believe the hype. Make a joke with someone, imagine everyone naked, sit on a whoopee cushion – whatever chills you out. Don't get end-of-the-world serious about it or you'll end up taking the ambulance home.

By the time the race started, I sensed the race organisers were barely tolerating my relaxed attitude. By the look on their faces, they didn't expect me to finish so it was good of them to give me the benefit of the doubt, I guess.

When the race got underway the small field of about 100 runners ran through the village towards the mountains in the distance. Then we turned sharply and started heading up a steep hill. At the top you could see the enormous Talybont reservoir, which we ran alongside, a giant sea of water sur-rounded by hills. It was quite a sight. The views in the Brecon Beacons are something else and I felt fresh enough to really enjoy them that day.

The next few miles were generally uphill, but with some downhills thrown in for good measure on the way. The run had over 4000 feet in overall elevation, some of which you could tackle only on your hands and knees. It was tough going, but there was some respite at the first-aid station, about 7 miles into the race. Shot Bloks were on offer but I'd never tried them before so I had a banana instead and the few jelly babies from my pack.

The views in every direction were stunning. Green,

treeless mountainsides, with nothing to obscure your view in all directions, were topped off by moody, gathering clouds. Rain looked imminent and I worried that if those clouds had as much water in them as it appeared, then we might all get washed off the mountain.

The race continued up to the first peak, Fan-y-Big (curiously named when you consider it's the smallest of the Pen y Fan set of peaks). Past that we came steeply down the other side before we started climbing again. All these ups and downs were what made this race 'brutal'. It was relentless and seemed to have been designed by a sadist – or an SAS squadron leader, which is probably much the same thing. My legs were really hurting now, my muscles screaming at me to stop.

Push on, Rob, I said, push on. It's just a bit of running.

It was then I went the wrong way and got lost. It could have been a disaster, but I figured out quite quickly that I'd gone wrong and doubled back on myself. Fortunately, I'd gone only about 500m in the wrong direction, so it wasn't the end of the world and wouldn't be the last time I'd end up on a detour during a marathon.

After climbing another peak, Cribyn, we started up the highest peak of the lot, Pen y Fan. We were totally exposed to the elements and, though it was mild that day, the wind was all over us. I had to use my hands at some point and walk for quite a bit of the ascents, but I was making progress and it never felt desperate. When I reached the peak of Pen y Fan, it signalled the halfway stage of the race and a medical check point. I was good to go and didn't linger up there for too long.

The rest of the race was more of the same, running up and down steep hills, walking for much of it but making progress. It started to get cold and dark, and by mile 20 I was ready for my tent floor until one of the race directors offered me a Shot Blok, which perked me up right away. Then it started to rain, as though the dark and the fatigue and the steep mountain descents didn't make it dangerous enough. Not long to go now, though, keep pushing on.

Soon enough I was on the Taff trail running along the reservoir again and down into the village. I was soaking wet and stumbling occasionally on the uneven ground, but in no doubt that I would finish. I got to the start/finish just before 11.30pm, with one more marathon still to run that weekend. Most of the field had finished already, but I hung about to cheer in the remaining runners and to swap stories with some of the guys. I really loved this event, despite the tension at the start. The organisers are some of the best around and the course was well marked and marshalled, with good aid stations. I'd encourage anyone looking for a tough run to give this marathon a go. You won't regret it.

Eventually, I left to find our tents in the field behind the race HQ. Dustin and William were already fast asleep in their tent, so I got out of my wet clothes and into some dry ones before zonking out in my tent for a few hours.

At 5am Dustin woke me up: 'Rob, Rob! We've got to get moving.'

'In a minute,' I replied.

'But we have to go now. How was the race anyway? Did you finish?'

We got up and threw the tents into the back of the car any which way. By now the car was a jumble of carrier bags, wet clothes, sleeping bags and tent poles. Finding what you wanted was a case of endless rummaging by now. I got in the back seat with the intention of sleeping some more, but we were on the move and there was I-Spy to play and sunrises to watch so that never happened. I was tired, but I was used to that so my body didn't go looking for those missing hours' sleep like it once did.

At about 7am Dustin, to his credit, pulled over at a mini-market and said we needed to get some food inside me. I don't know why but I wasn't hungry. Perhaps my body gets confused with all that it goes through, but I had no desire to replace the countless calories I'd burnt up in the last 24 hours. I should have eaten anyway, forced the food down. In the end calories-in have got to try to measure up to calories-out or you're going to get exhausted and slump. So I nibbled on some chorizo slices as we went along on another beautiful, summer's day. And we were off to the beach, too, in Rhyl on the north coast of Wales. How I would have liked to have laid down on that beach for the day.

I say that now, but at the time I wouldn't have allowed such thoughts to enter my mind; I was focused on the mission at hand. This was my dream and everything was riding on it. Though it was tough much of the time, having a clearly defined and challenging objective each day makes for a very peaceful life. Run a marathon, eat, rest, survive, negotiate people and repeat. That was all I had to do. It was taking all I had, but maybe that was the secret. By giving my all there was nothing left: no worries, doubts, thoughts of more or less, or what if. There was nothing missing. I was happy like never before.

Fortunately grace was on my side, too, or so it seemed. I said earlier that it would take a few miracles to achieve my goal, and I would need things that were out of my hands to go my way. Though I'd fail to get at least one of the world records I was after (and fail to raise the kind of money I'd hoped to), enough things went my way for me to feel like someone was watching over me.

That morning was an example of this. Waking at 5am looked enough time for us to reach Rhyl in three hours. It was 150 miles and some of it was on the motorway, but even without getting lost we still got to the HQ with only minutes to spare. I hurried to get my race number and join the other runners at the start on the beach front. It was all fine margins, but I was always on the right side of them.

The Runfest Wales marathon was, on paper at least, a straightforward one. We were to run along the beach front on a flat, half-marathon course, and then repeat. It should have been the easiest marathon of my entire year. I'd just run up and down the SAS training routes at night in the pouring rain, so what threat could this beachfront run possibly pose?

In a word, plenty.

I can't tell you much about the route or the occasion because about ten minutes in I was in trouble: I needed food. The aid stations on the route had plenty of drinks, but no food on offer, and I needed a couple of buckets of fried chicken and rice. I hit the wall at about mile 2 – there was nothing left. I think having my legs bent up in the car hadn't helped. Where was Dominika when I needed her to massage me? Where was a burger van? And where was my wallet to pay for those burgers?

Nowhere to be found, that's where.

I just had to drag myself around, as I had no idea where Dustin and William were. I wanted them to get me some food, but I was running away from them now. I felt like I'd just set sail for America but forgotten to pack the sails. This would be a whole new experience for me – a slow and painful one.

When I finally returned to the start point 13 miles later, I couldn't see Dustin anywhere. I had no cash on me or I would have jogged into town to buy a burger. I thought about asking someone for some money, I was so desperate to eat something. The aid stations didn't have what I wanted in terms of food, so I was stuffed, and not with food, unfortunately. To make matters worse, my kilt was wet from the night before and weighed a ton. I stopped and changed into some shorts, laying out the kilt in the sun by the beach; Marathon Man would have to run without his kilt today. It was an emergency situation and even superheroes have to adapt.

I'd pinned my hopes on finding Dustin and getting some food, so for the sake of politeness let's just say I was 'extremely disappointed' to be starting my second lap of the course on an empty stomach. It was a case of grin and bear it now. The second lap was a never-ending torture, so by the time the finish line loomed up I was dead on my feet. This time Dustin and William were both there and looked relieved to see me.

'Are you all right, Rob? We thought you'd failed to finish. I've been calling around all the check points to see if you'd retired from the race.'

'Where were you at the halfway point? I was looking for you everywhere,' I said.

'Shit! Sorry, man. We were on the beach.'

It turns out one man's journey through hell is another man's beach holiday.

The race had taken me more than five hours. A simple flat road marathon, one where runners come to record a personal best, had become for me a hugely unpleasant ordeal, my toughest marathon to date when I finished 108th out of 118 who completed the race. After the other two epic marathons that weekend, I'd made the mistake of thinking the worst was behind me. How wrong could I be.

It shouldn't need saying, but I'll say it anyway: if you're going to run multiple marathons then EAT PLENTY OF FOOD. Still, I had finished. I had gone through hell and kept going, and this is part of why we run marathons.

There are many reasons not to do a marathon or an ultra marathon. There are risks of injury and pain, a loss of your spare time in order to train and the expense of getting all the kit. But if you want to do one, then decide to do it and don't look back, that would be my advice. Decide to go through whatever it takes to get to your goal. It will hurt up to a point, but then it will go numb and it won't get any worse after that. When you eventually cross the finish line, the feeling of success will overshadow all that you've been through to get there. And that was my emotion when I finally completed my third race of the weekend.

But before I could get something to eat, I had to find my kilt. I returned to the spot I had left it, drying in the sun, but it was nowhere to be seen. I asked at the race HQ, but no tartan of any kind had been handed in that day.

'Someone's nicked my kilt,' I said to Dustin. 'What kind of a person steals someone else's kilt?' I was tired and hungry and in no mood for being philosophical. We headed off to the nearest fried chicken restaurant and got some takeaway.

It had been a triumphant weekend, or so everyone kept telling me. We'd managed to get to every race in time for the start and I'd handled the running well until the end. My decision not to eat much on the Sunday morning had been a big mistake and had made things a lot harder than they'd needed to be, but at least I had got round and in one piece.

I was pissed off about that kilt, though.

CHAPTER NINE
Solving the Enigma

29 June–6 July 2014

The drive back from Wales was a long one and I had time to think about things. I loved these weekends away: they were an adventure and I was thriving on how much they tested me, but I missed Joanna and Buddy. I wasn't seeing them enough and I didn't know when I could change that. I also missed my daughter Olivia, and wasn't sure when I'd get to see her next. Dustin dropped me off at the flat and I went in to find Joanna and Buddy. I had called them from his phone earlier in the day, so they knew I was OK and still in one piece. I gave Joanna a big hug and scooped up Alexander, who was smiling with everything he had.

'I'm exhausted,' I told Joanna.

'Let me get you some food,' she said. 'You lie down here with Buddy.'

I did as I was told. I felt my left leg, which was badly swollen and needed Pippa to get onto that. Alexander didn't want to lie around; he wanted me to play Lego with him on the floor. So, by the time Jo came back with my dinner, Buddy and I were playfighting on the living-room floor. She looked at me like I was being naughty.

'You're meant to be resting,' she told me.

'He wants to play,' I said. 'He won't leave me alone.' She gave that look again, only more of it.

'I lost my kilt,' I said. 'Someone stole it in Wales. I took it off because it was wet. And a couple of hours later and it was gone.'

'What are you going to do, then – get another one?'

'I wonder if it was an Irish thief?' I said. Joanna looked puzzled. 'An Irishman stealing the Scottish kilt of an Englishman in Wales.'

The next morning I was back in Richmond Park for my usual marathon. It was tough, as I was beginning to grow worried about my left leg. I ran a quick time in the end, but after about mile 16 my leg was really killing me and I had to limp the rest. I still finished in under four hours, so it didn't slow me down too much, but I knew I couldn't go on like that, so I called Pippa to arrange some physio and Dominika to book in a massage.

Pippa agreed to see me the next day and I went to her clinic in Richmond after I'd run a marathon in the park. I'd limped much of the way around again, and called work to say I'd be late as I needed to see her first for some advice.

Pippa was great, but she was very concerned. She told me I needed to ice the swelling and elevate my leg, as there was no magic wand to make it better, though she did have a tennis ball and a Geko device to help. She wanted me to roll the ball on my sore heels to work into the sore areas and alleviate some of the tension there. I can't say I used it that often, but when I did it seemed to do something. The Geko device helped a lot. It's not an actual lizard (they're useless for physio), but a strap that you attach to the back of your knee. It emits electrical pulses that stimulate blood flow to your leg when you are at rest. So it helps the knee to get more blood into it and so to heal. It's not a life saver, but I reckon it's helped me quite a bit since I started using one.

Even with her help and equipment, Pippa looked at me as if to say: you're not going to be able to keep this up for long, are you? But I knew I could; this would pass and move along – it usually did. I just had to keep going and keep the Geko nearby.

At work, when I finally got in, my boss was clearly annoyed with me. His patience for what I was doing outside of work was wearing thinner and thinner. I didn't know what to do about it, because I wasn't going to stop running. I could see that we wouldn't be able to go on like this for too long, and that something was going to give eventually.

That day, I found a kilt on eBay that was similar to the one I'd lost and bought it for about £30, which was a bargain. The weekday Richmond Park marathons continued as usual, and friends and others who had heard what I was doing kept turning out in the mornings to run or cycle with me. The World Cup was on at the time and people wanted to talk about that, but I had no idea what was going on as I hadn't seen a single match. I soon learned that England weren't going to win the World Cup, which of course I already knew.

I had another hectic couple of days on the road lined up for the weekend. The Enigma marathon was on Saturday and after that I had to get up to the Lake District for the Coniston marathon on the Sunday. It would have to be trains and buses this time as nobody had volunteered to drive me around. Fortunately, I had my Virgin Trains pass and a few quid in my pocket, so I was confident it would all work out fine one way or another.

On Saturday morning, I got up early and found my way to Milton Keynes for the Enigma marathon in time for the 8.15am start. There was a very friendly atmosphere at this marathon and I liked it from the moment I got there. Every marathon has its own unique feel, in my experience. Some feel like they've been put on by non-runners in an attempt to make money, or by a council who are required to do so. They don't have much of a soul, although the participants inject what they can into it. Then there are the ones put on by marathon enthusiasts with lots of nice touches and every detail thought about, the runners' needs met in every possible way.

The course was really simple but beautiful. Basically, it was seven and a bit laps of Caldecotte Lake just outside Bletchley (where the German Enigma messages were decoded in the Second World War). It was a pleasant route – I always like running by water, for some reason. There were no epic views to take in here, but at the same time no dangerous slopes to overcome either. This was a mild marathon, perfect for anyone wanting to take on the distance for the first time. After the scrambles and dramas of the weekend before, I was glad for the gentleness of the course and the incredibly supportive runners around me. Marathon Man UK gives you a vote of approval!

My left leg was still hurting and I was running with a noticeable limp for the last six miles, but I finished in 4 hours 11 minutes – a good time, all things considered. Running the entire year without injuries wasn't realistic. I'd have to learn how to get through marathons by managing my injuries, altering the way I ran at times, and doing things to look after myself (like using the Geko). Under Pippa's and Dr Kipps's advice, I had been trying to land more on my mid to front foot, rather than on my heels, which I tend to do in the latter half of races as I start to tire, or intentionally slow things down to begin my overall recovery. It was a question of listening to my body's feedback and trying to work around the aggravated areas. And if all that failed, I just carried on regardless, pretending everything was fine. It wasn't a sophisticated plan, but it worked for me.

The key, I'd come to realise, was that I needed to stay positive all the time. If you have an injury, don't dwell on it: tell yourself it will be fine tomorrow and keep saying it, and it will help you recover quicker. It's a question of fighting your own doubts and fears, even when you're running. I found if I stayed positive and light, made a joke about the situation, and used my mind for my cause, rather than letting it turn against me, that it helped. And I tried to remember that everyone else was going through the same thing as me, even though I might not have been able to see it.

When that race was over I did my usual thing, standing at the finish line encouraging other runners over the last 100 yards. I had a bit of time before the next race the following day, though it was a good 250 miles away by public transport. There was another race, the Enigma ultra marathon, starting at 2pm, run over the same course only more of it, over 30 miles this time. I was tempted to try to run it as well. In the end, after chatting with other runners there, I decided against it. It might not have left me enough time to get up to the Lake District for the next day's racing.

I hung around at the race HQ for a while longer and had some lunch at the café there before watching the ultra race get underway. I had the rest of the day to get up to Coniston, so there didn't appear to be any hurry. In the end a nice lady, Alison, offered me a lift to the train station in Milton Keynes, so I got on my way. It had been a great event, really friendly and I'd recommend it to anyone.

I don't prepare for journeys much, just as I don't look at course routes before I get to the races. That's partly because I'm so tired all the time. When I'm not busy I'd rather disengage and rest my mind. Wrestling with a course map is the last thing I'd want to do, but I also like to make it all a surprise on the day. When I got to the station, I started trying to work out how I would get to Coniston. I learned the best route was a train to Preston and then another train to Ulverston; a bus would take me the rest of the way to Coniston. It sounded straightforward, and I thought it should have taken me about four hours – a bit longer than I'd reckoned, but I'd still be there for about 9pm and have a good night's kip ahead of me.

It didn't turn out that way.

It ended up being quite late by the time I finally got to Preston, and I was lucky to catch the last train to Ulverston from there. So far so good, though. There were a lot of drunks on the train that night and it was an interesting ride. Some women started chatting to me and were being very flirtatious. One got a bit carried away and suggested I could stay at her house near Coniston. Tempting as a warm bed sounded, it probably came with strings attached so I politely declined.

We pulled in at Ulverston and I began looking for a bus station. I asked a taxi driver where the nearest bus station was (which strikes me now as a pretty dumb move). He told me there were no buses at that time of night. The only way to get to Coniston, he assured me, was by taxi, which would cost about £45. Not a huge amount of money for most people, I realise, but a fortune when you have only £20 on you. So I asked how far it was to walk there instead.

He laughed: 'You can't walk it. It's a good fifteen miles.' He didn't know me.

'In what direction?' I asked.

So he told me the best way to walk to Coniston. I had a heavy backpack and my feet were a bit sore, but I could walk 15 miles in the moonlight. It might even be nice.

'You'd better get some food here if you're hungry,' the driver said. 'There's nothing open in Coniston at this time.'

I thanked him and found my way to the nearest Indian restaurant and ordered a takeaway. While my meal was being prepared, I went to the Tesco on the same street and stocked up on food for the next 24 hours. Soon I was on my way: bulging rucksack on my back, Tesco bag in my left hand and Indian takeaway bag in my right. I thought about stopping to eat my food on the way, but I wanted to get to the race start first. I knew how these things can end up taking longer than you think, especially if you get lost.

I had some pretty specific directions from the taxi driver which took me along a quiet road to Lowick. This was a short cut, he had assured me. It was a long walk but not unpleasant. The weather was a little colder now than I'd have liked, but I made steady progress. After three hours or so, the road passed Coniston Water. It was about 2am by then and it was magnificent, this huge body of water, shimmering in the moonlight.

My left leg was sore, so I was glad when I finally reached Coniston, but finding the race HQ ended up being the trickiest bit. I had to cross some big fields to get there. I was relieved to have made it to the start of another race, my epic journey successfully completed. It was probably not the ideal preparation, truth be told, and I put up my tent in about a minute, in typical Rob fashion, so it was barely standing.

It must have been about 3.30 in the morning by then and time to eat dinner. Not-too-warm chicken tikka masala was on the menu. Yum! I gobbled it down and topped it off with a little chocolate milk and a can of coke. Delicious! Then I crawled into my tent to get some sleep. With the roof of the tent practically in my mouth, I passed out like a light.

I slept so well that I woke up in a panic. Had I missed the race start? I hurriedly pushed my way out of the tent to find a hive of activity outside: runners getting ready, stretching and filling up their water bottles, cooking up sausages on gas stoves, while others struggled to pin their numbers on. I was just in time.

First up, breakfast. I looked in my Tesco bag to see what lay in store: some pasta in a pot and a big bottle of water. That would do it. I ate my food, dug out my kilt and fresh socks and started to get ready. It was a beautiful, clear morning in the Lake District, about as wild and beautiful a place as this country has to offer. It felt good to be alive and on a mission. I made my way down to the race HQ to get my race number and register. I said a few hellos and chatted to a couple of runners about the race, who told me it was 'hilly, very hilly', with over 2500ft of elevation. Here we go again, I thought.

The HQ was at Coniston Hall, a big old country pile right on Coniston Water itself. It was a bit like Skyfall, James Bond's house in the film, except on a lake – a beautiful setting and you couldn't help but be knocked out by the perfect running conditions and scenery.

This was my 90th marathon in 84 days of running. I didn't

want to pat myself on the back (you could dislocate your shoulder trying to do that), but I did allow myself to think that was pretty good going. I hadn't always been 100 per cent certain I'd get this far and I think it was touch and go at times. There had already been a few nights when I went to bed thinking that I couldn't go on, but my body always recovered well enough as I slept for me to feel able again in the morning. And so here I was. Marathon Man was starting to live up to his moniker. What I wanted now was to get 100 marathons under my belt. That would be something. I should be able to reach that milestone at least, I thought.

The race got underway and it was perfect. I felt really fresh in my spirits and the warmth of the sunshine was doing wonders for me, despite the fact that my left leg was definitely swollen and hard to run on in the beginning. The first few miles were a bit of a wake-up for my tired old muscles, but after that I was in the flow and felt ready for anything.

The views in every direction were stunning. I could see how it got its reputation as the most scenic trail marathon in Britain. It was tough, though, with lots of hills to get over and down, and varying surfaces underfoot: loose shale, smooth road, bog and bracken, grassy hillside and, towards the end of the run, a load of gnarly tree roots which needed some careful picking between to get over safely.

I was in no hurry during the race; this was one to savour and enjoy. I took the time to stop to chat with marshals and other runners as I went along. I was even photographed doing a few of my trademark fairy dances, which involves spreading my arms out like wings and doing a ballet jump now and again while running along. A little bit of silliness goes a long way (26.49 miles on this occasion).

There was an infectious, small-marathon spirit to the event, and I think we felt like the privileged few, with the hills to ourselves on this perfect day. When I finally got to the finish, 4 hours 38 minutes after setting off, I wanted to hang around and socialise. That was one of the most enjoyable marathons I'd done to date, but I had a long journey home ahead of me so I couldn't stay for too long. One of the runners offered me a lift to the station and soon enough I was sleeping on a train again with another medal around my neck.

I don't remember the name of the first care home I ever went into, or the ones that followed. Forgive me if this is all a bit vague, but it's all blended into one now. Perhaps, at some level, I never really wanted to remember any of it too much. As far as how I felt about going into care, let's just say I wasn't too happy. I can look back now and see that my mum was struggling. I certainly don't bear her any hard feelings or resentment. She was just trying to survive, like we all were, but at the time I was eight years old and I'd thought things were starting to get better. I thought we could be some kind of family and things might find their way to some kind of normal. Going into care wasn't what I'd been lying in bed dreaming about.

And, if truth be told, it scared the shit out of me.

But that was the way it went and I had to face up to it. I had to survive and make the most of a bad situation, find a way onwards and hopefully upwards. However, that wasn't the way I saw it back then. That's an adult's perspective. At the time I was just angry and scared, and I wanted to fight back at the world. From the moment I got there until I was about 12 years old, I was always in trouble. I got moved from care home to care home, always being uprooted and having to find my way in a new place. Here comes Rob, the new kid, they'd say. Watch out for him: he's a loner, a loose cannon, someone to keep a watchful eye on. That's not to say I was the biggest troublemaker in any of the homes. I wasn't by a long shot, but I was no angel either. The thing about those places is the trouble always makes its way right to your doorstep, whether you're looking for it or not.

The worst thing about those places was sharing rooms with boys much older than me. Some were almost twice my age. The bullying used to be pretty bad at times and when the lights went out at night there was no one around to protect you. I did some dumb things in those homes back then, things I'm not proud of at all. I was bullied a lot, and pretty harshly, so I fought back and ended up making those bullies regret thinking they could pick on me.

There was a strange coping mechanism I used to do back then. When things got really bad I would just explode. I would go absolutely nuts and hit out uncontrollably. It was like I wanted people to know if you messed with me, they'd get a crazy man. Groups of boys would start picking on me, I'd lose it and fight them all at once. It was a strange thing to do but it helped at the time, made the bullies scared to pick on me again. It probably helped to let off some steam after many years of frustration, too.

It's strange to remember myself like that now as I'm so calm and mild these days. It takes an awful lot to get me even slightly angry, and even then I tend to quietly speak my mind or retire into my own space to calm down. I don't like confrontations much these days.

Something significant happened back then to make me change my ways and stopped me from going further down a bad road that might have led to a more violent life. I'll never forget it.

Everyone knew everyone else's story in those places and one time I was involved in a fight and a girl said to me, 'You're going to end up just like your father, Rob!' That was like a punch in the guts. And it scared the life out of me, too. Straight away I saw she was right. That was exactly where I was headed. It was like I was sleepwalking and someone had thrown a bucket of cold water over me. I woke up that day, and from then on started finding other ways to deal with the violence around me rather than joining in with more of the same.

As I said before, in the first couple of years I was moved around a lot. I stayed in a whole bunch of orphanages – it was like the Rob Young tour. So my schooling got broken up quite a bit. I was trying to learn to read and write at the time, to catch up on everything I'd missed. In the homes I'd read all the books I could and some people there saw what I was trying to do and helped me.

Looking back I realise there were always a lot of people helping me out, even in the most difficult years, from the couple on the road who bought me the delicious burger to the people in the homes helping me to read. It was always just a few little things that they did, but in the end it amounts to a whole lot. There are so many people I wish I could thank now.

I remember I was starting to compete at that time, too. We used to go over to the local parks and, when I wasn't fighting with other boys, I'd be racing against them. I loved to race, but even more than that I loved to ride bikes. My dad had a bike when I was younger and I wasn't allowed anywhere near it. He kept it in the outhouse where I wasn't allowed, but I was fascinated by it. I used to sneak out and turn the pedals on it, sit on it even. I once tried to ride it, when my dad was out, but I was so nervous as well as being too small for it. I ended up falling onto the crank and cutting my leg. I got blood all over my trousers that day. That didn't go unpunished, I can assure you.

At one of the homes I stayed in, there were a couple of bikes that we were allowed to ride. I was so happy. We'd go out with one of the staff and I would let rip. He couldn't keep up with me, though. I'm not sure Chris Froome could have back then. I used to fly by cyclists on their expensive racers and they'd look at me on my rusty old bike, a ten-year-old, and wonder what on earth was going on.

Eventually, I got moved to a better orphanage, in London, and I settled down there. I think I'd got a few things out of my system by then and I was big enough not to feel so vulnerable to the other boys around me. After years of asking to go to school, I finally got the opportunity. I remember my first school uniform and feeling proud, like I had won the lottery or something.

School was hard for me, as I had to catch up on all the stuff that other children knew already. I worked pretty hard though, I liked learning, and I was bright enough to do OK. But it was the sport that was the big excitement for me. I used to rush out into the playground at break and fly around non-stop for the whole time. I often missed lunch because I didn't want to stop playing. And I was competitive, too – always trying to win races, hit the ball the furthest in rounders, get the most baskets in basketball. I wanted to win at whatever I did.

Making friends wasn't all that easy for me at school. People knew I didn't live in a normal home, so I got stick for that. And I didn't really trust people that much, I suppose. I'd been used to fighting my corner on my own for too long. Things were moving forward, but I was still a handful and I needed someone to give me a proper home and show me the right ways in life and some real love. Everyone needs someone to do that. I don't know how anyone can make their way without it. Growing up, like running multiple marathons, is not something you can manage on your own.

By the time I was 12, going on 13, I was doing lots of sport and getting less angry with everyone around me. I was raw and undisciplined, still pissed off with the world, and my patchy education meant there were big gaps in my understanding. As much as anything, I lacked a proper moral upbringing. I didn't know how to behave or what was important in life. But I was lucky. Someone came into my life around that time who would fill that gap; he saw something in me and wanted to help – enough to rescue me from that home and give me a fresh start. I've always called him my godfather. His name is Peter and I think he, more than anyone, is responsible for me becoming the person I am today.

CHAPTER TEN
Reaching my Century

6–16 July 2014

That Sunday night after the Coniston marathon, I got back in time to give Alexander a bath before putting him to bed with a story, so I was in Joanna's good books. Almost. When we sat down to dinner she wanted to know why I hadn't called her the whole weekend. We had the usual semi-playful conversation about it and I promised to try to text more, but first I needed to remember to take a phone with me. Apparently, Ali Parkes had been trying to get in touch with me the whole time, too. The truth was that I was struggling to keep up with any aspect of my life beyond running marathons, and all that was involved in doing that, so I wasn't giving enough attention to everything else.

Ali had decided to turn his Twitter page into a fan page for me to drum up awareness for what I was doing, hoping to reach big hitters such as Richard Branson, and try to get them involved somehow. We even talked about finding sufficient sponsorship so that I could stop working and concentrate on the running and the recovery between races. He was always on my case to go to some meeting or to re-tweet something – in short, exactly the sort of thing a good manager should do. It was what I'd asked him to do, but more and more I just wanted to switch off in between races and couldn't face the non-running aspect of my challenge.

Joanna suggested I gave Ali a quick call to chat about the weekend (which is easier said than done as he always has plenty to say), but we ended up talking for half an hour. We discussed the focus for the coming week, and how the fundraising and profile-building were coming on. He was concerned about my leg and checked I was doing all the exercises Pippa gave me. Ali mentioned that he had the attention of a journalist at *The Times* who wanted to cover my story. It was clear that no one was pressing more for my cause than Ali. If only we could work out a way to get the donations to pour in. It would be easier to run knowing that all my efforts were making a difference to the children I was trying to help.

Joanna wasn't best pleased as our conversation went on – I'd been away for the whole weekend, and now I was ignoring her. After I finished on the phone, we were able to relax together for a while and enjoy each other's company, but before I went to bed I looked on Facebook for a while to see how my page was doing. I always take the time to reply to my followers' comments. A simple reply lets them know they're appreciated and I'm listening. That evening my knee was still troubling me and I knew I needed to get more help with it. I put on a Geko strip to help it through the night. It was gone midnight by then, so I got in beside Joanna and was soon fast asleep.

I awoke the next morning and headed off for my 91st marathon. After some nice weather at the weekend and the week before, this time the rain came down. Splashing around Richmond Park in the early morning was cold but fun; I just had to be careful not to slip. I got through the run OK, though I was still limping along at times. Closing in on the 100 mark was a big deal for me. If my leg grew worse, I had already decided I would crawl to the finish if I had to, but hoped it wouldn't come to that. Crawling in a kilt might be a bit undignified.

I had the Wales marathon in Tenby lined up for the Sunday, but hadn't managed to find a marathon (that would have me) for the Saturday. I was enjoying my weekends away, running more and more official marathons. It wasn't for the shiny medals, but for the credibility that came with them. If I'm honest, I was also becoming a bit addicted to the whole marathon scene and the adventure of getting across the country between marathons, by whatever means possible. It gave me something different to look forward to, beyond the relentless routine of pounding out the miles round Richmond Park.

So I put the word out on Facebook to see if anyone knew of any marathons/ultra marathons I could do on the coming Saturday. Someone quickly told me about the Harden Hard'un, an ultra run in Yorkshire. It sounded perfect: boggy terrain, 27 miles long and 4000 feet of elevation! That should put me to the test, I thought. I gave them a call. It turned out they'd heard of me and were happy to have me along. The weekend promised to be a challenge logistically, with the marathon on Sunday in south Wales, 250 miles from Harden. I'd just have to deal with that when it came.

That week's running went well and my times were consistent, especially given my sore leg. However, the weather was rain and more rain. At first it was a nice change from the heat, but then it started making me cold and miserable. A bit of rain I can handle, but the big downer of the week was having my bike stolen from outside Richmond train station. I was really pissed off about that. It was an old rust bucket of a bike and couldn't have been worth anything to anyone but me – I needed it to get around each day. It meant travelling would take even more time out of my day, which I really didn't need, as I'd have to run to Richmond Park for the Thursday and Friday marathons, adding another three miles to my tired old legs.

On a brighter note, I was cheered up that week by getting to meet some key people from the NSPCC, along with the Dreams Come True representatives. I came away from that meeting confident my fundraising was in safe hands – it seemed we had a plan in place to spread greater awareness about what I was doing and get the donations pouring in.

Soon Friday night had arrived and I was packing my ruck-sack to the brim with clothes, towels, food, Geko strips, tent and all the rest of it. I said my goodbyes to Joanna and Buddy and gave them both a big hug, then I was on my way to Yorkshire for another adventure!

Largely thanks to Virgin Trains it was an easy (and partly free) journey north. It still took a while to get there, as I had to catch a train to Manchester, then a connection to Leeds before hopping on a bus to Bingley. So it was gone midnight when I finally arrived at the race start and assembled my tent, in ramshackle fashion, and crawled inside it for a few hours' sleep.

I went out like a light but ended up waking early, probably because I was so hungry. I got up and dug around in my bag for some food, finding some chicken sandwiches Joanna had put in there. Delicious! I had a can of Sprite, a bag of Doritos and a chocolate bar. There's nothing like a good hearty breakfast to start your day right (I guess that was nothing like a good hearty breakfast, but it would do).

It was a lovely, warm day but the run itself was tough right from the off. It didn't help that I went the wrong way after only two miles and had to double back on myself to find my way back onto the course. Nice one, Rob. What made the running so difficult was that a good half of it was across moorland that had become boggy thanks to all the rainfall we'd been having. Sticky and muddy underfoot, it slowed everyone down. We went up a lot of hills which then dipped back down across the valleys. It was a tough course, but it did grant some great views across the Yorkshire moors. We were exposed out there in rugged and beautiful countryside, and it was exhilarating, when you stopped long enough to appreciate it. There was some variety on the course, some big jumps across muddy expanses as well as barbed wire to negotiate, which I liked. It keeps the mind fresh when you have a variety of terrain and some obstacles to grapple with during a race.

At about the halfway point, we climbed up a big hill and I was reduced to walking. My mood began to darken; I wasn't in the best frame of mind by then and quite looking forward to getting this one out of the way. I spoke to some runners who could see I was struggling. Marathoners are always quick to encourage you when you start to flag and need a word in your ear or an arm around your shoulders.

I got lost again (somehow) at a set of crossroads when I took the wrong turning. Things grew a little quiet and I soon realised I was all on my own. Eventually I had the good sense to about-turn and return to those crossroads (by then they were not the only things that were cross). I ran at least an extra three miles that day, in addition to the official 27, which was not ideal. What is it with me and going the wrong way? I think I must drift off thinking about cakes and ice cream and Doritos.

People sometimes ask me what I think about when I'm running. The truth is anything and everything, like anyone else.

Running-wise I try to manipulate my mind, so I often tell myself I'm at mile 3 of the race. It never feels bad at mile 3. I do that till I reach mile 13, when I tell myself I've done six miles. Come on, Rob, you've only done six miles, you can do a few more. Then it's mile 20 and I tell myself: 'It's only a couple of five-k park runs left. You can do a park run, can't you?'

When I'm not thinking about the race, my mind will wander all over the place: 'How am I going to pay that gas bill? It's been due a while. Dog shit, watch out. If I jump over dog shit, does that make me a CrossFit athlete? What exactly is CrossFit anyway? Must remember to google that later on. Look, there's another runner, I'd better wave. Shall I wave? Yep, I'm totally gonna wave. OK. He didn't wave back, that's not very nice. I'm never waving again. Little fairy jump over the stone. So Parkour! Another runner, should I wave again? No, you'll get burned again. OMG she waved first. Hello! Did he just say it's a forty-mile race today? I thought it was thirty miles. Oh, well. That's just twenty miles each way. And I can do ten miles. It's only two five milers and I can run five miles easy. I think maybe I'll wait till the final reminder and then pay the gas bill. Or I could live in a tent. There'd be no more bills then. Joanna wouldn't like it, though. I wonder how Olivia's doing? Does she even remember me? Are we only three miles in? That's OK then . . .'

Fascinating stuff! Generally, I try to focus on the running, but sometimes I get distracted into other topics. That's probably when I get lost.

But at least I reached the finish. And there was a pub lunch after, which was awesome – fish and chips! It had taken me six and a half hours in all, so I think the course record was safe. I had met some great people here, like Sam and Andrea, a young couple who had helped me over the barbed wire. I came away feeling pretty good as it had been a challenge and I'd got through it. I kicked back at the pub for a bit, getting to know a few people and chatting about life and running, then I realised it was growing late and I needed to be on my way.

Once I'd completed it, I recognised it had been a cracking event and a real challenge. Going off course spoilt my day a little, but that was nobody's fault but my own. The food stations were great, plentiful and spread nicely throughout the run. I'd recommend it to anyone who likes to run up and down hills in beautiful surroundings and who wants a bigger challenge.

I had a long old journey ahead of me to reach Tenby for the next day's Wales marathon. How I would have loved a lift there and a couple of fast-food stops along the way. I managed to get a ride to Leeds station from Sam and Andrea so I could catch a train to Birmingham. By the time I arrived in Birmingham, I discovered I'd missed a really important connection and so wouldn't be able to take the last train across to Tenby. It was only a minor setback, really, but at the time I felt like crying. I don't know why, but I was becoming really emotional. Maybe it was losing my bike or maybe it was just exhaustion, but I was becoming convinced that things were going against me. They weren't, of course, I was just tired and my leg hurt. It was a moment of weakness and I quickly pulled myself together.

The lady at the information desk told me I'd have go via Bristol to get to Swansea now, and the next train was in two hours. I looked at my watch; I could already tell things were going to be a bit tight. It was then I had the brainwave of catching a taxi over to the Birmingham bus station to see if I could get a bus to Wales. It felt like a good idea at the time, albeit one born out of panic, but when I got there the bus station was deserted, with nobody to speak to, just a bunch of self-service ticket vending machines. And from what I could make out, every bus was headed either to London or Manchester.

I thought about finding the motorway and hitching a lift but decided against it. In the end, I started running back to the train station, but I got a bit lost, so I flagged down another taxi to ensure I didn't miss another train. I was running in circles like a headless chicken.

I spent the next 40 minutes sitting in the station, playing games on my phone, eating out of a supermarket bag and watching people come and go. As it was late, I was worried I might fall asleep, so I started walking around trying to keep awake. There was nothing for it but to keep moving forward and have a little faith that I'd reach my destination in the end.

Eventually, I caught that train out of Birmingham and a couple more trains later and I was in Swansea – it was the right country at least. It was about midnight by now, and I thought I might have to run from there, little realising it was still more than 50 miles away. Fortunately, I caught the last train to Carmarthen, which took me some way towards Tenby. When I looked it up on Google maps, I saw my destination was 26.2 miles away – just a marathon to go! It felt like I was jumping across a dozen stepping stones. I couldn't believe how difficult one journey could be.

Unsurprisingly after all that had happened, I drifted off only to wake up with a policeman looming over me, his sniffer dog at his side. It took me a moment to get my bearings.

'Everyone off. Come on, son. That means you as well.'

'Where are we?' I managed to ask.

'Carmarthen,' the policeman said. 'The oldest town in the Wales and the end of the line.'

I got my things together and stepped off the train into the cold night. It was 1am, and the race started in about eight hours' time and I still had to reach Tenby. Outside the train station there were lots of transport police wandering around. I chatted to one about what I was doing and how I needed to get over to Tenby for the race in the morning.

'I'll probably have to run there,' I told him.

'But Tenby's about twenty-five miles away!' he said.

'Yeah, I know, but I'm not getting another taxi. I've already paid for two of those today.'

I'll never forget the look on his face. He couldn't believe I was going to run all the way to Tenby. I might as well have told him I was going to fly to the moon. I didn't want to run there as I was in no mood for that, but I couldn't see any other way. It wouldn't be that bad. I might even get there in time to have a bit of sleep before the race. I walked away from the station and put my bag down to take out some water. I was just having a sip when a police car drove up alongside me, stopped and rolled down its window. It was the same policeman I'd just been talking to.

'You're not walking all the way to Tenby. Or running. I'll take you there. Hop in.'

So there I was, in a police car, bombing along the motorway to Tenby. At first I thought he was a bit angry with me and that he must have felt I'd given him no other choice but to give me a lift, but then he relaxed. I was really grateful, getting a police escort, any kind of escort, into Tenby in the middle of the night. I tried my luck and asked if we could put on the siren, but he wasn't up for that. He said that in return for the lift all he wanted was for me to let everyone know that the British Transport police are a good lot. That was the least I could do, I told him.

Half an hour or so later, we arrived in Tenby – at last. He asked me where I was staying and I told him I was booked into a hotel in town, as I didn't want him to worry about me or feel he had to pay for a hotel room. He'd done more than enough already. Those British Transport police guys are a really good lot. I said my goodbyes and thanked him for his kindness. It was just another example of a complete stranger going out of their way to help me out during the year.

Now I had to find somewhere to sleep.

I spent ages looking around for somewhere suitable to lay my tent down, but I couldn't find anywhere I thought I wouldn't be disturbed. I ended up chatting to some young women who were staggering back from a big night on the town. They were quite drunk but good fun with it. I quickly moved along and continued my search for a pitch. Eventually I found my way to the sea front and ended up throwing my tent down on some concrete between two boats parked there. I crawled inside my barely standing shelter and, though a little cold and uncomfortable, I was soon in the deep kind of sleep that only the truly exhausted know.

Morning arrived too soon, with seagulls landing on my tent and making a whole lot of noise. I looked at my watch; I had about an hour till the start of the race. I knew I needed to eat to make sure I didn't run out of energy again as I had done in my last marathon in Wales. I could do without that experience again.

It was a beautiful morning and it was lovely to feel the sea breeze on my face and hear the sound of the ocean. I made my way to a bakery in Tenby and had some chocolate croissants and an orange juice. Marathoners were descending on the town in great numbers. This was the Wales marathon after all, a big event.

If I had to choose, I tend to prefer the smaller events, with a couple of hundred people or fewer running them. They're more intimate and it's easier to get to know people there. But the big marathons have a different appeal; it's a bit like a carnival and sharing that experience with so many runners, as well as all the members of the public who come out to support, is pretty awesome.

I left my bag at the race HQ and made my way to the start line. Soon we were off and running through the town. The race was all on roads and fairly flat, with a few tasty hills thrown in, but nothing too hard. There were no great challenges or surprises out there, and you couldn't get lost so that was a bonus, too. The way my leg was feeling, I didn't fancy any extra miles. I'd been doing what I could to ease the pain, using a foam roller to ease the tightness in my legs, and a tennis ball on my sore heel, but I felt like I needed a professional massage to help more. Dominika would get a knock on her door later on, that's for sure.

The run was going well until about the seventh mile when I got to an aid station and decided to try some energy gels. I quite enjoyed the taste of them. I liked to have extra gels and food bars on me to give out to other runners who looked like they might need it. I had a few of them, but I was soon regretting it – my stomach felt awful. At about mile 15 I had to throw up by the side of the road. Somebody gave me a bottle of water and I chugged that down gratefully. I ended up stopping to throw up a couple more times before the race was over. Those energy gels clearly weren't for me.

Being repeatedly sick was unpleasant, but it didn't slow me down. If anything my empty stomach seemed to make me lighter and I flew through the final miles to record another sub four-hour marathon. After a slow run the day before, I was pleased with how I'd run, especially on only one and a half legs. The sun shone and I had some fun on the course with a few people, made some connections, and had some good conversations. Tenby puts on a fun and well-organised marathon, so if you want a big marathon on the coast and can get over there (by car preferably) then this race is well worth it. You will never forget the best finishing straight of any marathon I've ever done. The road is lined with red carpet for about 400m to the finish line. Trust me, no matter how tired you may be, as soon as you step on that carpet it turns you into a sprinter.

Fortunately, the journey back was easy enough and I had some sleep on the train. I wanted to go and see Joanna and Buddy straight away, but I needed to stop in at Dominika's first to see if I could have a massage. Fortunately, she was there and she was happy to get out her massage couch and work on my legs (I did wonder quite how happy though, with me turning up at 10.30pm on Sunday night). It was a very painful session, but it felt like it was doing a lot of good. She made the mistake of putting on some relaxing music, and by the time she'd finished I was fast asleep.

I woke up in the dark, face down on the massage table in the living room. I wanted to get up and start making my way back home, but I was just too tired so I lay there for a little bit. The next thing I knew I was waking up again, having nodded off for a second time. It was 4am. Shit! At least it wasn't 4pm – I think I could have slept that long if I'd been on something more comfortable. I got up and grabbed my shoes and things and slipped out the door without waking anyone. I walked up the road to Richmond Park and started that day's marathon, my 98th so far.

*

I first met my godfather, Peter, when I was nearly 12 years old. I enjoyed athletics and had joined a local club, going to training at the track every Tuesday and Thursday with competitions every weekend. It was a nice change of pace from the children's home, and a chance to get some head space. In those days I was a hammer thrower, mainly, with a bit of shot putt and pole vault thrown in, too. I wasn't particularly big for my age, but I had quick feet and I was stronger than I looked. Spinning around in a tight circle and letting it rip was something I really enjoyed, even though I was on my own more often than not, as it wasn't the most popular event.

I wanted to have a go at every event at the time, so I'd often wander over to the long jump pit and try that, or run with the sprinters for a session. I didn't care what the event was, I just liked to compete. If we went to a meet at the weekend and someone didn't turn up for their race, I'd always offer to take their spot, whether it was the steeplechase or the long jump, the 200m or the 1500m. I once ended up competing in eight events at one meet. Looking back now, I can see an appetite for lots of exercise was always there.

The hammer throwing area was right by the high jump, and there'd often be a session going on there at the same time. Peter was a high jump coach at the club, so he'd be down there helping them with their technique, giving advice and encouragement. He was a quietly spoken guy, but he had a good way with the kids and people felt they could trust him. He didn't put up with any nonsense either. Over time we began chatting and we started getting to know each other from there.

When he found out about my situation and my background, he wanted to know more. He was easy to talk to and soon I was telling him things I hadn't told many other people. He listened to some of my frustrations at the time, mainly around my lack of education and my difficulties at school. He worked as the deputy headmaster at a private school, so this was something he knew all about.

Eventually, he started inviting me out at the weekend to do things with him, in order to give me a break from the children's home. He didn't have any family of his own and we enjoyed each other's company. I was glad to be out of the home and I liked being around Peter. He was always explaining how something worked or why it was how it was. It seemed there was nothing he didn't know. I was hungry for learning so I lapped it all up.

Once he came to pick me up from the home I was in and saw at first hand what it was like: the noise, the chaos, the lack of privacy and, always, a hint of menace. He could see right away it wasn't somewhere you could be at ease. It made a big impression on him, I think, so he started trying to help get me out of there. He contacted social services and asked them if I could stay at his place from time to time. They had to do all their usual checks on him, of course, which seemed to take a long time, but eventually he received their approval and I started staying over for weekends with him.

It was relaxing to have a quiet place where I didn't have to watch my back all the time. And Peter's was always quiet. Unless there was classical music playing, there was just the sound of your own thoughts. After the noise and outbursts of aggression in the home, it took a bit of getting used to. We got on really well and spending more time with him was easy from the start. I had my space and he had his, if we needed it. We became like a father and son, although I worried it could all disappear at any moment so I didn't rely on it. I just took it for what it was: a better thing and an opportunity to have some peace.

By the time I was 13, Peter had applied to be my legal guardian so I moved into his house and out of the children's home for good. That was the end of that chapter of my life in a care home. There wasn't a single thing I missed about it.

Peter was working on my education full time now. I'd missed so much school that there were huge gaps in my basic understanding. He taught me everything from how to read and write better, to history, geography and also moral lessons, understanding about values and how to conduct myself. It was probably a bit like being at a finishing school, except with most things Peter had to help with the start and the middle before we could get around to the finishing.

I remember how he used to let me sleep in an extra hour on the weekend before waking me with a nice cup of tea. He had some really old-fashioned but good ways. This was how he had been brought up. I felt safe now, for the first time, in a room all to myself, with someone around to look out for me and show me what life was about.

He taught me everything from how to set a table for a five-course meal to how to listen to classical music and what programmes to watch on TV. He liked *Antiques Roadshow* and *Mastermind*, which was fine by me as I enjoyed them, too. I remember he got almost every answer correct, before the contestants could even open their mouth. I told him he should have gone on those shows, and felt sure he would have won.

From Peter I'd learn about respecting others and how to look after my appearance (I know it doesn't show, so he clearly didn't do a good job on that one). It was an intensive period of catching up on all the things I'd missed. Without those evenings, studying and learning things, under Peter's careful supervision, it's difficult to say in what direction my life might have gone.

*

I ran my 100th marathon/ultra on the evening of Wednesday 16 July 2014, 94 days after starting out on this challenge. It hadn't been easy, but I had reached my first really significant milestone. A lot had changed in those 94 days. I'd lost quite a bit of weight, and a few toenails. I'd raised about £10,000 for good causes. And I'd discovered a passion for endurance running.

To be honest, I don't think I'd ever been happier in my whole life.

Ricky from Up & Running had rallied a good crowd of local friends and their family to come out for my 100th marathon, which I was doing in the evening after work so others could more easily join me. There was a pretty good turnout, with about 30 to 40 people there in all. Most of them I knew, but there were a few new faces there as well. I felt a bit awkward to be at the centre of all this attention, but really pleased at the same time. Quite a few children came along, some to run and others on their bikes. I liked to see kids get excited about what I was doing. That was probably the most gratifying thing of all.

Dominika's massage on Sunday had really helped and the pain in my leg seemed to have gone – only to turn up lower down my leg. Still, I was glad it was on the move. Maybe it would slip out through my toes and into the ground eventually!

For the first few miles it was, as always, a case of getting my jelly legs awake and out of their slumber. I was chatting with the little gang of cyclists and runners who were joining me, and it was fun. The occasion and the support gave me strength and I felt good throughout. As I've said, I usually taper off in the second half of a marathon, after running a quick first half, but knowing there was cake and champagne at the finish I pushed on at pace and finished in 3 hours 26 minutes, which is pretty quick for me.

A few more people were at the finish to see me. It was a real moment – sipping champagne, sharing all this excitement that others had for what I was doing. Physically I was hurting, although I didn't show it, and I was disappointed about the fundraising I'd managed so far, but this made it all worthwhile. Every step. Sharing moments with others and seeing that my efforts have reached people is why I run – to make those connections and bring people together. I can't think of a better reason.

And I was chuffed to reach 100 marathons/ultras. I'd always told everyone about the 367 that were my goal, but the more I ran the more I realised that would require some kind of miracle. I kept my mind positive, but the fact remained my body was falling apart with the stress and the sheer mileage I was putting it through – and I was only a little more than quarter the way through my challenge. There was never any time to rest before I was back running again. How long could I go on for like this? It was hard to tell, but I knew it wasn't going to be forever. Could I really last as long as 365 days? I told myself, repeatedly, that I could.

I was going to need all of that positive thinking, because I had my toughest challenge to date ahead of me. That coming weekend I'd be running my first ever 100km (63.75 mile) event, the legendary Race to the Stones.

CHAPTER ELEVEN
It's All About The Times

17 July–3 August 2014

The Race to the Stones is a 100km race in the south of England, following a route used by travellers for thousands of years. Starting in the Chiltern Hills in Oxfordshire, it goes through two designated Areas of Outstanding Natural Beauty on its way to the finish at the ancient circle of stones in Avebury. By all accounts, it was quite an undertaking. Signing up for it was a big moment for me. I knew it was going to be tough, but I wanted people to know what I was capable of, to see I was for real. Crazy as it might sound, I still felt I had something to prove.

I'd signed up for it only the week before. People in my camp thought I was mad to do it – and with good reason – but I was sure this was for me. I was made to do this, I thought. To prove it, I was going to put extra miles all around it. I felt unstoppable.

The weekend properly got underway at 12.20 on the Saturday morning when I met up with a friend, Samantha, who had agreed to cycle with me while I ran the 30 miles to Lewknor for the start of the race (which I count as one of my marathons). While the record I was chasing was always going to be 'unofficial', as not all of my marathons were run in official races, with chip timings, marshals and other competitors, it was important to me that I had my own rulings for them. I had decided a marathon had to begin and end on the same day for it to count, so I always started after midnight or finished before midnight. And when I was running a long ultra, such as this 100km race, I counted it as only one marathon, even though it was more than double the 26.2 mile distance, because it was part of the one race.

It was a warm night and it was great having Samantha for company. We wore down the miles, stopping once at a McDonald's for some burgers. People in the running community don't usually have much good to say about fast food, but I feel you can't beat it for calories intake. When you're doing multiple marathons, you need to replace those calories. Healthy eating alone won't get you there, so you need to mix it up. The great thing about fast food is it has lots of calories, but then you're hungry again quite soon after. That's the time to add your healthy foods: lean meats, rice or pasta and vegetables. If you can eat both these types of meals in balance, then you're in the best position to handle multiple days of marathoning. I had the fast-food side of that diet sorted, but unfortunately I still needed to work on the healthy bit.

I was pumped, as I say, and kept a nice pace up for that 30-miler to the race start. I arrived there by about 5.30am and had a couple of hours' sleep in a quiet corner of a field there. It was warm, so I was comfortable and drifted off easily.

There were a couple of different races: a one-day event and a two-day, more leisurely affair, for walkers as well as runners, so the start line was a real mixture. Among them were hardened ultra-runners, still with sand on their desert caps from their last Marathon des Sables, as well as sprightly groups of walkers, with walking canes, ready for the two-day hike. The contrast was amusing.

There was a good atmosphere at the start of the race. Many in the group were nervous, as some were taking on the distance for the first time, and wondering what they had let themselves in for. I was tired after my morning running, but chatting with the others livened me up and got me in the mood for a race (that and the cup of coffee with nine sugars).

Soon the klaxon had sounded and we were off.

There was a great variety of terrain during this race which kept things interesting, with paths through fields, rutted trails and rockier throughways along the way. Although the overall elevation for the race was over 4,000 feet, there were no ridiculously steep ascents to take on – just a whole lot of undulating hills and the course was almost never completely flat. We ran through muddy ditches and across vast poppy fields, over the River Thames and through forests and down chalky hills. It was a hot and humid day, so we were all struggling with the heat as much as the mileage.

Fortunately there were plenty of aid stations, evenly spaced out over the course, so you were never far from some refreshment and a chance to have a breather. And the marshals couldn't have been more keen to help. I joked with them and other people on the course and there was a very friendly, light spirit among runners once it was all underway. My body was in good shape, all things considering, but I was mentally tired. The lack of sleep was catching up on me. That and the hot weather combined to make the first half of the race quite hallucinatory at times.

By the time I'd reached the halfway point, the sky had grown dark and cloudy. It looked like rain was imminent. I ate some sandwiches and pasta, and took on some water before getting going again. Pretty soon those clouds opened and the rain came down. Only it wasn't rain – it was hailstones the size of pound coins pouring down on our heads – all accompanied by great booms of thunder and blinding flashes of lightning. It was epic!

The drop in temperature that came with it was a welcome relief and the hail was, well, interesting. I carried on running while others sought cover. Running while getting pelted with hail was a bit like having some sort of pressure massage on the go (I took a few blows to the skull but luckily there's not much to damage under there). As long as I wasn't knocked unconscious I'd be fine, and at least it kept me awake.

After the downpour, the rest of the course was covered in puddles and thick mud. It became really hard for me at about the 75km point and I needed some encouragement from others to carry on. I remember I stopped and sat on a log for a while to get out of the rain. It turned out I just needed a rest and then I felt fine again. My body was OK, and apart from the usual aches and general soreness I was in good shape.

Eventually, some 13 hours after setting off, I saw the famous stones in the distance and the finish line. I was relieved to have made it around in one piece. Apparently someone fell and broke their arm on the course, which is always sad to hear. I chatted to some great guys at the finish and shared what food and drink I had with them. Some of the finishers looked pretty beat up. I probably didn't look a million dollars myself. So that was my first 100km race, run and done. Not a bad feeling, I can tell you.

Now I needed to get home. We were in the middle of nowhere and I needed a lift back to civilisation, and preferably all the way to London. Luckily for me, I asked around and someone was going right past my flat. We set off and I was home by about midnight and in a hot bath. Then I slid in beside my sleeping fiancée.

At 5am the next morning, I was up. After grabbing some fresh clothes for my bag and kissing Joanna and my son, I was out the door for the next leg of the weekend's adventure. My legs felt very stiff still and sore, but they would hold up fine for a few more miles yet.

A tube, a train and an hour and a half later, I was in Stevenage at the race HQ for the Fairlands Valley Challenge. Ahead of me was a 50km trail race. Everyone kept talking about how easy it was to get lost out there. They were studying their maps and trying to work it all out. This was not what I needed. I could get lost in a two-bedroom apartment, so I would have to keep another runner in sight at all times and hope they knew where they were going. They gave me a map, but I put it in my bag and never took it out again.

Fortunately, once the race got underway, I teamed up with a guy who had run the race before and knew what he was doing. He was going my kind of pace (not fast), so I stuck with him and watched the miles tick away. It would be a just-get-around race for me. My legs were like jelly and I clearly hadn't eaten enough to be doing this. A bit like the Runfest marathon in Wales, I'd bitten off more than I could chew here, but I was making the best of a bad job.

It was a race across bridleways, footpaths and tracks in the, by all accounts, beautiful Hertfordshire countryside, but it was just plain nightmarish for me. I finished, though. I was cold and tired and just wanted to get back, though you probably wouldn't have known it if you'd spoken to me at the time. I am an expert at looking OK when feeling the opposite and saying everything is fine. I certainly wasn't going to share my anguish with anyone there, but inside I was hurting like crazy.

After a night's recovery in a warm bed, I was back out running my 107th marathon/ultra in Richmond Park on Monday morning, 21 July, like clockwork. Did I feel more tired than usual that morning after the weekend's exertions? I don't think so. I was tired and sore all right, but that was a given. I think I felt rejuvenated by the knowledge that I was able to run as far as I had. It had given me a boost. I wondered what else I was capable of doing.

I'll admit that at this stage I started getting slightly carried away. Whether you call that being over-reaching or exploring my vocation is a matter of opinion. All I knew was, I was loving the challenges, and had plans to run further. The more daunting the races I set myself, the more it put me on my mettle. And the more alive I felt, which explains why, that night, I signed up to a 100-mile race – the North Downs Way 100 – which was taking place in three weeks' time. It was an off-road race across the Farnham hills, and it had the reputation for being the toughest 100-miler in the UK, and I hoped to cover those 100 miles in 24 hours. In fact, I'd need to if I was going to do another marathon the next day. It didn't leave much room for things going wrong.

Now that was an exciting prospect.

Later that week, Matt Dickinson, a journalist from *The Times*, turned up to run with me. It turned out he lived locally and had heard what I was doing. So I told him about my background and why I was running, and answered his many questions. He was good company and I felt he understood what I was doing and why.

Dominika and Pippa both saw me that week, too. I'd

come to rely on both of them for their strong hands and words of advice – more and more my running was becoming a team effort. That weekend I had two regular marathons to run, one on the Saturday and one on the Sunday – nothing ultra, nothing very sexy. How could I make the weekend a little more interesting, I wondered?

The first marathon was in Northampton. I thought: why not run there? That would add an extra challenge to the weekend. A bit of drama. Like I said, I was getting carried away by then.

So that Friday started, as usual, with an early-morning Richmond Park marathon, followed by a day at work. Afterwards, though, instead of heading home I hitched on my backpack and laced up my shoes for a through-the-night run to Northampton. I left work at 5.30pm and got the Metropolitan line from Finchley Road to Watford. I'd figured that running straight from work was a bit of a risk. Northampton was almost 70 miles away and I might not cover that many miles in time for the race start the next morning, so I got to Watford first and started my running from there. It was at least 15 miles closer to the race and gave me a cushion. I thought I might even arrive in time to put my head down and sleep before the marathon began.

From Watford, it was straight up the A roads passing through the occasional town or village. They were busy roads and surely even I couldn't get lost on them. It was pretty noisy, of course, with all the cars whizzing by my ear all night, but I made great progress. I turned my head torch on when it grew dark. I was in a really good mood that night, bouncing along like a kid with a brand new toy.

I began to think about what my next challenge would be when I had completed this one. All sorts of crazy ideas for adventures flashed through my head as I made my way along: swimming the Amazon in a kilt, walking to the North Pole backwards, swimming the Amazon backwards.

I stopped at a Chinese restaurant somewhere on the route and ordered a couple of portions of rice to go. I walked and ate the rice as I went – eating on the move is part of the ultra marathon way. I ran through the night to Northampton and for the last few miles, once I'd left the safety of the A roads, I did manage to get lost. I don't quite know how that happened, but at five in the morning I wasn't thrilled about it. I ended up going down a winding road for a mile or two before realising I was meant to be on a larger road parallel to it. I was in no mood to turn back on myself, so I decided to try to cut through some fields to get there. I jumped over a barbed wire fence and weaved my way through nettles and thorn bushes. Then I came across a small river. 'Are you serious?' I thought. I realised it wasn't a great idea to keep going, but I was stubborn. I waded through the river, up to my knees in water, then there were more nettles and thorns on the other bank. Finally, though, I saw the road I was looking for. Thank God!

I ended up arriving at the race HQ, a Holiday Inn, at about 5.50am, having run over 56 miles according to my GPS watch. I was pretty tired and tried to sleep in the reception. I managed to zonk out for an hour, but there were too many people coming and going after that.

I had some breakfast there and chatted with a few guys who I'd seen at various marathons over the summer, Tiago, Steve, Denys, Lance and Jez. They were knowledgeable marathoners with lots of races under their belt. They'd been doing this far longer than me and had lots of great advice, about nutrition and running strategy. I listened carefully to what they had to say. They were passionate about sharing their knowledge and were concerned that I could be helping myself out more than I was. I don't imagine any of them thought my way of getting to the race was the best of ideas! If you're going to get into this world, then seek out those kinds of guys at the races. You'll be glad you did.

The race itself, Summer Around the Reservoir, was six laps around the Brackmill reservoir. It was a pretty featureless course, but flat as a pancake and having challenged myself by running there, I thought there was nothing wrong with one of those on my schedule, I can tell you.

After completing that without any problems, I took a train down to Bath and began the task of finding somewhere to stay the night. I met a student on the way down who said I could probably rent a room in halls at the university for the night. That sounded cheap, so when I arrived I went to the university and had a good night's sleep in some modest but adequate student digs.

The Bath Running Festival marathon the next day got underway at 9am. Bath is a beautiful city, as everyone knows, but it's also very hilly – at least the area surrounding the city is. I knew the course had more than 2,100 feet of elevation so it was going to be a tough afternoon. I didn't realise just how tough, until we began. The klaxon sounded and we rushed off into the woods. After a bit of a loop around the university grounds, we wound our way through woods and fields before heading downhill. I was in the leading group at about the two-mile stage and going well. Then there was a bit of confusion as we reached the bottom of the hill. Someone said it looked like we were off course, so we turned back and went looking for other runners.

We were now heading uphill. On the way up we bumped into some more runners, as lost as we were, coming towards us. It was chaos and I couldn't stop laughing. I love that kind of stuff; I find it hilarious. It was like we were all in a Carry On movie. Carry on Running.

Eventually we found the course again. Now the faster runners were behind the slower runners, which was interesting. I made a big push to get back up into the lead and went by a whole lot of runners. It was all very scenic and flat as we ran along a canal. Then came the first uphill: Fosse Way. It started off as tarmac and then regressed into gravel, then dirt as it kept on going up and up for a good mile or so. When we got to the top, it levelled off for a while before heading steeply down through some woodland.

Then we reached the real hill.

That second hill was seriously steep. I'd learn later it had a 25 per cent incline! I clambered my way up it. All the way up, you could hear nothing but the pants of the racers, mumbling to themselves, cursing under their breaths. We were all humbled by that gnarly, muddy, rocky gully and glad to eventually reach its summit. We weren't halfway into the race yet, but I was pretty tired already. At the top was an aid station and I had some cakes and drank some coke. I stopped for a while to get my breath back, while other runners sat on the dusty ground, looking ruined. This wasn't a marathon – it was an assault course.

I got going again and there were more downhills, uneven ground and steep inclines. Eventually I stood on top of Little Solsbury Hill and looked out over the whole city. We had covered some ground by then, that's for sure. I chatted to some great people at this race and was my usual sociable self. I remember someone telling me that if I liked hills I should go to the Cheddar Gorge marathon in a few weeks' time. I made a mental note.

I was never meant to be a runner –
I'd always preferred cycling. Here I
am on the way to a bronze medal
in the European triathlon.

Early days in my challenge,
and after all I'd been through
in my childhood I knew I
wanted to raise money to help
children.

However, when you ask children
for advice on what to wear
during a race, you don't always
get the most practical suggestions.

Where it all began: Richmond Park. The marathon course here would become very familiar to me over the year.

After a lucky break the night before, when we'd been offered some wonderful free accommodation by the beach, I was able to relax and enjoy myself at the end of the Endurancelife Flete marathon in May.

Things weren't always so luxurious. This was one of my better attempts at putting up my tent the night before a race.

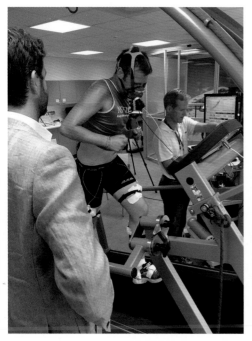

Dr Kipps looks on as I do some tests on my running style.

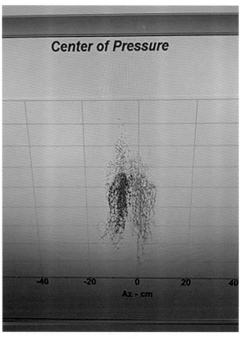

This chart shows how my running economy and foot placement was the key to my ability to keep on running as I have a perfect strike.

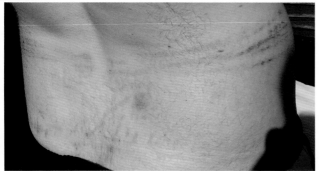

Sadly, while my footwork might have been good, my kilt did cause some problems, leaving some painful reminders.

Ali Parkes, me, Mo Farah, Joanna and Lorna Parkes. Ali and his wife did so much to help me.

The Scafell Pike trail was a really tough ultra – made all the more difficult after I had a spectacular fall. That evening, Ricky Lightfoot gave me some great advice about running downhill.

In serious pain during the North Downs Way 100 in August, after being stung by a lot of wasps – as if the race wasn't tough enough anyway.

After the Enigma Reverse marathon, when John Edmonds had to force me to get out of bed, and I realised that I had so many people backing me to complete my challenge – it was a real team effort.

After a long journey to get there, I was proud to be among the leaders in the challenging Ennerdale 50k race that took us through some spectacular scenery.

I accumulated a huge pile of medals during my year of marathons and ultras, but it was never about that.

All together at the start of the Race Across USA – but not everyone would be able to reach the finish line.

I ran with this lion for many miles, but in the end I had to leave it by the roadside for someone else to find.

The Race Across USA was also designed to encourage children to get involved in running – so when we had some kids come out to support us, it made it all worthwhile.

Jup Brown and I ready to take on our latest challenge in Arizona: paddling across the river on a mattress.

Near Roswell, and the conditions became almost impossible to run in as the roads became like a skating rink.

But it was all worth it, as there waiting to greet me were Joanna and Alexander. It was time to go home again.

Richard Branson joins in a publicity shot I did for the London marathon – the event that had first inspired me to take up my challenge.

Rob Hutchings gave me a lift on his motorbike to and from the London marathon to ensure I could keep on my schedule.

The sign in the background during the London marathon spells it out: 370 marathons in 365 days. It was just a bit of running.

The race continued steeply downhill before we reached the turning point. Knowing we were halfway was a comfort, but the thought of running the same inclines again was not. I do love a challenge, though, and this was certainly that. Somewhere along the way I got fully committed to this one. It needed all I had and that's what I gave it. I was used to resting in the second half of the marathon, beginning the recovery process – but not today. Today was a case of leaving it all on the mountain (or on the hill in this case).

Soon I was cutting through the university and breaking the finish line. My 115th marathon/ultra was done and it had been a good one, right up there with the toughest courses I'd ever raced. A time of just shy of five hours was respectable, too. I'd run flatter courses in the same time, so my fitness and endurance levels were clearly growing.

On 29 July my story went national, and it became the beginning of a week of media for me. I started off running my usual morning marathon, but this time with a twist. On finishing my run, an ITV news team turned up to interview me for a slot later that evening. The reporter and the whole crew were great. They were fascinated by what I was doing, though again it was a bit awkward for me, being the centre of attention. I think I coped OK, joking about with the reporter, asking him to join me on a run one morning. I tend to turn the questions on the reporters in my interviews, perhaps as an attempt to divert the focus onto somebody else. I think I'd rather be the one asking the questions than answering them.

Being interviewed is one of those things you get better at and I was just starting out – I'd never done something like this before and was unsure of myself. I felt like I was stumbling, saying some dumb things and getting tongue tied, but I tried to get the main message across and just hoped they'd focus on the charities in the edit. The interview meant I was late for work, and I was dreading explaining it away to my boss. I was certain that doing interviews for national TV would only make Ken even more annoyed than he already was.

As if that wasn't enough, Matt Dickinson's article about me came out in *The Times* the same morning. He'd written a full-page piece all about what I was doing and why, about my background and my fundraising goals. All this in one of the most important newspapers in the world – it was a great read and I couldn't have hoped for more. Again, I was a little embarrassed to see myself spread all over the paper like that, but I knew it was good for my fundraising goals. I just hoped Ken was reading another newspaper that day.

Everyone at work soon found out about the article and I spent the rest of that day getting my back slapped and being told how 'it was all going to take off now'. I didn't see my boss, though; Ken was in his office that day. A storm was brewing, I could feel it.

I was worn out from the weekend and all that extra attention wasn't entirely welcome. Don't get me wrong, I was grateful and pleased at the same time. This was what I had wanted after all, but the media side of things, the spotlight being on me, would take a bit of getting used to and I'd always be happier when the cameras were off.

Marathon Man media week continued the next day when I was interviewed again in the park, this time by the National Forces TV channel. As an ex-Royal Signaller, they were interested in what I was doing and why. It was the same old rigmarole, but I think I felt a bit more comfortable this time.

Beat up as I was, physically, looking back I think all that

media exposure gave me a bit of a boost and some added purpose. I felt pumped up all week and was always on the lookout for more miles to run. It was as though I had extra energy I needed to expend. My times around the Richmond Park course got quicker, too. The best effect of the publicity was that I got a lot more visitors to my website and a fair few more donations to my charities.

On the Thursday that week, after my morning marathon in the park, I was invited to the Institute for Sport, Exercise and Health (ISEH) in central London to undergo some tests. Dr Kipps and his team were going to look at my running stride and my physical capacity to see if anything interesting could be learned from me.

I turned up with Dominika, who had asked to join me for the session to see what she could learn from it herself. We met Dr Kipps and head physio Bruce Paton who soon got various sensors and wires clipped to me to measure my performance on the treadmill. I was interested what they might find out.

They ran a number of tests that day. They tried to do some muscle testing, but because of my sore knee it was difficult to measure both legs as they would have liked. They did a VO2 max test and a cardiopulmonary exercise test, which meant doing a fair bit of running on the treadmill, wearing a mask to measure oxygen consumption, carbon dioxide production and so on. I ran at different speeds for them to see what difference that might make.

I looked like Bane from the Batman film *The Dark Knight Rises* in that mask. We had a few laughs about it, but apparently it was not the first time that joke had been cracked. After a fair amount of exertion, the results came out. They were interesting.

The VO2 max test measures your lung capacity and is one way of measuring your fitness levels. My results showed I had a decent level of fitness, what you might expect from your average 3-hour 30-minute marathon runner, but there was nothing exceptional there at all. I was quite fit, but not ridiculously so.

Next up, were the results of the cardiopulmonary exercise test. This measured how well my lungs, heart and muscles worked together when I exercised, how efficient I was at using the oxygen I breathed while running. It turned out my anaerobic threshold was pretty high, which means I'm pretty efficient at using oxygen and can exert myself for longer than most people without getting a build-up of lactic acid in my bloodstream. That's what gives you that burning sensation when you run (and makes you want to give up and eat chocolate in the bath instead). Here, apparently, I'm better than average, but still not outstanding.

There was one aspect, however, where I really did stand out, where I'm top of the class, and that was in running economy. The treadmills at the institute have sensors on them that measure exactly where your feet land each time and with what degree of pressure. When I was asked to run at my favoured 3-hour 30-minute marathon pace, then I landed in almost the exact same spot under my body each time. There was almost no variation between each step. And that was exceptional, apparently. When I had to run a bit of faster or slower, the consistency of my feet placement decreased, but at my most comfortable pace I had an incredibly uniform stride pattern, which was comparable to elite runners, so they told me.

So that was it. I wasn't particularly fit, but my body used oxygen pretty efficiently and my running style wasted very little effort. I was like a running machine. Wind him up and off he goes – not superhuman, just super steady.

How disappointing is that?

Dominika and I left the institute that afternoon and went back to Sheen. I'd taken the day off work and done my marathon, so I had this big thing ahead of me I barely recognised: free time. It made a nice change. Now, what to do with it? She said she was off to do some hot yoga in Richmond, which sounded interesting, so I joined her.

Hot yoga is hot, I can confirm. It was quite a workout, too, and a whole different kind to the running I was doing. All that stretching and bending probably did me a lot of good – it was exhausting but also energising. I came out thinking, 'Right, what's next?' I wanted to run somewhere, but Dominika told me not to be so silly and to go home and rest.

You know she's really no fun. No fun at all.

With no official race for me on 2 August, I ran the Richmond Park marathon route in the morning before completing a 5k park run after that. As I've mentioned, I love the spirit of the park runs which were encouraging so many to take up exercise, and I also knew a few of the regulars, so I tried to get along to as many of them as possible during the year.

After running that, I popped in to see the boys down at Sheen Sports and then went to see Ricky Wood at Up & Running. I probably got in their way and made their busy Saturday period even more hectic, and ended up giving away free laces, though the way Ricky looked at me suggested he hadn't factored those into his marketing budget for the day.

I went home to shower and then packed for the Dovedale Dipper race, which was up in the Peak District. I had a big lunch, with lots of chicken, pasta and salad, and a bowl of ice cream for after. I was now race ready! After taking the train up to Stockport, a taxi driver told me I was still almost 30 miles from Bakewell and the race HQ, which would cost me £60 at least. Well, that's never going to happen, I thought.

I decided to run to Bakewell. Inadvertently, I took the scenic route too (not the best idea when you're running through the night) after I got lost, so what should have been only a little over 28 miles ended up being almost 40 miles according to my GPS. It was a pretty eventful night all in all. I set out at about 10pm from Stockport and I was quite keen to get where I was going.

About an hour into my running I passed through a village and stopped in a pub to fill up my water bottle. While I was standing at the bar, looking a bit of an odd man out, drenched in sweat and with a lamp tied to my forehead, some guys started talking to me. Needless to say they'd had a few to drink. I filled them in on what I was doing and where I was headed. They insisted I have a drink with them, so they ordered me an Amaretto and coke. I didn't want it, but I didn't want to offend them either.

'I probably shouldn't,' I said. 'Seeing as I've got a long way to run still.'

'Just the one then, come on,' he said. 'It's Friday night, man!'

'OK, then, just the one. Thanks.'

It's Peter's fault for teaching me to be so polite.

I thanked the guys and wandered outside with my bottle of water and my Amaretto and coke. I paused to get some crisps from my bag. Then I got chatting with another guy and a group of women, who said I should come out partying with them. I told them about my running, of course, and that prompted the guy to pull out his mobile and ring a friend.

'You've got to meet Derek,' he said. 'Hold on a second. This guy's a runner like you. A crazy guy.'

I was still 20 miles from where I needed to be and I really just wanted to get away, but in the end I went to meet Derek in another pub across the way. This wasn't in my plan, but for some reason I was going along with it. Derek was a local soldier and we chatted about running for a couple of minutes before I decided to carry on and not get involved in some big party.

I continued on my way and pretty soon it got very dark going down country lanes with no lighting and thick tree canopies overhead. It was like being in a tunnel at times. It went on like this for a while, with me hoping to God I was going the right way and wishing my head lamp worked a bit better.

Then I heard what sounded like a woman's scream. I heard it again, only more muffled this time. It could have been a man or a woman, I wasn't sure. I was terrified and a cold shiver ran down my back. Now I just wanted to find a taxi and get out of there, but I was in the middle of nowhere and there were no cars around for miles.

I stopped for a second: what was out there? Unsure, I turned around and started to make my retreat. Then I stopped again: you don't have time for this, Rob; you've got to keep moving. So I plucked up the courage to run into the darkness towards where the screams had come from. In the end, I ran as fast as I could, not looking back, and just put the burners on. The dark country lanes were making me really jumpy and I wanted to be at the race. Then I saw a campsite to my left, probably where the scream had come from. It all looked quiet and peaceful. I was obviously being paranoid: too much running, not enough sleep. I was shattered by now and swerving as I ran at times. I remember stopping by the side of the road and lying down for a minute. I even tried to sleep, but I was too cold, so I got up and kept going.

A few miles later, the sun came up between the hills of the Peak District. It was absolutely stunning. I was freezing cold, though, and stopped to put on all my clothes at one point. I had everything on me, including my blanket over my head. If you know the movie *Cool Runnings*, there's a scene when all the Jamaican guys get out of the airport in Calgary. They've never been in cold weather before and they're so cold they put on all their clothes. Well, that was me in the Peak District. I probably scared the life out of all the people driving by in their cars.

It took me over seven hours to get into Bakewell and I was glad to arrive. It was about 5.30am when I finally reached the race HQ in the little village of Hartington. I went inside the village hall and tried to warm up, then I had some food to eat, and chatted to runners as they arrived to register for the race.

The race itself was a good one, with beautiful surroundings and lots of hills, all on trails. I was starting to take that kind of scenery for granted, but sometimes you'd turn a corner and the sun would be shining a certain way and you'd just be blown away by a view. Occasionally, you'd be hurting too much to appreciate it, though. That's the yin and yang of marathon running for you. I wanted more of it and, less than four months into my challenge, I was sure I was going to get it.

CHAPTER TWELVE
One Hundred Miles and More

4–10 August 2014

I'd kept on trying to push myself harder and harder, but now I had to get ready for the 100-mile race coming up on Saturday 9 August. That meant massage and physio, healthy eating (plus fast food) and, best of all, hot-tub breakfasts!

Hot-tub breakfasts were a treat that summer and something that really helped keep me going. Ali had a hot tub in his back garden. He and other MMUK team members (including Ben, Johnny, Paul, Dustin and Lorna) and their children would join me for the last lap of my marathon runs, on bike or by foot, and then we all went back to Ali's for a hot tub.

Ali's wife Lorna would make us toast and eggs and bacon while we all chatted and joked in the hot tub (she was an absolute star all year, and I couldn't have made it without her amazing food!). The weather was usually good that summer, but even when it rained we'd still all pile in. I think we overstretched its capacity at times and I got a telling-off from Pippa and Dominika for 'risking infection' at one point. I don't know what she meant. How could six sweaty men in one small pool of hot water possibly be an environment for germs?

I even did some radio interviews on the phone from that hot tub. If you can't come across as relaxed in hot water and with jet-propelled bubbles massaging you, then you really do need a holiday.

I also saw Dr Kipps that week to have my left leg looked at, which was still sore and had become an issue. It turned out my sore knee was because of bursitis, which meant I had a sack of fluid on my knee that had built up from the trauma of running and now that sack had ruptured, leaking fluid into the muscles in my leg, which made them swollen as well. Dr Kipps opted to drain what fluid was left in my knee in the hope that would help. He said I should have an anaesthetic for this, but I didn't have time for that, so he just put the needle into the back of the knee and drew out the fluid. 'That'll reduce the swelling and should alleviate some of the pain and the stiffness,' he assured me.

Of course, I should then have rested my leg for a few days before resuming any exercise. Maybe I could have hired a cottage somewhere, with a sea view and sat with my leg up all week, watching the ocean, while someone brought me freshly cooked food and tended to my every need. In some other version of my life, in some other corner of the universe, that's exactly what I would have done. As it was, I had marathons to run and donations to raise.

An old friend, Adam, came down that week and ran his first marathon with me. It seemed as though almost everyone I knew wanted to run one now – even Ali had pledged to run one before the year was out. It was the summer of marathon fever and I was loving being part of it.

That was the fun side of things, but I also had a bit of a

showdown at work that week. It had been coming for a while now, so it was no surprise. From my point of view, things had been going well at work. I'd been arriving and finishing on time and getting things done in between. OK, I did nod off on a few occasions, but it wasn't often. The rest of the time I was as productive as ever and profitability continued to rise. We were taking on more work than ever, so it was a fraught time and stressful for everyone concerned at times.

My boss felt that my running was a distraction from the business. His point was that if I could do what I was doing while running all those miles, then how much more could I contribute if I wasn't running. I believed I was still doing a good job, and the challenge of the running meant I was happy, too, so I hoped he would be supportive during this period. I felt we had become more than just employer and employee, after all. Ken was like a mentor to me, a friend and someone I'll always respect.

On the Tuesday that week, Ken told me I needed to choose between work and running. He said I couldn't do both. I snapped back and told him that was unfair, and we agreed to discuss it at the end of the day. As I waited I thought how much easier it would be to run without a job. I would have more time and could do more with it. I'd been living on an average of three hours' sleep a night for a few months by then, and it would be great to get a full night's sleep. Maybe I would be freed up to visit some schools to give talks. But how could I afford that sort of life? I could barely afford things as it was, so I needed the income from my job. Ali and I had mentioned sponsorship in the past, but realistically it didn't look like a viable option.

When we spoke, I felt Ken had already made up his mind.

I was on my way. If I wasn't going to stop running (and I wasn't) then that was it. He said I could work till the end of the month and that would be it. I said OK; I certainly wasn't going to beg him to let me keep my job. But I was upset. I believed I'd helped transform that company, modernising it. It felt like I was losing my own business. What was more, Ken was someone I looked up to and someone I once wanted to be like.

Anyway, that was that. There was too much of me glad to finally get a rest from my over-filled schedule to argue the matter. I was pissed off but relieved at the same time and I knew he had a point, too.

The running came first. This was my passion. I had to turn it into a career now, somehow. This year's challenge would come to an end, but I wanted to carry on after that, to find a way to make endurance sport a living. So here was my chance to take a leap of faith. I wasn't looking forward to telling Joanna, though.

For the moment I had to keep focused on the running ahead of me. I had the little matter of a 100-mile race to complete that weekend, which was new territory for me. I felt confident I could finish 100 miles, but just in case, I had decided to run a Richmond Park marathon beforehand, as a back-up. I wanted to make sure I had a marathon ticked off for that day if I failed to finish the 100-miler for whatever reason. I wanted to keep my main target, at least a marathon a day for a year, on track.

Then, after the 100-miler, my plan was to get over to the Salisbury 5-4-3-2-1 marathon and run that, which would bring my eventual weekend's running total to 154 miles, with only a few hours' sleep – if I was lucky. It would be my biggest weekend to date and would test me to the very limits.

*

It all started on the Friday after work. When I got home, Joanna made me an enormous meal. I had eaten a huge lunch that day, too, as I tried to get as much energy on board as possible. After all, I had run a marathon that morning already. My feet were pretty good considering, but both my knees still hurt. Unfortunately, the swelling hadn't gone down much since Dr Kipps had drained my knee earlier in the week, and now one of my ankles was painful, too. No doubt things would settle down as soon as I got going, I figured. I hoped.

I took a late bus to the park for my early-morning marathon and arrived just before midnight, so I had to wait a few minutes before I could start. Then I ran a quickish marathon in the dark. I didn't want to use my head torch, as I knew I'd need it for the 100-miler and I didn't have any spare batteries. You don't need one if you are in the open with good moonlight, in my experience. In fact, I feel like I see better without it at night, and of course I knew the path well by now.

Not that the run was without incident; I got spooked by a couple of deer who'd come onto the path. I think they were as surprised as me. Fortunately I managed to avoid a confrontation. They aren't aggressive so you're usually fine with them. Then the rain came down. It was pouring and soon I was practically swimming in it – massive puddles everywhere, mud and swirling wind. I had to stop and look around me at one point and wonder what on earth I was doing: here I was, running a marathon at night, in the pouring rain, as a warm-up for a 100-mile race – a distance I'd never yet run. I'd come a long way since my 5k park run days that was for sure.

Despite all the rain, the run went fine, though I felt cold during the second half of the marathon. I was grateful I wasn't wearing the kilt, which would have got soaking wet and heavy. I finished in just under four hours, by which time it had stopped raining. Lorna, my taxi driver for the day, was already waiting in her car to drive me to the race, as arranged. She looked wide awake, but I was tired. I towelled myself dry and changed clothes before getting in the car. She was chatting away, all excited as we headed off. I tried to stay awake and listen, but in the end sleep got the better of me.

The next thing I knew Lorna was waking me up. I'd been fast asleep and it took me a while to realise where I was. The clock in the car said 5.15am, and we had arrived at the North Downs Way 100 race HQ in Farnham. I got up slowly and gathered my things together, put my kilt on and got myself race ready. The sun was starting to rise and I was looking forward to seeing more of it. After more than an hour in a warm car, for some reason I was still really cold as well as being a bit stiff.

I registered and sat down for the briefing. I saw a few familiar faces in the room. Traviss Willcox was there and a few other ultra enthusiasts I recognised from other races, people I'd chatted to before. There was a bit of pre-race banter as usual at the briefing. Apparently a hurricane was on its way through these parts. Unless we were really quick, it looked like we'd get a soaking early Sunday morning. Or, as I liked to think of it, a nice shower to start the day.

The organisers came around to check on us all to make sure we had all of the kit required. I think I was short of a few items, but I assured them I was good to go. I had some warm clothing and enough gels and food and a head lamp. I thought the other stuff was a bit unnecessary, for me at least. I needed to travel light, but I understood why they were making sure we were properly prepared for what might lie ahead of us all.

'Are you sure you're up for this, mate?' the race director asked me. I looked back at him, unsure what he meant. 'Only I hear you've run four marathons already in the last couple of days,' he added. He was concerned about me, making sure I was OK to race. Perhaps I looked how I felt.

'Don't worry about me,' I said. 'I'm the last one you need to worry about. If I don't make a checkpoint then someone must have shot me. Otherwise I'll be there.'

It was a strange thing to say, I guess, but enough to make them give me the benefit of the doubt. It's important to put out positive vibes even when you aren't feeling it. Especially when you aren't feeling it. Put out good vibes and more good thoughts and feelings soon join them, then your confidence will grow in no time at all. I ate some last-minute food – four chocolate eclairs I found at the bottom of my bag and some fruit. I also had a big cup of coffee with umpteen sugars in it.

At 6am we lined up at the start. I was nervous and excited, like this was a competitive race. I'd first dreamed of 100-mile races while reading Dean Karnazes' book, *Ultramarathon Man*. His account of the Great Western States 100-miler in Colorado had given me goosebumps. If you finish a 100-mile race in under 24 hours, they give you a big old belt buckle. No ordinary prize for no ordinary achievement. Win one of those and you join an elite group of men and women. How I wanted one of those buckles.

The race got underway and we were off; a field of 180 diehard runners all hoping we could reach the finish line. In the end, as many as 70 of us would be disappointed.

We made our way through an assortment of country lanes and woodlands, across fields and up some inclines. Everyone was fresh and the early miles were no great challenge. It was cool but also humid, so by mile 5 I was sweating quite heavily. I reached the first-aid station at mile 7 in Puttenham with the leading runners. I had some big gulps of water and a banana and carried on, eager to keep up the pace.

Weather-wise it was a picture-perfect day, though later on it got a little hot for ideal running conditions, but you can't argue with blue skies like that and golden fields at your side. The North Downs were right up there with the very best of English countryside I saw throughout the year.

At mile 14 there was another aid station. As I gulped down some more water, I chatted with a guy there whose ankle was hurting him. 'Don't give up, buddy,' I told him. 'Even if you have to crawl, you're going to finish this.' I was worried for him, because it was too early in the race to be in trouble. The next 11 miles were pretty straightforward, across some rutted paths and fields, then some steep climbs. My knee was holding up OK, and my ankle too, while my energy levels were fine. I felt in good shape.

At Box Hill there was another great aid station, this time with everyone dressed in Hawaiian clothing. Aloha! I gobbled down some biscuits and took a chicken wrap to eat while I was going. After that it was over the river on some stepping stones and then a steep climb straight up Box Hill. From there on it was up and down some pretty punishing hills, but with amazing views as our reward. I was still doing OK and keeping a decent pace.

I kept chatting with other runners along the way. Some of them had already got lost and had to double back to find the course again. I'd had to make a few decisions at times, where the path diverged and it wasn't clear which way to go. Fortunately for me, I'd been lucky and hadn't gone miles off course. Yet.

After 38 miles there was an ice-cream aid station. How awesome is that! I had some ice cream and jelly and could easily have stayed for another bowl, but instead said thanks and got going, eager to keep up my progress. By about 40 miles, I was running along with a guy called Matthew (now a good friend), chatting about life as we moved through the rolling countryside. We then passed a field where a family was picnicking. Their two young children offered Matthew and me some jelly babies, pretzels and crisps. I took them gladly and the kindness (as well as the food) was energising for us both.

At about 4pm, ten hours after setting off, I reached the 50-mile point. I was on track to get this done in 24 hours. And I needed to really, if I was going to get to the next race in Salisbury. Of course I was going to get slower, but still, I had some time to allow for that. The worst of the day's heat was over now and I thought I might have been sunburnt, though I couldn't allow that to bother me.

Most runners I saw after that were in the zone with their headphones on, listening to their chosen soundtrack. I don't listen to music when I run and haven't for any of my marathons. I like to be awake and aware, present with the surroundings and fully focused on my body and my stride. I haven't met too many others who run without music so that seems to be my unique thing, though I do sometimes sing when I'm running. I'm not sure if that counts as listening to music or not?

We began to climb up a steep hill and my calves started to hurt, so much so that I could only walk for a bit. I'd never felt pain there like that before, and I began to grow concerned and tried a few stretches to work it through. Someone saw I was in trouble and stopped to ask if I was all right, but I told them I was fine.

Eventually we reached the top of the hill and it levelled off. The track turned muddy and lots of tree roots made it very awkward and slow going. My calves felt OK again now that we were no longer going uphill. Soon the muddy path came to an end and we were running through open fields again, full of sheep and goats. Then we headed into the village of Otford and from there on to Wrotham and the aid point at mile 60. I refuelled and chatted to the lovely volunteers there. I had a few comments about the kilt, including that old question about whether I wear anything under it. I told them it depends on whether I can find any clean underwear that day. I wasn't feeling very hungry, but I was glad to stop for a minute and have a chat. They told me I was looking good and that there wasn't too far to go now. The way they said it, they made it sound as though 40 miles was just around the corner.

As the light faded at about 9pm, I remember I went off track in the woods and ended up brushing past a wasps' nest. I didn't think much of it at the time, but a mile or so further on, I got a stinging sensation on my abdomen, a pain that then shot around to my back. The pain was getting worse and worse and I didn't have a clue what it could be. I thought it might be that I'd broken a blood vessel.

Eventually, I stopped and lifted up my top to have a look and found loads of wasps in there, some dead, a couple alive. I brushed them all away and then took all my clothes off, apart from my shorts, to see if there were any more. The skin was raised and I had clearly been stung several times on my abdomen and on my back. Another runner stopped to see what was going on and told me if it started swelling then I might be having an allergic reaction.

Shit!

The runner said he'd go on and tell the next aid station what had happened and to expect me. I thanked him and started walking now to get there as soon as possible. The pain was pretty bad and I was concerned they might try to stop me racing. I'd been stung by something in Cheltenham and had an anaphylactic reaction, with my throat closing up, which was awful, so I was worried that might happen again and maybe even worse, with the amount of bites I'd had.

I got to the aid station a few miles later and they sat me down and looked at my stings. I was made to sit there for about 30 minutes to see if I had a reaction or not. It was getting quite dark now and I could feel the weather was on the change. That storm they were talking about was definitely on its way. Fortunately for me, there was no allergic reaction, so I got the all-clear and off I went again. I'd lost some time, but apart from the soreness around my belly and back everything still worked. I was a little stiff, after having sat down for so long, but I worked through that and a few miles later I was running well again. I was just glad still to be in the race.

At the 76-mile aid station there were some pretty sorry looking runners sat down, retching or being sick, some with their heads in their hands. Words seemed pointless at this stage. Just looking at them, you could tell they weren't going to be leaving that tent. That was a long way to run for most people and if you've picked up an injury then you're pretty screwed. The drop-out rate for big runs like this is high.

It was about midnight now and pitch black as I went through the woods. I had my head lamp on but it wasn't helping much, and kept flickering on and off. The next few hours would be the toughest. If you got lost that would be it, I figured. I hoped that wouldn't be me. Then the rain started coming down in torrents. It was relentless. Running in that rain in the dark seemed really dangerous. I got to the next aid station and I was completely soaked through and freezing cold. People were huddled around trying to get warm, some suffering from hypothermia. It was a bit of a disaster zone. Apparently most of the 70 runners who quit the race finished here.

I stopped to wait out the storm. I decided to cut a hole in my foil blanket to make a vest of it and I put my head through that, then I put dry clothes on top of it. Now I felt warm and dry and fresh again. It really worked. I ran on and got to the next checkpoint at about mile 90, feeling better. People were being sick in the tent and it was all unpleasant. I told everyone how my trick had worked and that it had kept a lot of the rain off me, helping to keep me warm, hot even, and how this had raised my spirits and made me run better. But nobody else thought it was a good idea.

I ran on and reached the final aid station, just four miles from the finish. It was 4.45am by my watch. That gave me a little over an hour and a quarter to complete the race, if I was to finish in under 24 hours and get that buckle. Ordinarily four miles in an hour would be child's play for me; in fact I could probably walk it. I was tired, but surely not enough for that to be a problem. I had a coffee and hoped the caffeine would help me float to the finish line.

Four miles to go and this would all be done. My first 100-miler and in under 24 hours, too – I couldn't help but think about crossing that line now. I got to a crossroads and the sign said straight on. I saw it, but for some reason I turned right. I can only think I was so exhausted that my mind wasn't working properly. I went steeply downhill for a while and couldn't shake this sense that I was going the

wrong way. But I kept going anyway. After about five minutes or so I got to a crossroads, and there were no signs to
anywhere I was looking for, so then I knew I must have
gone the wrong way.

A few miles from the finish, what a time to get lost!

I turned back and started trudging up the steep hill. Now
I felt sure I'd blown my chance to finish in under 24 hours,
but still I would finish. I walked up the hill in the thick mud
with the rain pouring down. Eventually I got back to the
crossroads where I had gone wrong and was back on the
course again. I started running now, but slowly. I was pretty
dispirited because I'd made such a silly mistake which was
going to cost me achieving my goal. Then a couple of guys
came up behind me, going at pace. They stopped to speak to
me. 'Come on,' they said. 'We can still finish in less than
twenty-four hours. We're nearly there.'

'I don't think so now,' I said. 'I think we're too late.'

'Bullshit,' the other guy said. 'Let's keep moving. We've
still got time.'

So I dug in and picked up the pace to keep with them.
They kept encouraging me, telling me we were almost
there and not to give up. It worked and we covered that last
four miles in less than half an hour. Soon we could see the
finish area, a blur of activity in the early-morning light. We
had just one more muddy field to cross now. Seeing this, we
all ran as fast as we could. Our brotherhood had served its
purpose and now we were three competitors again, each
racing for his own piece of glory. Just seven minutes shy of
24 hours, I crossed the finish line. I couldn't believe it. I
was convinced it was over, but those guys helped me to
keep going. I wouldn't have made it under 24 hours without them.

In all, 180 runners started that race, only 110 finished, and just 36 of those made it in under 24 hours. I knew I was very lucky to be in that group. If there was any feeling of glory, then it lasted less than a few seconds. Lorna was waiting to whisk me away as I didn't have much time before the next marathon would start. I said a few goodbyes and thank yous and picked up my buckle and a bacon sandwich. Then it was straight in the car; I would get changed on the way and didn't have time for a shower, though fortunately the storm had pretty much washed me clean.

We had a two-and-a-half-hour drive ahead of us to the start of the next race in Salisbury. We would just about be able to make it there in time for the start of the Salisbury 5-4-3-2-1 marathon at 9am. Lorna was her usual excitable self, full of praise and concern, offering me food when not phoning people to tell them I was still alive and in one piece. I was exhausted, though, and had to sleep before I did anything else. She had brought a duvet for me and the warmth and stillness were intoxicating. Soon I was fast asleep.

An hour or so later I woke up with a cramp. I needed something to eat. I wasn't hungry, but I knew I was down on calories. I'd eaten plenty of gels and other bits of food but it wouldn't be enough; I couldn't have a repeat of the Wales Runfest marathon where I died after mile 2 and had to drag my corpse around the course. Never again. Lorna had brought all kinds of freshly cooked food with her, so I ate some chicken and pasta, but my appetite wasn't there. What I wanted now was more sleep.

There was no time for that, though, and we arrived at the race HQ soon enough and I was inside registering and picking up my race number. These marathons are the hard ones. When you've exerted your body to the max and then you ask it to start again, without proper rest, it really isn't interested. By my reckoning I'd had only two hours' sleep in the last 74 hours. That's no preparation for anything. I'd have to run this race on sheer willpower, one step at a time, wearing it down bit by bit.

It didn't help that the course was pretty hilly, nothing exceptional but not flat either. I hadn't eaten enough and it was painful all the way around. I had no energy and my legs felt very tight. I met some great people on the course, though, including Vicky and Adam, a couple who were extremely supportive when I was flagging. So many people recognised me and said hello. I heard later that my responses were slurred, but I didn't notice at the time. The support from those guys out there that day really helped me keep going and to reach the finish line.

The course ended up being longer than described which wasn't what I needed. Twenty-eight miles and change according to my watch, but at least I didn't get lost. I walked quite a bit of it and dragged myself round the rest. It took almost six and a half hours, but it felt like considerably longer.

Enough said about that one; it was not the best of memories. I crossed the line thanks to sheer willpower – and not just my own. Those on the course that day were so positive and encouraging that it gave me what I needed to get through it. What may sound like an individual achievement was actually the work of a whole group of people. I'm not sure I could have finished that one if I'd been out there on my own. I might still be running it now. So, in that sense, the race was special – it showed me how well people can work together and inspire one another to achieve what seems almost impossible.

Lorna was there at the finish line, again. I waited to see Vicky finish, as she had helped me during the race. She came in a few minutes after me. Not many others followed her because I'd finished 234th out of 245 who completed the race. I was pretty much the last man out there. Oh, well, so much for my moment of glory!

I was absolutely exhausted. I'd done 182 miles of running and two days' work, all on only two hours of sleep. Lorna drove me home and I slept all the way. It was more of a coma than a sleep, really. It was early evening by the time I got home. It was lovely to see Joanna and Buddy, but I was so tired I just lay down on the sofa like a dead man. Joanna had cooked me a big chicken dinner and I got a few mouthfuls down me before having a shower and going to bed.

My teenage years were the happiest years of my life until then. I had a good home and, in Peter, someone to give me the love and support I'd never had before. We don't need much more than that, do we? But without it, life is a very steep climb.

At school, I was progressing. With Peter's expert tuition and guidance, I was able to fill in the gaps I'd missed in my earlier years, to some extent at least. I wasn't about to ace my way into Oxford University or anything like that, but I could hold my own in a classroom without looking too stupid. I was becoming less aggressive and confrontational, too. I avoided trouble at school, rather than looking for it. Every now and again I got into something, either standing up for a friend or squaring up to a bully, but Peter was teaching me right from wrong so I knew when to make a stand. Bad things happen when good people do nothing to stop them. Bullies could never beat me, because what they couldn't understand was that I didn't mind being hit. No matter how much they punched me, I would always come back, grinning, for more. No bully can live with that.

I was a bit of a school counsellor, too. For some reason, people would come and tell me their problems. A girl once confided in me how her step-father was abusing her, so we hatched a plan together and I helped her get away to her grandparents in Birmingham. She told them all about it and the authorities were informed. We lost touch for a while and I'd always wondered what happened to her, but we've reconnected and happily things worked out for her. She now has a wonderful family and a great life.

After I'd finished school, I went to college and two years later came out with some A levels and a BTech. At that time, I wanted to join the armed forces, though I couldn't decide whether to go for the Army or the RAF. I remember the summer I got my exam results, going to an Armed Forces Recruitment Fair in London. The RAF guys there told me it would be a six-month wait before I could join up, but the Army boys said I could be training in a matter of weeks. So that made my decision for me. I was in a hurry, I guess.

I had an aptitude test a few days later to see what regiment would suit me best. I remember helping out the guy sitting next to me with some of his answers. He was finding it all a challenge. Once I'd finished the test, they told me they'd seen me helping the other guy but they'd let it pass. They gave me a telling off, but I could tell they were quite pleased at the same time. At least I was bothering to help someone out.

My spelling and grammar were still pretty poor, but I was quick at solving problems and seeing solutions. As a result, my test score was quite high so I got to choose almost any trade I liked. I was torn between the police, intel or comms. Communications appealed to me, and I liked the idea of working with satellites and sending secret messages, so in the end I opted for the Royal Signals.

Soon I was at basic training and living the army life. At that time I also started doing biathlons (run, bike, run) and triathlons (swim, bike, run) and got chosen for the GB Junior team, so the Army let me do full-time sports in the beginning. That meant I was pretty much training all the time, rather than marching and doing drills with the other lads. It suited me, as I love to compete, and though I wasn't exactly setting the world alight, I had my fair share of victories, too.

I stayed in the Army for five years, from 18 until I was 23. By the end, the Army had taken me off full-sports duty, so I was just doing the regular training with the rest of the lads. It was around then I started drinking with the guys a fair bit, trying to fit in, and misbehaving more than was good for me. I was going down a bad path and getting into fights. I wasn't starting trouble, but I was quick to protect friends who were, and when you're drinking with Army lads in local pubs it's never too long before a situation comes up. I hated those skirmishes and how they made me feel afterwards. I wanted to be away from that world by then.

In the end, I realised I wasn't happy and decided it was time for a change. Happily, a chance came up for me to cycle semi-professionally in Italy. I had no ties and it seemed like an exciting opportunity, so I left the Army and moved out to Italy. In the early days, I was riding for the team but not getting paid a bean. I was based near Milan, cycling every day and living off my savings. I was loving it, though, in a new country with a new challenge. The fact that my savings were disappearing fast didn't worry me too much, either.

Then I got a break and was asked to join a professional team as a *domestique*. That meant I cycled for the team, helping the main riders to do well. It was decent money and the life was good for a while. I was cycling a lot and then coming back to the UK every other weekend to see my girlfriend – not a bad old life for a young man. Not long into my riding career, my girlfriend fell pregnant, which meant I had a choice: either stay in Italy and not be much of a father, or quit riding and come back to make a go of it as a family man. It was never a difficult choice.

I returned to the UK in the summer of 2008. My partner and I moved in together near Watford, I got the job at the car parts company with Ken, and soon enough Olivia, our darling daughter, arrived. For a while everything went well. We got engaged, but things changed quickly. Various things happened, which I don't need to go into here, but the upshot was that before Olivia was even three years old, her mum and dad were no longer together.

I was devastated.

That was the beginning of a very difficult time for me. I took the break-up badly and I sort of unravelled. I ended up living in a shed in one of Ken's lock-ups for a while. It was winter time and there was ice on the inside of the windows. Every morning I'd wash outside in the yard with a hose pipe. It wasn't pretty. Soon enough, though, I turned a corner and got myself together and rented a flat. I got on with my life and saw Olivia at weekends. I was doing what I could to be the best dad possible under the circumstances, though I now realise it wasn't nearly enough.

Six months later I met Joanna via a dating website called plentyoffish.com – it was pretty much love at first type! She was, she says, attracted to me by the pictures of my bike.

Strange, because I wouldn't say that's my best feature. On our first date, I brought her a piece of fresh cod from the fishmonger, wrapped up in lovely pink paper with a bow on it. It was a plentyoffish reference, in case you're wondering. Chocolates or flowers might have been a better idea, though, but she seemed to like the joke.

We had a whirlwind romance that first year; we fitted perfectly and I was devoted to her. Of course, she won't let me forget it now. It's the yardstick by which I am (constantly) measured. If I'd only known what a rod I was making for my own back. I used to leave a trail of rose petals from the front door to the bath when she got home – and not occasionally, but all the time. I don't do much of that kind of thing anymore, though. I think she knows how to find her way to the bathroom by now.

Alexander was born a few years later and there wasn't so much time for that sort of romantic gesture. And it was then that my relationship with Olivia's mum got worse, and we had a big falling out; as a result I haven't seen Olivia since 2013. Allowing things to get that bad is my greatest regret. I'm doing what I can to be back in Olivia's life again and I hope we will eventually come to some arrangement, but these things can take time, and there are always sensitive matters to resolve.

But for now, my focus was on keeping going with my challenge.

CHAPTER THIRTEEN
A Fight with Mr Negative

11 August–3 September 2014

In the week that followed the 100-miler, I got plenty of attention. I think my achievement astonished a lot of people, and forced them to take me more seriously. My story was certainly more interesting because of it. However, I wasn't going to repeat that kind of distance anytime soon. My focus now was to get to the end of the year in one piece. I continued with a pretty set routine of hot tubs and massages to help me recover, marathons to keep me ticking along, selling car parts during the day, and spending my evenings with the family.

My next weekend had a novel twist to it, though. An old Army buddy of mine, Chris Dickson, had set me a crazy challenge that I was dumb enough to accept. The rules were these: on that weekend, I could take only a banana, a bed sheet, a single blanket and a pound in spending money with me (I could raise more money by busking, but I wasn't allowed to ask friends for cash). I wasn't to use any taxis or buses or even allowed to hitchhike. Oh, and I was forbidden from riding on animals at any point, too. So donkey rides were out. I had my Virgin Trains pass, so getting to marathons was feasible, and I could eat a fair amount of food at the events, but realistically I would need to eat more than that. Dinner, for example. I wasn't sure about the busking either. If you'd heard me sing you'd understand.

After an early start on Saturday morning, I got to the Lemmings Track marathon in Worthing within the rules of the challenge. I took a train to the outskirts of London where Emily Hannon, a fellow marathon runner, picked me up and gave me a lift the rest of the way. It was good to be arriving in comfort for once, rather than running to the event.

My 137th marathon/ultra was a novelty: 106 laps of a 400m grass track on the south coast. You'd think the sheer repetition would make for a dull race, but it was actually a fun event. You got to see the faster runners and the slower runners again and again, and it gave the race a unified feeling. We were constantly cheering each other on and horsing around. It quickly became more like a casual jog with good friends than a race. It was a fantastic occasion and I met loads of great new people. You were never far from an aid station too, which was nice.

After that, I had to travel 130 miles to the next day's race in Somerset, the Cheddar Gorge marathon. A succession of trains got me to Wells by the late evening, but I was starving by then. I'd eaten my banana and spent my pound and I was in no mood to busk. I'd been jogging and walking for some time and was getting fed up with the bet, to be honest. It wasn't as though I didn't have enough to deal with already, so I cheated. I went to Tesco and bought myself dinner with some 'emergency' cash I'd brought with me. And I thumbed a lift from Wells into the outskirts of Cheddar, too. Sorry about that, Chris. Now I just had to find myself somewhere to sleep.

As well as its cheese, Cheddar is famous for having the

biggest gorge in Britain, and it is also the site of the Cheddar caves. In 1903, the oldest complete human skeleton in Britain was found here, who became known as Cheddar Man, and he died over 9,000 years ago. It appears to have been a violent death, with a blow to the skull in these very caves. If it was good enough for Cheddar Man, then it would do for Marathon Man. I decided to sleep in a cave that night. What better shelter would I find around here anyway? So I ended up following signs to the nearest cave.

The town was alive with boy racers that evening. It was midnight but still garishly coloured cars with souped-up engines revved and raced around every corner. Was this what they did for fun in Somerset? I managed to cross the roads I needed to, dodged the cars and found my way to the cave. Once inside it was a little spooky. I didn't go too far inside the entrance before laying out my sheet and getting my blanket over me. Then I was good for the night. I could still hear those V8 engines roaring around the town as I lay there, but it would have taken more than that to stop me getting to sleep.

It's strange to wake up in a cave, but the kind of strange that's good in my book. It had been a little chilly in there, but I'd survived the night, which was more than Cheddar Man did.

Just getting to the start of the race required some effort – we had to climb to the top of the gorge for that. Once the race was underway, there were lots of undulations as the course took us up and down the Mendip Hills. There were some super steep ascents and a good variety of terrain to keep things interesting, with lots of amazing views to take in as I got to run around another of Britain's 'Areas of Natural Beauty'. It was a real privilege.

It was billed as a tough race and so it was. Not as tough as others I'd run, such as Bath or Scafell Pike, but challenging nonetheless. I'd recommend it to anyone who can handle the ups and downs and wants a breathtaking race. I finished in a little over five hours, then it was lifts and trains back home and a little catching up with the family before another week of Richmond Park marathons started again.

The following weekend was a case of near and far. To begin with, I had my local course, the Thames Meander marathon, which almost went past my door in Isleworth. After that, I had to travel to the Guernsey marathon on the Sunday. It needed a bit of planning, which runs contrary to my nature. I did think about swimming there for a minute or two, believing it wasn't far from the UK coast, but it turned out to be at least 50 miles away. Shame. Throwing a Channel swim in among the running would have got the social media channels abuzz. As I was pretty broke at the time, I booked a one-way flight to Guernsey in the end, and would have to worry about how to get back once the race was over.

The Thames Meander route was nice and flat, starting at Kingston and following the river path down to Putney bridge before turning back on itself. Later on in the year, in October, once the deer rutting season started, I'd end up running this course several times instead of the Richmond Park one. It was nice running locally and having my son and Joanna at the race, as well as plenty of other support. I even had time to run with Alexander on my shoulders for the last couple of miles and buy him an ice cream (which he dripped all over my head). Marathon 144 was a good one. But I couldn't hang around, as I had to catch a train to central

London, then another one to Southampton airport for my flight over to Guernsey.

That evening I met up with the race directors. With no hotel booked, I was expecting to be sleeping rough for the night. I asked them if they knew of any cosy caves in the area, which they thought was funny, then they realised I wasn't joking. 'We're not having you sleep outside before our race,' they said, and they got on the phone to arrange a hotel room for me. I was really grateful as I wasn't in the mood for a night in the cold.

Once in the hotel room, I contemplated sleeping on the floor rather than the bed. I'd learned that I felt better if I kept my body in a state of readiness. When I allowed my body to get too comfortable, it became sleepy and sluggish. Then it needed a few miles running before it woke up. Sometimes, however, a soft bed with a heavy duvet is just too tempting to resist. Tonight would be such a night.

I got a great night's sleep and arrived early at the race start. There were some bananas there for the runners, so I had a couple to get me going and a cup of very, very sweet coffee. The race itself was a good one. There were a fair amount of roads that needed crossing, so you had to watch out for traffic at times. We had a good nose around the island and passed through towns as well as countryside. The course took us up to the highest point of the island and on past sandy inlets and bays in the second half of the race. However, it was never too challenging, and I thought it was a beautiful place to run and I can imagine it's lovely for a holiday.

I hadn't eaten much in the previous 12 hours, so I was a bit greedy at the aid stations and hope I left enough for the other runners. At the end there was fresh, creamy Guernsey milk for every finisher, which was a novel touch. But in many ways, that was the easy part done: now I had to find a way off the island and get back home.

I went down to the ferry port. I can't remember how much a single ticket back to the UK was, but it was too much. I tried to negotiate a lower price, and was told the later ferry was cheaper, but it was still too expensive – it was the holiday season, after all. I even asked if I could work on the boat for free passage, but apparently that wasn't an option. The best I could manage was a staff discount, so I took that.

The boat shipped out at about 3pm and I was back on the mainland three hours later. I had almost no cash and no bank cards on me now, so the rest of the trip was a challenge. Fortunately, I got a lift to the train station, but it wasn't a Virgin route, so I had to persuade the officials to let me on the train to London without a ticket. I was very grateful for their help – it was these sorts of gestures that enabled me to keep going. The return journey was a bit undignified, begging for price reductions and free passage, but I had arrived back home, safe and sound, on Sunday night with my mind, body and, most importantly, my world record attempt still intact.

The following week was marked by an extraordinary face plant while running in Richmond Park. It was pitch black and I didn't have my head torch on, so I only had a little moonlight, as well as my knowledge of the course, to guide me. I was running down the biggest hill on the course, or rather falling in a controlled way. I had learnt to come quickly down hills, using my raised arms to steer me. I feel that there's no point in braking if you don't have to, and you might as well let gravity help you out when you can (see page 76 for more on this). But that night a deer was standing on the path. You'd think he might have realised by now that this was my route. I'd run it often enough at that time of the morning. I mean, really! He has over 2,000 acres to graze in and he needs to stand there?

It was only when I was just a few yards away that I saw him: a great big elder, with a good set of antlers on his head. I changed direction in an instant and managed to miss him, but ended up face first in a path-side bush. Ouch! I cut my face and muddied myself up, though considering how fast I was going I got away lightly. It could have been a whole lot worse. I decided that if I ever faced a similar problem in the future, I'd jump over him as if he were a steeplechase hurdle. I'd plant one foot on his back before sailing over. You never know, it might come off.

During that week, I passed another landmark when I ran my 150th marathon/ultra. I wasn't feeling very good, though. I was pretty low in spirits for some reason, either through sheer exhaustion or perhaps out of disappointment at the amount of money I'd managed to raise. Either way I was in need of a boost.

Fortunately, I got that one evening that week when I went to the Mo Farah Foundation dinner in Putney, a black-tie affair that I had been invited to through having met Mo's agent. It's not really my scene, in general, but I enjoyed it well enough. It was something different, and I met some top sportsmen that night including Chris Robshaw, Jermain Defoe and Mo himself, as well as the comedians Jack Whitehall and Jimmy Carr. All of them were great people, down to earth and genuinely interested in what I was trying to do.

Despite that, when I woke up early the next morning, I was still in a slump. Joanna prodded me and said I should be getting on my way. That was a first: she was usually trying to get me to stay rather than leave. I was meant to be heading over to Milton Keynes for the Enigma Reverse marathon that morning. I'd had enough, though. Enough of running and getting up early, worrying about how I could afford to get here or there. What was I doing? And why was I doing it? People weren't that interested, not enough to put their hands in their pockets at least. I was killing myself while the world turned. It wasn't changing anything.

Mr Negative had come to visit.

About 20 minutes later and I was still in bed, my conscience wrestling with my exhaustion. My exhaustion was winning. Then I heard John Edmonds' unmistakable voice at the door. Johnny was a New Zealander friend of Ali's who I'd met playing rugby the previous year. He and his wife were part of Team MMUK and he'd given me countless lifts here and there; he'd been a real friend and supporter of what I was doing. Joanna let him in and I heard him walk up the stairs towards my bedroom. He stepped in.

'What are you doing, buddy?' he said. 'Haven't you got somewhere you need to be?'

'I'm not going,' I replied.

'What's the matter? Are you sick? Are you injured? What is it?'

'I'm tired, that's all. I'm gonna sleep for a bit and then see about running later.'

He'd never seen me like this before – no one had. Even Joanna was worried. I found out later she had contacted the MMUK team that morning to ask someone to come around and get me moving.

'I'll tell you what we're going to do,' Johnny said. 'You're going to get dressed and I'm going to drive you down to

Milton Keynes for this race. When we get down there, if you still don't want to run then I'll just drive you back. How's that sound?'

'I'm going to stay here, Johnny,' I said. 'I need the sleep.'

Then I felt his great, big, Kiwi rugby-playing arms slip under my armpits and lift me to a sitting position. 'I'm going to take you, Rob. I'll dress you myself if I have to, but we'd both rather you did that. Come on, you don't want to let anyone down, do you?'

That was it – it wasn't all about me anymore. I was just the pinnacle of a team and under that was a whole body of support, willing me on. I knew I'd be letting a lot of people down if I quit now. I'd just given up my job for this challenge, and perhaps, deep down, I was worried about that, too. Who knows the reasons, but I was sure in a lousy frame of mind. I'm pretty stubborn, though, so this conversation with Johnny went on for a while. He wasn't backing down though, and I was awake now, so in the end I agreed. Looking back, I think I came pretty close to quitting that weekend. It was only thanks to Joanna and Johnny that I was still on track.

As promised, Johnny drove me up to Milton Keynes and I was 20 minutes late for the race start, but that wasn't an issue. This was a repeat of the marathon I'd run in July. I was slower this time, completing it in 5 hours 43 minutes and, crossing the line with two other runners near the back of the field, I felt more tired than usual. I recognised I was going to need more than a couple of hours extra in bed to get back to top form.

After finishing that race, I needed to get to the Halifax marathon the next morning. I was feeling in a better mood by now, though I wasn't exactly Mr Happy, and I was still heavy-hearted. I realised it was a slump that would take a while to get through. I took a train to Halifax and went straight off to look for the race start, which was near the football stadium. Once I'd found it, I went in search of somewhere to sleep that night. I was looking for somewhere quiet and warm that I could lay my sheet down and get some undisturbed rest.

I think I ended up in the wrong part of town, because I soon attracted the attention of a gang of locals. Three guys and a girl approached me and began asking a barrage of questions. What was I doing? Was I lost? What hotel was I staying at? What's in the bag? Too many questions. You didn't have to be a sniffer dog to know I was in a spot of bother. I was the prey being assessed for weaknesses. It was dark and late and I was pissed off, so I didn't need this.

I was close to flipping out, if I'm honest. It would have given me some satisfaction to put them on their backs right there, and to have vented some of my frustrations on them, but I wasn't about to do that. I might have hurt one of them and I would have hated myself for it afterwards. I stayed calm and looked for a way out of the situation. I told them I was staying in a hotel in the town centre and they said they knew a short cut. They asked if I had a bank card; I suppose that was meant to be intimidating. While batting off their questions, I was scanning the area for an escape route.

It reminded me of a similar occasion many years earlier. I was about eight years old and was cornered by three older kids in a shopping centre. They tried to steal my stuff and I just let them. A few weeks later, they caught up with me again and chased me across town. This time I ran into a dead end and there was nowhere to escape. They pushed me around a bit and called me names. I was angry but still scared. They told me to go and grab a lady's handbag and bring it to them, then they'd let me go. I told them I wouldn't do it. So they moved towards me as if to give me a beating, but that's not what happened.

I flipped. Crazy Rob appeared, and I became like my dad. I smacked two of them onto the ground and the other one ran off. Then I got on top of the ringleader, who was out on the floor, and I pinned him down and started to lay into him. He forced his way to his feet, but I wasn't finished yet. I headbutted him and continued to kick and punch him wildly. 'Think you can push me around? Think you can steal my stuff?' In the end, I was dragged off by several adults and I tried to fight them, too. If you're not for me, you're against me. And I'm not taking it anymore.

I really didn't want to get into that state again.

Eventually, I just bolted for it, running between one of the lads and the girl, figuring she'd be the least able to get hold of me. I got through the gap and I was away. I ran flat out for a couple of hundred metres and didn't look back. Then I found a bus station, with its lights on. I darted in there and ducked down in a little alcove. A bus out of Halifax would be a good idea, I thought. Or better yet, a train home.

Once the coast was clear, I'd had enough again. I didn't need this, so I decided to go back to the train station and return home. Sleeping rough in the bus station was an option, but I'd lost my faith in the locals and wasn't in the mood for any more surprises.

I try to avoid getting into unpleasant situations such as that as much as possible. What worries me most is what I might do to someone; I don't want to be violent, or be drawn into that world again. I hate how it feels and I worry I might get carried away and hurt somebody. I guess I'm always worried about wandering onto my father's path.

So I made my way back to the station, determined to head home, but it was gone midnight by now and I'd missed the last train back to London. So that was that: I was stuck in Halifax for the night. I contemplated my options before deciding to find a hotel room. Whatever I had to pay, I wasn't hanging around on those streets any longer. I was going to be in my room for only about five hours, so I was reluctant to spend good money on it. After failing to negotiate a reduced price with the receptionist, I accepted my fate and paid up. Soon I was warm and comfortable enough in bed, but I tossed and turned for most of that night, still worked up after my unfriendly welcome into town.

Happily, the next day I awoke on the right side of the bed. I felt like all the dark clouds had passed and I was looking forward to the day's running. I was back. The Halifax marathon was a good one, with the route taking in a mixture of urban and rural scenery, taking us on a tour of industrial Halifax as well as through the hilly countryside. I finished in under four hours, so I was pleased with how my body was holding up. After all the dramas of that weekend, I was delighted to have got through my low period with my challenge still intact.

It was September by now, and I was no longer working so I finally had time for other things. I had plenty of extra time to sleep and see the family, which was nice. I was also able to do a few school visits in the local area that Ali had organised, which I enjoyed. It was great chatting to kids about what I was doing – some of them practically had their tongues hanging out when I told them about all my running. They were really blown away and I could sense some of them thinking: well, if he can do that, then I can run 5km. It made running seem less scary to some, at least I hope it did.

I don't know how many people ran their first marathon, or did their first 5km run that year because of me, but it was a lot. Even if I didn't raise as much money as I'd hoped to, I did help get more people out running, cycling and exercising generally. It just became infectious. Whether they did it to support me or because I was making it look achievable for the first time, I'm not sure, but they laced up their shoes and got out there. And that's pretty much all it takes.

Even Ali, a powerfully built rugby player, was setting his sights on a marathon. Well, he was a little bullied into that, to be fair. I did a post on Facebook suggesting he run one and said that if the post got 250 likes then he would do one. We got 269. He accepted his fate willingly, though, I'll give him that. He really put his back into training for a few weeks, but in the end he got a nasty injury and had to stop. Or pause, as I prefer to say. I like to think he'll run one yet.

With that 100-miler behind me, and those few runs through the night to the beginning of races, I had got something out of my system. In September, I never ran more than one marathon a day (or race, I should say, as there were a few ultras in there, though none longer than 40 miles) throughout the whole month. I'd realised that all I needed to do now was run a marathon a day for the rest of the year and the record was mine, as by the start of September I'd run 153 marathons/ultras in 142 days. I might not have been even halfway to my target yet, but I had a few extra marathons in there just in case. As it turned out, I'd end up needing every one.

CHAPTER FOURTEEN
Setting More Challenges

4 September–28 October 2014

The Great Barrow Challenge in early September was a rarity in the UK marathon calendar – the only multi-terrain ten-day festival of running in the country. It gave me the opportunity to run ten official marathons in ten days, and I was looking forward to it. I was given a lift down to the event HQ, which was a small karate dojo/gym in a remote field in Suffolk. The event organiser, Glen Moulds, was a top karate instructor, among other things, and a bit of a character with a heart of gold.

Those ten days were spent running morning marathons and then idling for the rest of the day. Without a car of my own, I was too far away from home to return so, between marathons, it was a case of communicating with my family and Ali by phone and getting some rest. I didn't particularly enjoy either, if I'm honest. Overnight I'd gone from having an incredibly busy schedule to having almost nothing to do, and I wasn't used to it. The races would be over by lunch and then it was pure downtime from there, but I was hungry for more activity, more racing. So it was frustrating at times.

I met some great people at the Great Barrow Challenge, though, including a very talented marathoner called Adam Holland, who is one of the quickest in the UK. He's become a good friend and we have big plans for future events together. There were just 15 of us who completed all ten, including the slightly bonkers Kate Jayden, one of the most prolific female multiday marathoners in the UK and a terrific character. They were all serious runners, with great stories to share and advice to give. As we were marooned together in Suffolk for the duration, we had an excellent chance to get to know each other quite well and it helped ensure there was a good atmosphere.

To give you an idea, on one of the marathons Kate and I took a wheelbarrow around the course. We took turns to run with it and gave lifts to other runners in it. There was a bit of beer being consumed that day too, if I remember rightly. It was a lot of fun and gave me an outlet for some my surplus energy, as well as breaking up the monotony. It ended up taking us over seven hours to get around the course that day (my slowest marathon for the entire year). So if you're looking to improve your running times, my advice would be to leave the wheelbarrow at home! However much I enjoyed being with that group, I was ready to get back home once it was over. I had been away from my family for too long, and don't like being stuck in one place.

People often ask me if my background has influenced me, or whether dealing with the pain I suffered as a child has enabled me to cope with extreme endurance events, and the physical suffering that accompanies them, whether those experiences enable me to go through the pain barrier and keep on going. The honest answer is I don't know; I'm not a psychologist.

Having lost my family as a child, I think it might explain why I enjoy the 'greater family' aspect of the running community. The only people I call family these days are Joanna and Alexander, Olivia, Peter, and Joanna's parents in Poland. So I probably get more out of being part of the marathon-running community than those with all the usual parents, cousins and grandparents around them. They have become like a second family to me, for sure.

I've shared my abusive past with you because it's a fact of my life. But at the end of that day it's just that: the past, a story that's finished. I'm like that with my races, too. As soon as one is done, I think about the next one. I prefer to look forward rather than back. A lot of people get stuck in the past – not just those who were abused. I see people, whole nations even, getting hung up on the anger and the hatred over something that once took place and that takes over their life. I think if we were meant to look back so much, we would have been born with eyes in the backs of our head.

That's where forgiveness is so powerful. The best way to stop looking back is to forgive those who've hurt you. Then you no longer have to think about them. It doesn't happen overnight, but it's a journey with an end point and you can start any time. I was angry for a long time as a kid and, to be honest, ashamed, but over time I worked it out of my system.

If you're struggling with your past, you can try various techniques to learn about forgiveness – there are plenty of suggestions about how to go about this online or in books. Follow your own path or get help if you need it – sometimes a professional therapist can enable you to unburden yourself. Telling your story and sharing your anger and shame will help the healing process. I found it helped to get things in the open, and not to suffer in silence. The dark is where shame and fear lurk, so shine a light on them.

The most important lesson I have learned is that if you have experienced abuse, then you have to realise that WHAT HAPPENED IS NOT YOUR FAULT. Could I have stopped my dad doing what he did at my young age? No. Could you if you were being manipulated? No. So forget that shame you are feeling because IT IS NOT YOUR FAULT. You are now in the position of power. Remember that. We all have choices to make. Do we choose peace and happiness, kindness and honesty? Or do we choose victim-hood and hatred, anger and resentment? It's really just that at the end of the day: a matter of choice.

These days I carry no anger towards my dad. The last thing I knew about him he was in prison for raping my sister. I don't know if he's out yet, but I don't want to re-establish a connection with him. I'd just like him to know that I forgive him. At least he doesn't have to worry about that if and when he is on his deathbed.

What of my mum and my sister or anyone else from my childhood? In my twenties, we did briefly get in touch again, but that was only a disappointment, so we have gone our separate ways. As far as I'm concerned, my family tree starts with me and goes forward. I'm the creator of my life. I'm like Adam in the Garden of Eden – only with a kilt on instead of a fig leaf!

My 170th marathon/ultra was the Equinox 24-hour race, where I ran six laps of the course (37 miles), around a lake on the Belvoir Castle estate in Leicestershire. It was here I met Sid Sidowski on my final lap, or Ultramorph as he's sometimes known. You can't miss him as he wears a white, full-body morphsuit, so he can barely see where he's going. He's raised a fair amount of money for Children with Cancer UK and we chatted about that, among other things, as we ran the last 5km of that lap together. He followed my bright green socks to begin with, as he could make them out through his spandex suit. Then, when he struggled to see even those, I took off my vest and he held on to one end while I held on to the other and I guided him to the finish of that race.

It was good to meet Sid, a delightfully eccentric marathoner and part of what makes the community great. I couldn't hang about, as I had to get down to the Farnham Pilgrim marathon the next day. That was a gruelling one, running (or wading) up big sandy hills in the North Downs. It was a hot day and a beautiful course, but some of the hills were very tough, both going up and coming down. It was a friendly marathon and I enjoyed it, even though it took everything out of me.

The weekend after that, I headed up to Scotland for the Clyde Stride 40-miler and the Loch Ness marathon. The running was great and the people even more so. My kilt didn't look quite so out of place up there, either. The biggest challenge of the weekend, apart from a sore leg and ankle, was getting between the races, which took some doing. After oversleeping on the Sunday, I needed lots of trains and taxis and a mountain of luck to get to the start line for the Loch Ness marathon in time. But I managed it, somehow, before catching a flight back to London. It was another unmanageable weekend managed, and I was back home in time to read a bedtime story to my boy, too.

By October, I had started to do a few of my midweek runs on the Thames Meander marathon course instead of in Richmond Park, because it was the deer-mating season so the park was not a safe place in the early hours. The male deer became a little volatile at that time, to say the least. I had already noticed their behaviour starting to change, and on a couple of occasions things got quite hairy, with stags clashing antlers on the path in their bid to prove themselves the dominant male. If you keep your distance they won't trouble you, but running right into them (as I was in danger of doing in the early morning) probably wouldn't have been a good idea.

My 185th, 186th and 187th marathons were all run at the VO2 Atlantic Challenge in the first weekend in October. This is a three-day event taking runners and walkers, at their own pace, along the wild and rugged north coast of Cornwall. It was a tough three days, with the wind in your face and the ocean almost permanently at your shoulder. Some really steep climbs and almost sheer descents meant you had to keep your wits about you at all times. Exhilarating is probably the best way to describe it.

There were golden beaches and boulders, bog and muddy passes, granite ledges, coves and cliffs and fields to get past. I walked and clambered and ran and got around it. It was certainly a test, especially as my leg was hurting again, and I was struggling with it. I made a mental note to make sure I got some treatment on it later.

Runners who slipped were in danger of cutting their legs up on the granite surface. It was very unforgiving, and you had to try to lift your legs up to avoid tripping and falling. I fell once and split my knee quite badly. I used some of the acid which I had bought online to seal up the gash. It left a little scar, but it meant there was no risk of infection and that was more important. It didn't make things any easier, though.

I met a load of great people at this event and there was a terrific atmosphere among the runners. I can't commend the race directors enough for a very well-organised event. When I finally finished in Land's End, I was a broken man, held together by who knows what. It had been a really memorable race, though. I'll be back again one day, for sure.

The following weekend, I had the Lakes in a Day 48-mile race in the Lake District on the Saturday, followed by the Isle of Wight marathon on the Sunday. With 350-odd miles in between events, I thought it might almost be the case that the logistics were going to be a bigger challenge than the running – how wrong could I be? Fortunately, I did seek some help for the travel, but when it came to the first race it would all be down to me.

But first of all, I had to get through the Lakes in a Day race. Honestly, it makes me emotional just thinking about it. Starting at Caldbeck, on the northern edge of the Lake District National Park, the route takes you along the Helvellyn Ridges, along the shore of Lake Windermere and all the way to the southern-most point in the Lake District at Cartmel. It was tough ultra and a day I'll never forget.

I arrived late on the Friday night. After sussing out the race HQ, I looked for a place to bed down for the night. I found a children's playground with a big slide. Underneath that was nice and dry – that would do for my mattress – but I wasn't ready for bed just yet. I had arranged with some ultra runners, who I'd become friends with on the circuit, to go running that evening. They had devised a marathon course in the area and wanted me to check it out.

I called the guys to let them know I'd arrived and they picked me up from the playground not long after. After a brief chat, we disappeared across the hills into the night. Twenty-eight miles and a little over four hours later, we were back. It had been a good run with lots of banter and laughs. It must have been about 4am by the time I returned to the playground for some sleep before morning broke. My easy month in September was very much behind me now.

By 8am I was up again and dressed, with super-sweet coffee in my belly and a briefing ringing in my ears. The directors doubted my ability to run this race and wondered whether I should be allowed to run. Fortunately, I managed to persuade them I was up to the task. Somehow I got distracted and ended up totally unprepared by the time the race started. I was pretty much still in my underwear when the klaxon sounded, so I spent the first mile or so busily getting my kilt on properly and pinning my number on while everyone else disappeared ahead of me.

It was the perfect day for a long run, cool but sunny, with some cloud cover. Once we got out of the village, the views of this special part of Britain were exceptional. I was tired but wide awake at the same time. It was very calming running through that kind of country. The greens and browns and greys of the hills had a soothing effect on my mind.

I put in a big effort to catch up with the leading pack and gradually moved up the field. There were some really tough hills and it was horrendous at times. The race boasted about 13,200 feet of climbing in all, so I knew how it was going to be, but it was worse than I had imagined. Maybe running through the night a few hours earlier wasn't the best way to prepare, after all.

When the fog came in, things got even harder; I couldn't see more than about 20m ahead of me. One second the front runners were just ahead where I could see them, but then they were gone. After that, I just had to do my best to stay on the route on my own. I'd left my compass and map behind at the race HQ, so it was a case of relying on my instincts. I never like reading maps much (though I recommend you learn to!).

My Achilles had been an issue over the previous week or so, and early on it flared up again, which was a worry. I had some ibuprofen with me, which I stopped to take. I don't usually take painkillers, and you shouldn't when you run, but this was one of those times when I felt I needed them.

At one point, the trail went in different directions and I had to guess which way to go. I opted for straight on. Soon after that some of the descents got so steep I was sliding on rocks and having to dig my heels in just to stay on the hill. I bounced off a rock at one point and managed to stop myself falling. Then it got almost vertical and I knew something was seriously wrong. They'd have supplied us with ropes and crampons if this had been the route.

I realised I was in danger at this point. I was lying on my belly on this incredibly steep hillside, holding on, hoping the loose rocks beneath me wouldn't start slipping. I started inching myself back up in the direction I had come. Then I stopped; there was an eerie silence all around. I felt like I was all alone. How far off course had I gone? I was starting to get a little worried.

Eventually I clambered back up and was able to get back on my feet again. Using nothing more than guesswork I tried to find my way back on to the route. I kept calling out for help, hoping someone would hear me, but it seemed I had managed to find myself all alone on some remote corner of the hill, cut off from all the others. Then someone's voice called back out of the fog. What a relief! I followed the voice and met up with a whole group of runners, which was great news, though I was disappointed to learn that they were lost as well. Shit! You know you're in trouble when the search party is lost, too.

Everyone had a different theory about how we would get back on the route. We ended up splitting up and agreeing that whoever found the route would have to make a whole lot of noise to let the rest of us know which way to go. It worked and eventually we had all found our way onto the course again. That little detour had taken a good 45 minutes from start to finish, but at least I was where I needed to be now.

We reached the first checkpoint, at which stage some of that group had had enough and dropped out. I knew how they felt, I have to admit. I could easily have joined them. That big detour, coupled with the nagging pain in my Achilles, had me feeling pretty low. I thought about giving up, but I carried on and just slowed down to a gentler pace. I chatted with some of the other runners who were struggling too and tried to encourage them. It always helps to focus on others, to try to help them out. Then the sky cleared a little and there were rainbows and amazing scenery to see, which lifted my mood. I was suffering but I was in one piece.

I came across a grand hall at one point and wandered in. They seemed to be preparing for a big party and there was loads of food around. I was starving and they let me have a few bits to eat. I felt better after that and continued on, only to get lost one more time, in the second half of the race.

Some 15 hours 17 minutes after starting out, I dragged myself over the finish line. According to my GPS, all those off-route detours I'd taken had added an extra 12 miles to the 48 miles I was supposed to be running. Nothing like doing things the easy way, then.

Ben Thornton was waiting for me at the finish to give me

a lift to the next race. He looked concerned. He wasn't the only one – my leg was hurting really badly and I couldn't disguise my limp.

'What took you so long?' he asked.

'We can talk on the way,' I said.

I said my goodbyes and we got in the car to head off. It was around midnight and we had a seven-hour road and ferry trip ahead of us to get to the Isle of Wight. I got into the back of the car and curled up under a blanket to get warm. My leg was in agony, but I chatted to Ben for a while. After an hour or so, I drifted off into some kind of sleep. It wasn't very comfy back there, but I was tired enough to sleep on the roof rack by then.

That road trip ended up taking almost eight hours in the end, what with waiting for a ferry at Southampton. We stopped off at a McDonald's at one point to get some burgers, fries and chips, with lots of extra mayonnaise – and a chocolate milkshake. I'd been drinking energy drinks in the car, too, so I thought I was pretty well replenished.

We arrived at the Isle of Wight marathon just in time to register with the other runners. We got underway and, though I was tired and in pain, I'd eaten enough to have some energy. I ended up finishing in a little under five hours, which wasn't bad considering I had a limp in my stride. It was one of those just-get-through-it marathons that was difficult to enjoy, but I coped OK. A guy called Ian Culton went past me at mile 17 and then doubled back to see how I was. I must have looked a mess, because he was concerned enough to stay with me for the last nine miles to help me get around. So he sacrificed his race for me as we took 90 minutes to complete the course after reaching the 20-mile mark. What can I say about that? Except thanks, though it barely seems enough, but his gesture was typical of what you see all the time in marathons.

I was grateful to have survived another busy weekend. I was still in the game, though I knew my body wasn't in the best of shapes. I didn't let on to anyone just how tough it had been, and kept up the pretence that everything was fine. I was probably trying to convince myself as much as anyone else. I went to bed many nights certain that would be it, and I wouldn't want to carry on the next morning, but every time I awoke, I felt more encouraged. I knew if I could just get myself to that start line then I would make it around. So I kept going, wondering deep down how long I could keep this up. It went on like that for a while.

And on and on. Especially as another major problem was about to strike us.

The following week was perhaps the hardest I'd faced to that point. Luckily, I had physio and massage to help me recover from the weekend's exertions, and I had the time to get some rest now I wasn't working. But that wasn't the problem. It was my finances. Without an income, I just couldn't afford to keep paying the bills and rent on our flat in Isleworth.

Graciously, Ali and Lorna invited us to stay with them. Indefinitely, Ali had said. I was incredibly grateful, but I didn't like it at the same time. Joanna and Buddy needed a home of their own, and I was supposed to provide that. Initially, I didn't want us to leave our home, but Joanna and Ali were convinced it was the right thing to do and per-suaded me. I felt like I was letting them down, but I couldn't see another solution other than to accept the Parkeses' gen-erous offer. Joanna got on with it, thankfully. She could have kicked up a fuss, but she didn't. I hoped Ali and Lorna and their kids, Shaun, Sophie and Calum, wouldn't mind having another family in their midst for a while.

On a brighter note, that week also led up to my 200th marathon/ultra on 17 October, followed by my birthday the next day. Finishing my 200th marathon on the Friday morning was a big moment for me. I was over halfway there now and, apart from a sore leg, I was in good shape. What I hadn't counted on, though, was the birthday party at Ali's house that night.

I'd never had a birthday party before. Ali knew that from previous conversations, so it was touching of him to organise one for me. There were loads of people there, most of the MMUK team of willing volunteers, physios, masseuses, web designers, taxi drivers and so on – the list is long and distinguished. They were good friends and the sort of people you'd want on your side in a crisis – or at a party for that matter. I don't really enjoy situations where the attention is on me, so it was a bit of a strange night, but I was really touched by all the kindness people were showing me and I hoped I looked like I was having a good time, at least.

I had a couple of tough runs in the schedule for that weekend: the Trailscape North race in Essex on the Saturday and the Ennerdale 50km race in Cumbria on the Sunday. After the dramas the previous week in the Lake District, the one thing I knew I didn't want to do was get lost again. But, soon after the klaxon sounded for the beginning of the race, that was exactly what I did.

It was a really tough diehard trail marathon in challenging conditions, even without making things worse. The course was soaked through from the heavy rainfall of the previous week and it took us through never-ending muddy fields that were like treacle, while massive puddles dotted the course.

We were all filthy and in need of a change of clothes after the first couple of miles. Then everyone started getting lost. I was in a big group and we all managed to go in the wrong direction, somehow. I think someone must have turned one of the signposts around, otherwise I don't see how it could have happened.

We were lost in an isolated part of Essex. It took an age for us to find our way back to the course. By now I recognised that I wasn't very useful at the navigation, so I left that to the rest of the group and just stood there laughing about it. I couldn't help it, and I'm not sure everyone felt the same as me. Eventually, we did find the course again. After that it was OK; my leg wasn't too bad and I finished in a little under five-and-a-half hours. Considering my GPS said I had run as far as 33 miles, I was quite pleased, but I really needed to ensure I wasn't making things even harder for myself.

Then I headed up to the Lake District again for the Ennerdale 50k ultra race. A couple of trains later, I was in a Chinese takeaway getting some food before my last connection, a train to Whitehaven. I took the chance to post a silly message on Facebook to say I was heading to the Ennerdale campsite and if you were up there and saw someone putting up a tent very badly, not to worry as that would be me.

On the train, a group of about seven women got on and sat in the seats around me. Maybe they could smell my food, but they all started talking about how hungry they all were. I'd planned to eat my takeaway in my tent in Ennerdale but, of course, I offered to share my food with the hungry girls, and we were soon chatting away and munching down on my chow mein and special fried rice.

It was late now and the carriage became increasingly packed with people who'd had a few drinks on their Saturday night out. There was singing and people falling over and laughing. Fortunately, I was surrounded by these women, who appeared to be the most sober ones on there, apart from me (and hopefully the driver). I wanted to keep to myself as I was tired, but someone recognised me, and soon I was being interrogated about my running.

When I got off at Whitehaven, I heard a woman calling out my name and feared it might be one of the girls asking me to join them, but it turned out to be Barbara Nelson. She and her husband Pete were followers of mine on Facebook and Pete was running at Ennerdale too, in the 25km event. Barbara had messaged me a few days earlier to offer me a place to stay before the race. I hadn't replied because I was a bit shy, but they had seen my post earlier that evening and they knew I'd be on that train, so they came down to fetch me. Of course, I accepted their offer. I was really grateful to spend a night in the warm, in their beautiful home. It was yet another moment of kindness from the marathon-running community.

The next day came and the race itself was spectacular. I got around the 50km course in a little over five hours, finishing tenth overall, so I was pleased at how my battered and bruised body was holding up. I had the feeling things were getting better again, and that I had got past a difficult patch and I was back on track.

I was given a lift back to a train station, but by now I was really hungry, so I went to a McDonald's and got 12 hamburgers and two apple pies. On the train home, I started going through the burgers one by one. I ate ten of them! I couldn't manage the last two, so I gave them away, but I still made room for those apple pies. I was in agony for the rest of the trip, but at least I felt full.

*

The following week went smoothly. Living with Ali and his family was working out OK. They seemed happy enough having us to stay, and Joanna and Buddy were enjoying themselves. It was nice for Buddy to have other children around, and Joanna had some willing babysitters on hand, which gave her a break now and again. From my perspective, I was relieved I didn't have to worry about them, as I didn't have the energy for it at that stage. Despite my ten burgers, I was noticeably leaner by this stage, as my body had become honed by all the races I'd run, so my times were a bit quicker than usual too that week.

For the final weekend in October, I was booked to run three official races, starting with the Beachy Head marathon on the south coast on the Saturday. On Sunday I would run the Leicester marathon before catching a flight to Ireland for the Dublin marathon on the Monday. It was going to be a long weekend of planes, trains and automobiles.

The Beachy Head marathon has a reputation as a very hilly and challenging course. They were very clear it was not one for first timers. My friend Johnny, who had dragged me out of bed and taken me to the Enigma marathon back in August, had agreed to drive me there. He planned to spend the time with his wife and two children at the beach while I was running the race.

Both Johnny and his wife, Ceri, had been inspired enough by me to begin training for a marathon, but it was still early days for them. The furthest they had run at that point was a 10km race, and they planned to gradually build up to a full marathon by the end of the year. It was a sensible plan, but I did not think it was very ambitious. All that week, I had tried to persuade Johnny to run the Beachy Head marathon with me. I was sure he could do it, but he didn't agree. So instead I worked on Ceri and managed to persuade her to run the 10km event that day.

When we got to the race HQ, I told Ceri I would go in and register her for her race, and get her number, but they had no more places left for that event. However, there were a few places for the full marathon, so I registered her for that instead. When I gave Ceri her race number, she asked if it was definitely for the 10km race.

'For a short run, yes,' I said.

So she went off to get changed. While she was away, I told Johnny what I'd done; he was certain I was for it when she found out. 'You'd better watch it,' he warned me. 'She's not going to be happy.'

By the time Ceri returned from changing, she'd worked out what I'd done. She looked really flustered and not at all amused. 'You've entered me for the bloody full marathon, Rob!'

Ceri was adamant that she wouldn't run it. I told her she'd be fine, that she could always drop out if it got too nasty, and how she might be surprised by how fit she was. Full credit to her, she decided to give it a go. I ran the first 10km with her and she was moving well. I left her at that stage and hoped she'd manage to get all the way round.

They weren't wrong in warning us about the event – it was a tough race all right, around the clifftops, with lots of hills to get over. When I finished I was concerned about what I'd got her into, and realised it had probably been a bit irresponsible of me to push her into it. Eventually though, a little over six hours after starting, Ceri came into view. What a moment! She was dead on her feet when she crossed the line, but she had done it.

It just goes to show that we are capable of so much more

than we think. If we will only push ourselves, we might be surprised by what's there. Completing a marathon for the first time can give someone so much confidence. Admittedly, Ceri did give me a hefty punch on the arm at the end of the race, which wasn't very nice, but maybe I deserved it.

I said my goodbyes and left them so I could catch a train up to Leicester, where I stayed with one of my best mates, John. It was good to unwind at his home that evening before running the Leicester marathon the next day. I ran quite well there. After that it was off to Birmingham to catch a flight to Dublin. I had arranged to meet up with some top ultra runners when I arrived. They had found me a place to stay that evening, so I was fully organised, which felt strange.

The Dublin marathon was a good race for me personally, but many of the competitors struggled with it. I don't know if they had been drinking the night before or if there was some bug going about, but a lot of people were violently sick and looked very ill at that event. It made me realise yet again what a big deal a marathon can be, and how it tests people to the limits.

I'd become blasé about it all. By that stage, I'll admit that usually when I finished a marathon I tended to think it was just another race completed, no big deal, but it's clearly a huge thing to most, something they aspire to and celebrate like mad when they finish. I think I regained some respect for the distance after seeing the suffering people were going through that day to get over the line.

Maybe I was wrong, and it wasn't just a bit of running after all. I was about to find out as I soon faced up to the biggest threat to my record-breaking challenge.

CHAPTER FIFTEEN
Disaster Strikes

29 October–26 November 2014

The weather was still surprisingly warm as November arrived, but there was lots of rainfall and plenty more forecast for the next few months. Nice. I had quite a few official marathons coming up – nine in ten days to be precise – starting with the winter version of the Thames Meander, my local marathon, on a course I'd run a few times already. I had to run a quick time in order to catch a lift and make it for the start of the next race, the Spooky Halloween marathon, 160 miles away in Telford. I did it in 3 hours 20 minutes, pretty darned good for me, especially as my leg was very painful.

Then, and not for the first time, I found myself jammed up in the back seats of a VW Scirocco with my friend Paul, trying to get some rest on the way up to Telford. I was massaging my leg, which now seemed to be permanently sore. It wouldn't get any better for the rest of the month.

We found the Spooky Halloween marathon that evening, more by luck than by the directions we had been given. That was a different race, for sure. Everyone, except for me, turned up in Halloween fancy dress (Paul, though, was kind enough to say I looked like a zombie and would fit right in). There were ghouls and vampires and witches, with lit pumpkins everywhere. It was really cool, especially as night set in. I took it pretty easy and met some great people along the way, as well as some old friends. It was difficult to turn up to any marathon by now without seeing people I knew. I had become a part of the marathon-running community and I loved all that came with it.

Paul ran with me for a few laps, while we ate barbecued food from the grill they had there. It was a fun event and a nice change for me. People asked me about my limp during this run, which surprised me as I hadn't realised it was noticeable, but I just had to force my sore leg to keep up with the other one.

By the time we left, it was about 10pm and the weather had turned nasty. We had a couple of hours' drive ahead of us to get to Marsden Cricket Club in Yorkshire for the White Rose Ultra the next morning. It was like judgment day on the motorway, with wind and rain lashing against the cars. Driving in a gale-force storm was interesting, though Paul's permanently furrowed brow next to me said he wasn't enjoying it too much.

We ended up driving around Yorkshire for ages looking for the race HQ, which was not where the sat-nav had led us. In fact, I was asleep for most of it, but was woken up by Paul's swearing every now and again. With my sense of direction, it was probably best I didn't make things any worse than they already were. As it was, we seemed to be visiting everywhere in Yorkshire apart from Marsden CC. Eventually, after a McDonald's dinner of several burgers and a milkshake or two, we found the cricket club and put up Paul's tent. He went to the car to get something while I crawled into the tent, and was asleep in seconds.

The next morning, we were awoken by the sound of other runners turning up in their cars. I overheard a couple outside my tent talking about 'Marathon Man UK'. It was strange to hear them discussing me as if I were some kind of celebrity, and I felt a little uncomfortable if I'm honest.

The race was tough, as expected, taking us through the moody Yorkshire countryside. I walked it as much as I ran it, thanks to the pain in my leg. There were some serious ultra-runners there and at times I felt like a bit of an amateur in their company. I listened to their stories with interest and tried to pick up whatever hints I could get on how to run with an injury – they gave me some good advice on how to tape up my leg. It was a beast of a run, with lots of hills, that took me just over six and a half hours, but the people were amazing and I had some great conversations.

Paul, my faithful man-servant, was still on hand by the time I finished. What a star! We headed off soon after to get back to Telford for the November Nightmare series of marathons, run by Denzil Martin, the same guy who had put on the Spooky Halloween marathon a couple of days earlier. He had kindly offered to let me stay at his house for the four days I would be running up there, and he'd explained in detail where he lived as well as where the race HQ was.

However, my mind had become jumbled after a few days on the road. Somehow I had got it into my head that Denzil lived on the disused railway line in Telford. This was in fact where the race HQ was located, while his house was a few miles further up the road. For that reason, we spent a couple of hours late at night knocking on doors along the railway, asking bemused individuals if Denzil lived there. In the end, we went to a pub and contacted him on Facebook to get his address. By the time we knocked on his door, it was about midnight and he was half asleep. Sorry about that, Denzil.

The next few days were pretty horrific, running wise. My leg was now a real problem and though I was getting through these races it was very painful before, during and after. The marathons in Telford were all along a disused railway line, which had been concreted over, but not very well, so the surface was uneven, which didn't help. It was pretty wet, too.

I managed to complete four marathons in the series, but it wasn't pretty. The third day was the toughest. I came down with a cold and my eyes were burning throughout the race. My energy levels dropped to zero and I had no strength in my left leg at all. I felt like crying, to be honest, and had to fight the instinct to give up the whole way around. Each of those marathons in Telford took me an average of six hours to complete. They called them the November Nightmare marathons and I could see why.

My cold would pass, but I really had to get some help with my leg or I knew I would be struggling to keep going. I went back to my family on the Friday and visited Dominika for a massage. She saw how swollen my leg was and thought I should see Dr Kipps to get it properly checked out. That sounded like a good idea, but I decided it would have to wait. I had too many runs ahead of me, and I think I was too scared of what he might have said.

Next up was the Druid Challenge. This was a three-day trail event along the 3000-year-old Ridgeway path in the Chilterns, which is apparently the oldest road in Britain. I was running only the second and third days, though.

The highlight of those runs was meeting the legendary adventurer Ranulph Fiennes. He was running a marathon there in preparation for the Marathon des Sables the following year. At the age of 70, he wasn't showing any signs of slowing down much. We had a good chat, and he wanted to know what I had done so far and what I had planned once it was all over. I told him I wanted to do something nobody had done before, so he suggested an impasse in the North Pole that no one had ever crossed solo, because the weather was just too bad. I told him I'd do it if he lent me some warm clothes.

'Ah, but you'll need to get permission to run that one out there,' he said.

'Well, maybe you can ask on my behalf,' I replied. 'They'll never refuse you.'

'Are you serious?' he asked me.

'Why not,' I said. 'It's not impossible, is it? It just hasn't been done yet.'

He told me I sounded a lot like him when he was a young man. High praise indeed! We discussed various things that day. I really liked the guy, though you could tell he was a bit bonkers. And I mean that with the greatest respect. People such as him, who do extraordinary things, are not regular people. They're a little bit off-centre, and much better for it.

You won't be surprised to hear that I got lost again on this run. Really lost. A load of other people followed me this time, and it took us about an hour to find our way back onto the course after that. They probably thought let's follow Marathon Man UK, he knows what he's doing. How wrong could they be!

It wasn't ideal preparation as, in just three days' time, I was due to run marathons 230 to 234 at the Hell of a Hill event on the Lancashire moors. They were supposed to be the toughest five consecutive marathons in the whole world. But seriously, how hard could they be?

*

I had a few days at home before going up to Lancashire. I say home, but it was Ali's house, though we were being made to feel really welcome. I'd like to tell you Joanna and I were hitting it off and that we weren't arguing about how long I was spending away, or how I needed to sort out a home of our own for our family. But, sadly, that wasn't the case.

I felt under pressure from Ali, too. He was probably doing no more than usual to try to help build my profile, but I guess my leg was worrying me and pretending everything was fine was a strain. Whatever it was, I was looking forward to getting away from it all. I'm sorry to say that, but that's how I felt at the time. When I was running, there was peace from all the demands on me, but when I returned it all started anew.

On Tuesday 11 November I caught a train to go to the Hell of a Hill marathon series. The course was eight laps up and down the Rivington Pike, a steep hill on the exposed West Pennine Moors. That meant 6,000 feet of climbing a day, up 2,416 misshapen steps, in the wind and the rain. What could possibly go wrong?

I hadn't brought my tent with me this time, but fortunately they let me sleep in the race organisers' main tent, with all the t-shirts and medals. (Truth be told, I snuck in there the first night and after they caught me in the morning they agreed to let me sleep there the rest of the time.) It wasn't the most weather-proof of places, so I slept under a massage table to keep the rain off me. And it rained almost continuously that week.

There were about 20 entrants taking on all five days of the event, and I would get to know most of them well, while an additional 20 or so runners joined us each day for that day's marathon. The first one was a rude awakening. The course was unnaturally brutal; the cobbled, broken path was treacherous underfoot. It was incredibly slippery and you had to be careful where you placed each step. Coming down was as dangerous as going up. There was nothing uniform about the route. It twisted this way and that, and had death traps everywhere. Runners were falling all around me – you just couldn't keep on your feet. And falling on those rocks meant nasty cuts. I was lucky. I fell only a couple of times and after the first two days found a good route up and down.

I was in a lot of pain, but I had a little help with it. My strategy was to take 2 × 400mg tablets of ibuprofen and 2 × 200mg of paracetamol about 30 minutes before the race start. Then I'd take another paracetamol at the halfway point in the race. Whatever the thinking on running with medication is, those pills certainly helped make the whole thing bearable for me.

The second day was so windy I almost got blown off the hill. This was insane, I thought. Really good runners were struggling to get around. It was one of those events where you had to encourage and support each other as much as possible, but somehow I managed to get round in a similar time to the first day, just over five hours.

I met a bunch of good people at this race, including Mickey Dwyer. An Australian comedian living in the UK, Mickey livened up the post-marathon wind-downs in the tent at the end of each day. He was funny, obviously, but also very compassionate, the first to help anyone on or off the course who might need it. We'd sit in that tent chatting and sharing stories until it was late. The other runners didn't know I slept there, so at the end of the evening I was just waiting for them to leave so I could get some sleep.

Poor old Mickey. He was leading after three days, but he didn't have much luck after that. On day four, I found him picking himself up off the steps halfway down the Pike. He'd fallen and cut his knee very badly. I joked about it with him and told him to get up and get on, but it was really nasty and he could barely move. I suggested he sealed up the cut with a bit of acid, but really it was too deep for anything like that. He needed stitches.

I decided I needed to get him off the hill and out of the cold as soon as possible, so I lifted him up on my shoulders and piggy-backed him down the most treacherous bit. Then the trail turned right and I managed to find a guy with his bicycle who let me use it to wheel Mickey down the hill. He ended up free-wheeling the last half-mile on his own, while I continued on the marathon route and met him again at the bottom of the hill where we waited for the ambulance together. He was cold and agitated, and I just tried to keep his mind distracted. To be honest, for at least an hour on that hill, I think I was the better comedian of the two of us.

Later we learnt that a helicopter ambulance had been called out onto the hill for him, but he'd missed the ride because I had taken him to the bottom of the hill. He'd never been in a helicopter before, so he later he ribbed me mercilessly for robbing him of that opportunity. (In December, Mickey and his comedian pals would treat me and my friends to a special comedy performance at Ali's house, as a way of saying thank you for helping him off the hill that day. That was a lot of fun, though really unnecessary. Thanks, Mickey.)

Mickey's injury was the worst of many that week. Almost everyone was carrying some kind of cut or knock by the end. It was tough to see so many people struggling and in pain. For myself, I had to take plenty of painkillers just to get through it. At a time when I should have been giving my leg a chance to heal, I was giving it more reason to be distressed and angry. Looking back, I'm not sure running those races was a very good idea.

But I got through it. By the final day I'd completed my 234th marathon/ultra and I was a wreck. The combination of five freezing cold nights in that tent and all the running had left me exhausted and in need of a break. I was looking forward to getting home, but the rest of November was equally tough for me. I was taking a lot of painkillers to help me through the running – maybe as many as 15 or 20 ibuprofen every day. It was getting to the point where I was being woken up in the night with the pain. My left leg was swollen from the ankle all the way up to the thigh. Something wasn't right, but I was carrying on. Everyone could see there was a problem, so eventually I was forced to visit Dr Kipps to be checked out. I felt a bit bullied into it, to be honest.

I remember Dr Kipps's look of concern when he saw me. He said I looked thin. After a brief examination, he booked me in to have MRI scans that day, on both legs, and rushed it all through. He said it would take a few days for the scans to come back, and I told him I was going to keep running whatever the results showed and that he should know that. I returned to Ali's that night and I wasn't feeling good. I fell asleep on his couch and then was woken up from a deep sleep.

'What is it, Ali?' I said. 'What time is it?'

'It's about midnight,' he said. 'Kipps just called. You need to hear this.'

I sat in the dark of the unlit living room. Ali turned on a light. 'What did he say?' I asked.

'He's got the results of the MRI scan, Rob. And it's not good news. You've got four problems in both legs, but it's the swelling in the bone in your left leg, in your tibia, that's the real issue. If you carry on running on it, it'll fracture. You'll break your leg, Rob.'

'It's swollen. I knew that before,' I said. 'This doesn't change anything. It'll get better, you'll see. I'm gonna keep running and that's that.'

I lay back down to go to sleep; I had a marathon to run the next morning.

'You've got to stop, Rob,' Ali said. 'He was very clear. If you run any more you'll break your leg. Do you hear what I'm saying?'

It turned out Dr Kipps had been concerned enough to have the scans rushed through immediately. My first reaction was just to ignore it and carry on; I wasn't willing to face the prospect of everything ending like this. I'd always said I'd keep running until I could run no more – and I hadn't reached that point yet. But deep down I knew that was madness. My leg had been getting worse for a while, not better. Slowly I started coming around to the fact that I might have to stop, and who knew for how long.

The next day was 26 November, and I ran my 241st marathon in the morning, as usual, on the Thames Meander marathon course, and it hurt every step of the way. Then I went to see Dr Kipps again. I wasn't sure what I was going to do, but by the time I saw him I had decided I wasn't going to fight him. I accepted his diagnosis and got on with the idea of resting up for a while before getting back on the road.

It was a dark day. The *Daily Telegraph* immediately announced my failure to the world. Messages of support came in for me. I would be back, I assured them all. This was a pause and not a stop. We tried to be upbeat, but it was hard. It felt like the whole world had caved in on me. And I had no idea what would happen next.

CHAPTER SIXTEEN
Getting Game Ready Again

27 November 2014–13 January 2015

After speaking with Dr Kipps and making my decision, my left leg was fitted with an aircast boot. Dr Kipps then told me what the road for recovery looked like. He said I shouldn't run or walk on it for six weeks to let the bone stress heal. Then it was a case of building up strength in the gym, doing physio, and slowly, over the next couple of months, building up my running till I could run a marathon again. But I didn't have that kind of time. The world record for consecutive marathons was gone now, but I could still get the record for most marathons run in a year – if I got back to running in the next few weeks, that is.

'Statistically, that's simply not possible,' Dr Kipps said kindly. 'You need to rest for a good while to let your bone recover, or you'll just run the risk of injuring yourself.'

But it had to be possible. Everything is.

Dr Kipps tried his best to help me. Pippa Rollitt had me doing exercises to flush out my legs. They found a Game Ready machine for me, which was invaluable. Using that every day really brought the swelling down. A Game Ready is a piece of state-of-the-art medical equipment, featuring NASA space-suit technology. When attached to the leg, it pumps ice-cold water and air onto the damaged area, keeping it iced and compressed, to aid healing and recovery.

At home everyone was full of sympathy. 'You've done so well, Rob,' they kept saying as if it was all over. It wasn't. I could get back, I knew it. The experts didn't know me, they didn't know my body. They knew only the average for all people, and that wasn't me. By staying positive, I knew I would recover quicker than any statistics could predict. So that was that for a while: rest and recover. I visited a few schools and gave some talks, which was great, as the kids helped to keep me positive. It was a tough time all in all, but I made the most of it. I got to hang out with Alexander and to see much more of Joanna, which helped make things better between us now I finally had some time to be with her.

It was around then that I learned about the upcoming Race Across USA marathon series which took place every year. The 2015 event started in January, and would take a group of runners on a four-and-a-half-month journey from one side of America all the way to the other, from sea to shining sea. It would mean 117 back-to-back marathons, all of them official. The event also aimed to raise awareness and funds for a fantastic organisation, the 100 Marathon Club, which was set up to combat childhood obesity by encouraging children in the United States to exercise more.

I wanted to run in that race, but wasn't sure if it would be possible to make the necessary arrangements. It was coming up soon and I'd need a visa and sponsorship. Then there was Joanna. She'd probably hit the roof if I disappeared to another country for the best part of five months, but I couldn't get the idea of it out of my head. Thinking about it gave me something to work towards – but first I had to fix my legs. Even after just a few days' rest and use of the Game Ready machine, I was feeling better and the swelling in my leg had gone down considerably. Soon I would be ready to put some weight on it.

While all this was going on, I attended the BBC Sports Personality of the Year presentation evening, thanks to Carl Doran. That was quite a night and took my mind off the problems I was facing. Ali and I dressed up to the nines and spent the evening having selfies with the great and the good of the sporting world. I even met Eddie Izzard there, who had famously once run 43 marathons in 51 days. The first thing I said to him was, 'Wow, your skin looks amazing, how do you get it like that?' Then he came alive. He pretty much did a one-man skincare sketch for the next few minutes. What a funny, funny guy! It beats talking about running anyway. Can you imagine how many conversations I have to have about that?

On our way out at the end of the night, after plenty of beers, Ali and I somehow ended up on a coach with the women's rugby team, instead of getting a taxi. We'd been invited back to their hotel. I couldn't believe they knew the words to the rugby songs they were singing on that coach. Then it was my turn. Reluctantly (with a capital R) I sang my standard. 'I love you baby, and if it's quite all right, I think that maybe ...' Fortunately, they all joined in to help me out. Then it was bags of chips and back to their hotel, not for anything saucy, I might add. I can imagine the headlines now:

MARATHON MAN UK BEDS HOOKER

The following day I spoke to Pippa about an anti-gravity treadmill I might be able to use. I had heard about them being used by Mo Farah and other athletes to come back from injury. They used NASA 'unweighting' technology to allow recuperating athletes to run with only a fraction of their weight going through their legs. As you become stronger you can adjust the percentage of weight you are bearing, until eventually you are back running under normal conditions again. I believed that the sooner I was running again the better, even if it was on some kind of futuristic treadmill. Pippa told me they had one in the changing room at Twickenham rugby ground, the home of the Rugby Football Union, but she thought it would be next to impossible to get permission to use it. She and Dr Kipps said they'd try for me, which was all I wanted to hear.

And, as always, Pippa came through. So somehow, someway, on 9 December, a little over two weeks since my last run, I found myself being strapped into a space-age treadmill in the hallowed heart of Twickenham. It's testament to my team's resourcefulness that a plodder like me had got access to this thing, which they believed would be able to accelerate my recovery by as much as three weeks.

The first time I used the anti-gravity treadmill, I ran 5km on about 20 per cent of my bodyweight, the second time I ran 20km and the third day I ran a full marathon on it. Dr Kipps had urged me to build up slowly over the next few weeks, but I just didn't have time for that. By 18 December I was out running unaided again. It was just a short 5km jog to ease back into things, and everything felt fine.

The next day I ran a half marathon and the day after that, on 20 December, just 23 days after stopping my challenge, I was able to run another marathon. My legs felt great and as far as I was concerned I'd recovered fully. Of course my medical team had urged caution and wanted me to wait longer. Pippa had suggested I run 10km that day, but I knew

I could do more. I ran the full Thames Meander marathon course instead and felt pretty good.

Of course my body had slipped back and it was no longer the running machine it once was. It had embraced the easy life for the previous three weeks and was lazy and resistant to effort. I was back on that difficult curve, whipping it into shape. In a month's time it would be trained up again and ready for anything.

My goal now was to run more than the 366 marathons/ultras in a year that Ricardo Abad had achieved. At that point I had run 242 marathons in 251 days, so I was behind schedule, but as long as I remained fit I knew I could do it. I'd only need to run a few double marathons to get back on course.

Marathon Man UK was back!

I went down to the south coast for the Portsmouth marathon the next day. It was a hard race and I felt sluggish. It would take a lot of miles before I would be back to optimum fitness, but I got through it, completing the race in 4 hours 8 minutes. With the Race Across USA series on the horizon, I knew I had to put extra miles in to be fit and ready for it. So after the race I went out for another ten miles on my own. I just felt that's what was needed to get my body into condition again.

It was nearing Christmas and good will was in the air – an ideal time to speak to Joanna about the Race Across USA series, I thought. It was a tough conversation. She could see why it would be good for me and what I was trying to achieve, but she didn't want me to go. She was concerned about the effect it would have on our relationship – I wasn't being a father or a husband. I told her I couldn't give up now, and nor could we. I had to finish the challenge and this was the best way to do that. The Race Across USA would effectively give me a support team for the rest of my challenge and help me to the finish line. I knew it was my best option at that time and something I had to try to join.

Fortunately, and typically, in the end Joanna gave me her blessing, and I started to put the wheels in motion to join the RAUSA team in January. It meant a lot of hustling and organising. I needed to get funding and to know Joanna and Buddy would be OK without me. She decided to go back to Poland to stay with her mum for a while; Buddy loved it there and they could live cheaply and well. It was a good plan and would mean I didn't have to worry about them too much.

Then I had the small matter of raising the money to enter the race, which, including flights and everything else, came to about £10,000. I got some money through from my sponsor, Sense Core, which covered most of it. Then two local sponsors, who wish to remain anonymous, stepped forward to help me with the rest. I couldn't have done it without them and am incredibly grateful to them both for their generosity (they know who they are). Ricky, from Up & Running in Sheen, got me some kit from Salomon and Brooks to take to America, too. Not for the first or last time, he came to my rescue (as did the guys at Sheen Sports, too.)

It was getting very cold in the UK at that time and that was taking some getting used to. Running on Christmas Day was a first for me, too. It wasn't easy finding someone to join me for that run, I can tell you. Pulling crackers, watching end-of-year quiz shows and eating turkey and Christmas pudding was all anyone wanted to do. And I couldn't blame them. Hopefully that would be me next year.

On Boxing Day I messed up. I was running downstairs at Ali's place, in too much of a hurry, when I clattered into an open door. My left foot, protected by only a sock, smashed into the leading edge of the door. It was a really violent collision and I lay on the floor in agony. Eventually, I took my sock off and looked at the damage. I couldn't touch my little toe or the one next to it. I hopped down the stairs, furious with myself for being so stupid.

Joanna was there at the time but apart from her I didn't tell anyone in the team what had happened. Instead, I went out and ran that day's marathon, which wasn't easy. My time for that marathon shows how tough I found it. It took me over five hours (I'd completed one the day before in less than four) and by the end of that day my toes were red and swollen and I went to the local hospital to have them checked out. They soon confirmed what I suspected: I had a fracture in the bone just above the toes and two small fractures, one in my little toe and one in the toe next to it. Of course I was told to rest, but I knew how to take care of them. I iced them when I could and otherwise just got on with the running. They were sore for a couple of weeks, but after that they were fine. To be honest, it was only during the first few miles of a marathon that they were sore at all, then they just became numb.

I continued to push hard in my Richmond Park marathons through that last week of the year, trying to get back into peak fitness. The other runners in the Race Across USA series sounded fit, experienced and capable. I felt like I needed to be at my very best in order to be able to live with them. It wasn't until 29 December that I was able to run two marathons in a day, and that felt good. My legs were getting stronger again, more resilient. I could feel the progress.

I had two official marathons in Liverpool, the Liverbird marathons, to help me see in the New Year. One was on New Year's Eve and the other on New Year's Day. I would be meeting up with my good friend and fellow runner Adam Holland and our buddy Graham Clarke for the races.

The first run on New Year's Eve was a good one for me. It was a flat course up and down the Otterspool promenade in Merseyside a few times. With almost zero elevation it was a chance for a quick but steady run, and I managed a time of 3 hours 29 minutes. Adam won the race with a time of 2 hours 38 minutes, making me look a bit ordinary, while Graham came in shortly after me. That night we'd managed to find a self-contained flat in the heart of Liverpool. It was New Year's Eve, so despite having a race the next day, we decided to go out and enjoy ourselves. We all knew it would probably get a bit out of hand, which it duly did.

None of us was used to drinking, especially Adam and me. We almost never drank, and especially not before or after a race, but that night we went for it. We were drinking cocktails followed by wine and beer – whatever we could get our hands on. Whatever had the highest alcohol content, that's what we ordered. It was ridiculous, really.

Graham and I took it upon ourselves to try to find Adam a girlfriend that night, which meant embarrassing him and ourselves in front of several groups of girls. Then came the sambuca. I don't know whose idea that was, but it turned out to be the final straw for Adam. Moments after necking it, he disappeared out of the bar and threw up all over the pavement. It was truly torrential. I felt bad for him as he had to run a marathon the next day. Happy New Year!

By about 3am, we returned to our apartment and Adam and Graham crashed out within seconds of hitting their beds.

I went to the toilet to put my finger down my throat to make myself sick, but nothing wanted to come out so I accepted defeat and went to bed. The next morning we woke late and rushed around the apartment trying to find clean clothes. It was chaos. Eventually we got ourselves together and out of the apartment to head off to the race. On the way we passed a McDonald's and popped in to grab a coffee and a couple of burgers.

At the race start Adam looked as white as a ghost, like he was in a state of shock. Poor guy. That night he'd probably drunk as much alcohol as he had in the entire year before that. I remember him eating a Mars bar at the start line and looking like death. I thought he would struggle to finish that race – I knew I would. But he didn't look in any condition to do anything remotely athletic – not even a game of frisbee, let alone a marathon.

When the race gun went off, Adam responded like the champion he is. The course looped back on itself repeatedly, so we passed each other several times, with him in the lead and me way back. Every time we saw each other we shook our heads at each other as if to say 'Never again!' After drinking way beyond his limits and projectile vomiting only a few hours earlier, Adam won that race in a time of 2 hours 57 minutes. That's got to be some sort of record for a drunken athlete, surely. I, on the other hand, would need over five hours to get around the course. It was awful. I can only repeat what I said earlier: 'Never again!'

I was due to leave for America on 14 January. So those first two weeks of the year were spent getting things in order. Joanna and Buddy had their tickets booked to go back to Poland later in January. Ali and I had booked tickets out to

America (he would be there just for the first couple of days to help me get settled in) and my visa was on its way.

It was a stressful time for me and some cracks began to form in my relationship with Ali at that time. Little things became magnified during those weeks leading up to my departure. He had worked hard for months to make a lot of things happen for me outside of the running and I was grateful for that, but it had taken its toll on him, I think, and he knew that. Now he wanted to step back a little and spend more time with his family, who he'd probably neglected while he'd been making me his priority. I didn't want that for him anymore. He and his family had done so much for my whole family, opening up their home to us when we were most in need. It was time for the Parkes family to get their lives back, and for me to make more decisions on my own.

Before we left I had a couple of tests to see how far I'd come, how fit I was and how ready I was for this race across America: the Trailscape South marathon in Kent on Saturday 10 January was followed by the Martello Marathon on Sunday, also in Kent. The Trailscape South marathon was a challenge, largely because I got lost again. Then there was an electric fence that a group of us got stuck behind, which none of us could work out how to open. We spent ages trying to figure it out before somebody showed us – at least we didn't electrocute ourselves. I spent six-and-a-half hours out on those trails – some of it actually running and on the right course, too. Still, I got around and had some laughs with other runners despite the frustrations of the day.

The following day's race, the Martello marathon, was a good one. Flat and simple, with no chance of getting lost or electrocuted (barring a freak lightning strike), I went flat out

229

for the first ten miles to see what I could do and then eased right back after that. My time of 3 hours 22 minutes told me I was race ready. I'd got back to where I needed to be and finally felt confident about going to the United States to race. When I returned home that evening, I went straight out to the park to run another marathon. That second marathon really took it out of me and I ended up resting the following day, which was fine. I knew that once things got underway in America there'd be no chance for a break, so this was a good moment to take a breather.

I spent the day with Joanna and Buddy. It was my last chance to pause from all the running and say goodbye. Once I got to America I wouldn't see them again for a couple of months at least. We didn't do anything special, just kicked around the house for most of the day and went to the park, but we got to chat and take some time, which we both needed. I hoped she'd find a way to come out to visit me in America, but didn't know how that would happen exactly.

I was going to miss the pair of them in the coming months, that was for sure. There would be no home comforts, no hugs before getting back on the road again, but this was the home straight and nothing would distract me from finishing what I'd started. The next day I ran a double marathon on the Richmond Park course. I was almost back to marathon-a-day status again – running my 275th marathon/ultra on my 276th day of the challenge. I felt strong and confident.

Marathon Man UK was ready for America and hopefully it was ready for me.

CHAPTER SEVENTEEN
Taking on America

14 January–23 February 2015

At Heathrow, Ali being Ali managed to sweet-talk the British Airways crew into giving us a free upgrade. So it was first-class all the way to LAX, which didn't hurt. On that first day in Los Angeles, we took a taxi from the airport out to West Hollywood to see a chiropractor who had been recommended to us. He was a bit of a celebrity healer and had treated all the movie stars and the top athletes in his day. Somebody in the team had put us onto him and it seemed like a good idea to get a tune-up before the racing began. He clicked my spine and I felt a bit lighter after the session and my shoulders a little looser.

It was late afternoon by the time we got out of the clinic and realised we didn't have a room booked for that night. We wheeled our bags around the block looking for a motel, but Ali didn't like the look of what was on offer, so we kept walking. It was an exciting adventure to be in a foreign country, not sure what might be around the next corner. Ali was grinning from ear to ear; he was a big kid just like me. Eventually, we got chatting to a couple of guys outside a gym and the next thing we knew they were offering us to sleep in their gym for the night. I'd slept in caves, under slides in children's playgrounds and in a dozen half-assembled tents, so a night on a yoga mat in a gym sounded like five-star accommodation to me. Ali was reluctant at first, but he went along with it after a little persuasion.

The next morning we left the gym early before the first customers started to arrive. The sky was blue and the sun warm, even in the early hours of the morning. It made a nice change from the grey skies, cold and rain we'd been used to in London. We made our way over to a clinic in the city to have some medical tests done by Bryce Carlson and his team. Bryce was racing in the series, but was also its research director. An assistant professor of anthropology from the University of Purdue in Indiana, Bryce was interested in seeing what could be learned from all our exertions in the coming months.

So I had agreed to be subjected to a variety of tests before, during and after the race series. Bryce had organised quite a team for the task; alongside him he had experts in human biology, physiology, sports medicine and sports psychology, all determined to learn how we would cope with the five months of physical and mental stress we had ahead of us. That was what they called it anyway. Five months of running is all I would call it. After all, I wasn't trying to put myself off before I'd even started.

Dr Aaron Baggish was part of the medical team. He was one of the heroes of the Boston marathon terrorist attack, an experience which had left its mark on him. Dan Liebermann was there too, an endurance-running specialist. These were top guys in their field. They measured us for various things, did heart scans and injected dye into my blood. I was a willing guinea pig, only too happy to be able to help these guys try to learn something useful out of our crazy bit of running.

I met some of the runners for the first time at that clinic, too, people who I hope will be lifelong friends. There was Bryce, of course, who was impressive in almost every way. Intelligent, open, warm and humble, he was all you could hope any human being to be. And then there was 'Barefoot' Alex Ramsey and Jup Brown. I was introduced to them, we had a handshake and hug, and it was like we were old friends right away. It was uncanny – I guess we all had something in common, so there was no time needed to get to know each other. We could have stayed all night talking; we'd read about each other online and now we were face to face, so there seemed like so much we wanted to say.

Eventually, we went to the hotel where we were being put up that night and to the race presentation there that evening. It was great to meet everyone at last: the runners, the support crew, the faces who'd become so familiar in the coming months. For the next hour or so, we were introduced to the key personnel and briefed on the race itself and what we should expect. It was all very exciting.

The next morning was race day 1. We assembled on Huntington Beach and the getting-to-know-you continued. All 12 core team members were there, those who were attempting to run the entire race series from coast to coast, as well as a few other runners, including those who were doing just the ten California marathons. We all paddled in the ocean, which was freezing. One of the runners, Patrick Sweeney, even had a swim, but he was the only one brave enough. Some guys bottled up a bit of Pacific water to pour out once we got to the Atlantic on the other side. I remember Patrick telling us how he liked to search for and find treasure along his runs, little toys and plastic shovels, all kinds of discarded stuff. He said he later gave them away to friends as awards, which we thought was a lovely idea.

The core team was a varied bunch, but each of us was as enthusiastic and excited as the next. Here's a little introduction:

Newton Baker – the oldest of the group, he was celebrating his 73rd birthday on that very day. Newton was a wise, poetic and relaxed guy. He was really witty, too, and we'd have some great moments together in the coming weeks.

Nancy Bennett – the mother figure of the group, I grew to be really fond of her. She was a real Texan girl and tough with it, but she was always looking out for the best interests of the group, and if someone got low Nancy would always be there to help.

Jup Brown – the sweetest, funniest, most free-living guy of them all. He is up for any adventure that you might suggest. While he stuck around, he brought everyone together. He'd run the length of New Zealand and Japan before, so we knew he could put the miles in.

Bryce Carlson – he brought some academic scrutiny to the event which could only give it added credibility. He's a top-quality endurance runner in his own right, too. He mellowed out in the second half of the race and, I think, started to live for the moment a bit more. We became closer for it and shared many happy, funny moments.

Steven Cooper – 'Coop' was a great guy and an intelligent one, too. His company serviced SpaceX and Tesla, doing things too advanced and technical for my little brain to comprehend. When the first man lands on Mars, Coop will be behind it.

Jessica Hardy – tough as nails. A bit like me, she likes to mess about but underneath is resilient as hell. She's also very kind and loving, always looking out for those around her.

Chris Knodel – a war veteran and an all-round great guy. A bit of a fellow nut-case is Chris, and like me he wears a kilt sometimes.

Linda Mazenko – a really soft, loving lady who I respected a lot. However, she was also on the board of the event and somehow I think that put a barrier between us and the other athletes at times.

Alex Ramsey – Barefoot Alex is pure Hawaiian sunny vibes, as mellow and colourful as the tie-dye t-shirts his company makes and that he's always wearing. No one could possibly say a bad word about this guy, least of all me. One love, always.

Patrick Sweeney – a very mellow Californian dude and a good runner, too. He's laid back, down-to-earth and good to be around. We could all use being a little more like Patrick, I think.

Darren Van Soye – the race organiser as well as running the event alongside his wife, Sandy. His heart was in the right place and he was a really nice guy, but running in the event as well as being its main organiser might have put a little too much on his plate at times.

As you can imagine, this was a big day for us all and there was a real feel-good vibe on the beach. We posed for a few photographs and then it was toes-to-the-line time. Newton had been so impressed by Patrick's story of finding cool little trophies in the sand that he was distracted, still looking for a memento of his own as we lined up for the start. Then his eyes lit up as he found something and picked it up. I thought it was hilarious that we were about to start this epic race and he was more intent on finding a bit of plastic on the beach, but the look of joy on his face when he found it was priceless.

I hadn't run for a couple of days now, so I was keen to get going and to see what the rest of the field had in them. I had read that a few of the guys were sub-2.45 marathon runners, so I was interested to see if I could keep up. All the talk at the start of the race was about conservation of energy. Restraint was the key (apparently) to running 117 back-to-back marathons, but surely not if you wanted to win the thing. It was a race after all, and if there was a chance I could win the race series and be one of only a few Europeans to do so in the event's history (since the 1920s) then that was my goal. I'd spent seven months running marathons without winning a single one, so maybe now was my chance.

The race got underway soon enough in the 70 degree heat. I went out pretty quick. A couple of runners gave me the impression they didn't quite believe I could have run the number of marathons I had in the times I'd stated, so I wanted to let them know from the off I was for real. I led the race for the first few miles as we ran along the beach before turning left and running up beside the Santa Ana river. There were a fair few people out to wave and support us, so I loved that. The excitement of it all must have distracted me because, somehow, I managed to miss a right turning over the bridge. Even now I'm still not quite sure how that happened.

So, just a few miles into a 3,080-mile race, I was lost again, freewheeling down the LA sidewalk, heading who knows where. I ended up running into a dead end, thank goodness, otherwise I've no idea what would have happened. Then I turned back on myself and went looking for the race. Luckily for me, I soon noticed a couple of runners on the other side of the river. They motioned that I should get myself back to the bridge I'd run past a mile or so before to rejoin the race on the right side of the river, which I soon managed to do.

So much for showing them all how quick I was. Or how intelligent. I think I might have let my country down a bit that day. Still, at least I found the route again and made steady progress. It was another loss of concentration for me and I finished in fourth place, but I had survived the first day and we were underway. There was plenty of time to make my mark on the event yet.

*

After our first marathon in the series, we drove out to Linda Mazenko's home for a big slap-up dinner. It was both Newton and Patrick's birthday that night so we had birthday cake, too. There was a happy vibe and we were all floating on this wave of optimism, but things wouldn't always be this cosy in camp.

The next day was a big one as we got to pause in the middle of our marathon to visit the 100 Mile Club head-quarters in Norco. I was excited to meet the kids and hear their stories. It was such a great initiative they had set up, something the UK would do well to replicate. The idea is simple: kids sign up to take part at their school and then for the rest of the year they have to run (or walk) a total of 100 miles at school, which is measured and verified by a teacher. They get rewards for hitting various goals on the way, and at the end of the year they get a certificate and that feeling of success and accomplishment that all children thrive on.

It cost only $10 per child to take part in the initiative, but not everyone in America has that, so our job was to raise some funds for those children to take part, as we ran through the country, as well as spread awareness about the initiative. Being part of that was a real privilege. I love hanging out with kids anyway, so this day was a real bonus. Logan was the epitome of the programme's success. He ran his first 100 miles five years ago and every year since he had added another 100 miles to his year's goal, so in 2015 he was running 500 miles for the year. That's pretty impressive for a 14-year-old!

We had a great lunch with those guys before rejoining our marathon route to the finish. I got lost again, although just briefly this time, and I ended up finishing in first place that day. Although where I finish has always been the least important thing to me, it still felt good finally to win a mar-athon at my 277th attempt. I enjoyed that day, despite my ears getting a little singed in the hot weather. That night we went out for American pizza, which was the best!

The third day went well; I was finding my stride with the running and getting quicker. The scenery was breathtaking in an entirely different way to the UK. The huge skies and the ever-expanding landscape were something else. We were heading out towards the Joshua Tree National Park and I had heard the stars shone like diamonds out there. I was really looking forward to seeing that. As a bonus, this was also the day I learned that I was able to run faster than a car, too – or at least quicker than our support vehicle.

The way each day worked is we would get up early in the morning and ready ourselves for the race. We'd start running by about 8am, when the support vehicles would also set off, so they could set up the first-aid station at about mile 5-7 in the race. But I got there before they'd arrived. Apparently, I was running too fast for them to get there in time, as they couldn't keep up in the traffic. They finally reached me at mile 17, by which time I'd already needed some tap water at a fast-food restaurant to keep me going. After they'd checked I was OK and given me some food, I carried on with the race. Then things got interesting; I got lost again. By the time I realised what I'd done, I was running on the wrong side of the Santa Ana river. I knew I had to get across the river to rejoin the race, but how? I should have turned back to find the small bridge that I'd clearly missed, but I noticed there was another one right in front of me. Only it was a railway bridge.

I had a good look up and down the track in both directions: nothing but silence. It must have been only a couple of hundred metres to the other side. I looked again up and down the track again: still clear. So I set off across the bridge, but soon worked out it was narrow with nowhere to hide if a train did come, so if that happened I'd have to jump in the river, which was a good 15m drop. I decided to hurry along.

Then I heard it – quiet at first, but getting louder in a hurry. I looked back, just once, to see the train far in the distance, so I sprinted as fast as I could. By now I could hear the lines whirring and the noise of the train growing behind me. It wasn't far to the other side, but it seemed to take forever. Only a couple of seconds after I'd crossed the bridge and jumped to safety, the train flashed by going at some speed. I realised how stupid I'd been – that was far too close a shave for my liking.

I found the race again and was still in the lead. I'd taken a little detour there, and ended up running further than if I'd stayed on course. I came in first again, but later that evening the race directors spoke to me about how I was running. 'You're going too fast,' Sandy Van Soye said. 'We can't crew you if you run that fast. We can't catch up in time. You're going to have to run with the other runners behind you.'

I was in a race but was being asked to run slower, which seemed crazy, but what other choice did I have? From then on, I ran a bit slower. I didn't mind too much, but it did have an impact on my legs over the next week, almost like I was relearning how to run, because I was no longer running at my natural pace. So I just hung back and chatted with Juan Carlos Calderon, a really nice guy who was the second quickest runner at that point. He was a sheriff who was only doing the California leg of the race. Having to run slower meant I could go into shops to get drinks and ice creams for the guys and share it out with them en route, which I liked.

That evening was our first night's camping and I hadn't yet bought a tent. Fortunately, we all went to the Super Walmart in San Moreno where I managed to find one for the princely sum of $14. I can't tell you the dollar/pound exchange rate at the time, but I'm sure that would have been a bargain even during the Gold Rush era. Now I was ready for anything.

We camped in the Lake Perris State Recreational Area that night. It was pretty epic. A skunk, who smelt even worse than us, came sniffing around at one point. Later, while we prepared our food on stoves by the tents, we could hear coyotes howling in the distance. This was the Wild West all right!

The next day was hot once the sun rose, but I didn't mind. I was running well and everything felt good. We were heading off down Highway 10 now towards Palm Springs and the desert. I saw a couple of monster trucks by the road, as if to further remind me what country I was in. Sadly, when I asked the drivers wouldn't let me get behind the wheel. That night we stayed in a hotel with a pool and a spa, so you can imagine how well that went down. Then it was out to dinner and a brief visit to a casino with the guys.

I took $20 with me and figured I had to have a gamble. I was a few hundred miles from Vegas, so I thought when in Rome . . . I sat at the blackjack table, which seemed to offer the best chance of success, other than blind luck. I don't think I was doing anything exceptional, but before long I was winning and Jup and the rest of the guys were whooping up a storm. I was on a hot streak and everything was going my way. Pretty soon I had turned that $20 into $800! Someone told me that, as a non-US resident, if I won over $1,000 I'd start to lose a chunk of it in tax, so I cashed my chips in and left while I was ahead. I used the $800 to buy everyone's dinner the next night and still had some left to add to my kitty for the coming weeks.

The next day we ran along Highway 62 towards the Joshua Tree National Park. It was our first taste of some hills, with well over 3,000 feet of climbing throughout the day. For those among us not used to running this kind of distance every day, it was starting to get hard. We finished the day at the park, setting our tents up on the sand and had great fun playing ultimate frisbee for an hour or two. As it got dark, you could see all the stars, large and bright, in between the clouds overhead – awesome. Then Jup got out his camera and started taking clever shots, using a flash light and adjusting the shutter speed to capture our names in lights in the night sky. It was a great end to a great day.

The next morning it was very windy and I almost lost my tent to the wind while trying to pack it away. Which gave me a great idea: let's fly it like a kite! Jup got involved too and together we tried to get my tent up in the sky, where it wanted to be. We managed to lift it only a few metres off the ground, so it just wasn't to be.

We were booked in to visit a couple of local schools that day and split off into two groups to get it done. Jup and I and a few others went to Yucca Valley High School to talk to them about what we were doing. Hearing the kids' stories about what they were up to and how they were getting fit was really inspiring. We messed about in a gym there for a while, which helped to take everyone's mind off the running. After that, I had to break away from the group to go and run the same route as the day before again, only this time on my own. I was still behind on marathons for my attempt to run 367 in the year. Fortunately, the crew were happy to help me out and I ran a decent time, pretty much the same as the day before. My count was now up to 281 marathons in 283 days.

The next four days were spent running across the desert, a straight highway through wide open land, under a hot, hot sun. There was little traffic now, so the support vehicle was better able to get ahead and set up the aid stations, and I could run as fast as I liked, which was important. I took a piece of chalk with me one morning and at about the 17-mile stage I stopped to write some messages for the runners behind me ('GO ON, JUP' and 'RUN, COOPER, RUN' for example). I hoped they'd see them and be encouraged at that, often rather miserable, point in a marathon. When they finished later, I was pleased to hear most of them had seen my messages and they had given them a boost.

From here on in, I would use the technique that had served me best in multiple marathoning. That meant starting out quickly and running the first six miles in about 30 to 40 minutes, then I'd try to get to the halfway point in about 1 hour 30 minutes or quicker. For the second half of the race, I'd taper off and walk and jog, depending on how I felt. This meant I was already starting to recover in preparation for the next day's running. If I wanted to improve my time, I might switch up the pace for the last few miles, but generally I'd just cruise in. For anyone trying to run more than a week's worth of daily marathons, this is the technique I'd recommend adopting.

That afternoon we camped again in the Joshua Tree National Park, surrounded by desert sand and boulders. It was strange to think only a week ago I was running in the British rain with the whole world on my shoulders; now I was in cowboy country, with new friends and nothing but the open road ahead of me. Having all that company, during and after races, and being with people who got what I was trying to do was making a big difference to my spirits.

A group of us decided hike up a hill to watch the sun set. Sitting at the top, supping a beer and taking in that view, we felt free. We chatted easily with one another and I felt among friends. It was a perfect, magical moment. It makes me well up just thinking about it. Usually when I told people I was running a marathon a day, their response was: 'What! Why would you do that?!' They'd react as if I were some sort of crazy person. To the average guy, I guess that's how it looked, but to these guys I was just one of them. There was nothing I needed to explain; they got what I was doing and why, and that made all the difference.

The next day I found a cuddly toy lion on the highway, so I named him Leo. We picked up all sorts of things; it seemed this was where teddies came to die, or to be rescued by marathon runners. I was pleased to have discovered something myself, but after a couple of hours of running with Leo, I had to release him back into the wild as he was a bit of a pain to run around with. It was a shame, as I felt sure Buddy would have loved him. Thinking of him was a painful reminder of just how far Joanna and Buddy were from me, on a map at least. However, since landing in America, they kept on turning up vividly in my thoughts. Their smiling faces and the silly things we had done together may have been unremarkable memories, but they now seemed incredibly precious.

A couple of days and marathons later, we set off on a very overcast morning for our tenth marathon and our last run in the state of California. It felt great to have run across one state and now to be heading into another; we were making progress. The last part of the race was over a bridge across the Colorado river, which served as the state line. We were now in the town of Parker, Arizona.

California had been amazing: hot, dusty and empty for much of it, but beautiful, wild and epic. For the state runners it was the end of their journey, and we said our goodbyes that night. Juan Carlos, Ryan, Jack, Alfa and the rest had been a big part of the team and they had all stood up to the task of running a marathon every day. They had some truly awful blisters to show for it and a sense of pride, and in some cases astonishment, at what they had just done. It goes to show that if you put your mind to something you might well surprise yourself. Next up for the rest of us: 15 marathons across the desert state of Arizona. Bring it on!

The following day was a rest day. We got up early and some of us were messing about by the river, playing with Jup's slack line, trying to balance on it. Then someone bet that I couldn't sail my blow-up mattress across the river to the other side in under 15 minutes. You know me well enough by now to recognise that was a challenge I wasn't going to turn down. Jup joined in and soon we had borrowed a paddle and were in the freezing river on a mattress furiously paddling to the other shore. There was a donkey on the other side and Jup wanted to bring him back with us, saying we'd get bonus points for that – more like a bonus kick in the eye.

We managed to get back to the shore, without the donkey, in under ten minutes, which is surely a state record (in both California and Arizona) for crossing a river on a blow-up mattress. Everyone had a good laugh and let off some steam. Jup's a real character with an infectious way about him that draws everyone in and I was enjoying being around him.

Doing silly things like that was a lot of fun and also an important part of the long-distance runner's survival kit. You need to break up the tedium of countless miles on the road by doing random things that bring a smile to your face, for no other reason than that. Happiness keeps the show on the road. Without those moments, your spirit will give in and your body will break apart. So keep it light out there, cowboys and cowgirls.

While everyone else continued their rest day, I had a couple of marathons to run. I needed to get some more under my belt if I was going to reach that world record of 367 marathons in a year. This time it was simple. I ran the same marathon as the day before, except in reverse, running from Parker back along Route 62 to where we had started the day before. Then I turned around and came back. It was pretty tough going, as it was a hot and cloudless day, and without the others around it was lonely. You realise at times like this how much you appreciate the support and company of other runners and crew. I managed to run the two marathons in under eight hours, which I felt was pretty good going. My body felt fine and, after a big meal, I was in good shape and ready for the next day's run across Arizona.

Sadly, Coop had to drop out at this stage to return back to work at SpaceX. Mars's gain was our loss is all I can say. He was a good guy and would be missed. We were now a man down, but he wouldn't be the last to leave us that week.

Arizona was dry and straight. We stuck to the highway for the entire route, so it was just the long, empty road ahead, broken up by the occasional cactus. Though it was pretty featureless, we were still unmistakably in America and it was all very exciting and novel, to me at least. My excitement was a little dented one morning when I got hit by a rock. Some idiot had thrown it from a car, along with word 'Faggot!' The rock bounced off my back and made me stumble to my knees. I was only bruised, but lucky not to have been seriously injured, and just a little shaken up and disappointed that someone who didn't even know me would do something like that.

It didn't take me long to work out the rock was probably thrown because I was wearing a kilt. This was redneck country and there'll always be a few idiots out there. I had a feeling that if men in skirts aren't appreciated in Arizona, my kilt might not go down so well in Texas either, which was where we were headed. It was a worry as I could do without feeling like a target.

I was rooming with Patrick Sweeney that night and he had some really cool running shorts in a stars-and-stripes design, so I asked if I could borrow them to run in instead. He said that was fine, so now I had a new running outfit. I had gone native. From then on, I got nothing but love on the highway. Plenty of drivers honked me and waved at me on my runs, all because I was wrapped in the flag. It was sad to put the kilt away, but it was out of its element here. It was goodbye MMUK, hello MMUSA!

Things seemed to be picking up in that first week in Arizona, despite Coop having left us, but then they got worse. Patrick and Jup had some disagreements with the race organisers and told me they'd decided to pull out of the race. They both felt passionately about the 100 Mile Club initiative, and were convinced they would be better able to serve that cause by heading off in their own splinter group. They weren't guys to kick up a fuss about nothing, but I think their departure was down to a failure of communication; sometimes that's enough to break up a team. At the time, I was as cross as they were about a few things and contemplated joining them. However, in the end I decided to stay with the race, after much persuasion from Jup and Pat (and Pat's support crew Vanessa and Shacky) not to throw away my year's ambition.

Jup said his goodbyes to the group that night. After only three marathons in Arizona, he was leaving the race and starting a new one of his own. His going really hit everyone hard, as you can't imagine a nicer, warmer and funnier guy to be around. He was really the good heart of the group and it broke everyone up to see him go. People understood the issues involved and respected his decision.

Although his mind was made up, Patrick hung around for a few more races with the rest of us. His friend Michael Miller was due to join us for four days of the Arizona leg, so Pat stayed to run those marathons with Michael before calling it a day and joining Jup. It was disappointing to see friends go;

additionally, Patrick was one of the faster runners and someone I was looking forward to racing against in the miles to come.

Lucky for me, it wasn't long before I got to see Jup again, as he and I had a special invitation the following night. Michael and his partner Kimberly had invited us to their home to share dinner with Vanessa, Shacky, Pat and Maria Walton. Maria had been the girlfriend of the legendary ultra-runner Micah True, more commonly known as Caballo Blanco, before he died in 2012.

Caballo Blanco has become a legend in ultra-running through his starring role in Christopher McDougall's *Born to Run*. The book tells how he ran with the Tarahumara tribe in the Copper Canyons of Mexico, a reclusive people who run vast distances, either barefoot or in simple sandals. Minimalist running, as practised by Barefoot Alex, for example, exploded off the back of that book. Maria was now one of the race directors of the Ultra Marathon Caballo Blanco, which Micah founded back in 2003. She is very well respected in the running community and it was a real honour to be able to hang out with her and the rest of the guys for the evening. We had some great food (though the hot sauce blew my mind!) as I listened to stories and shared my own with these beautiful people.

One story that evening, told by Michael Miller, made a big impression on me. It's not my story but I want to share it now because it manages to capture, better than anything I can say, how profoundly running connects us to the world of nature. Michael runs where he lives in Arizona, in the foothills of the McDowell Mountains. It's desert country, searingly hot of course, but alive with life too – snakes, scorpions, mule deer, skunk pigs and hawks, including Michael's favourite kind, the red tail hawks.

As a lover of the majestic red tail hawk, Michael told how

over the years he had enjoyed passing one particular Saguaro cactus, which he called 'Old Man'. As an ancient cactus it was impressive enough, but what made it special was that it was used, year on year, by red tail hawks as a nesting spot. Each spring Michael told how he would enjoy running by and glimpsing a baby hawk in a nest in the arms of the 'Old Man'. Mama hawk would be circling overhead, keeping an eye on her little ones down below and Michael would always cast his eyes skyward and reassure Mama that he was just a sweaty runner passing by, and of no threat to her darlings.

Then, a couple of years ago, he was heading out towards the 'Old Man' on a run, but as he approached he failed to notice its distinctive silhouette, as he usually did. As he ran closer he discovered that it had been the victim of a lightning strike, its once impressive size cut down by half. What remained was no longer a fit home for baby hawks to nest in. Amid his shock and sadness, Michael was initially concerned that the chicks might have been harmed by the strike. He looked for any evidence to this effect and was encouraged not to find any. He told us how he stood for a while at the base of the massacred cactus, with tears in his eyes and his heart full of sadness.

When he did run on, he soon saw as many as five red tail hawks perched on bushes in the vicinity. Before that day they had never let him run so close, and he had only ever seen one adult before and that was the Mama flying overhead. Now he saw five of them, all untroubled by his proximity. For him it was a special privileged moment. It almost felt like they were there to comfort him in his loss, to share their grief with him. A silent communication passed between them and it was something he would never forget.

Some months later, at an arts festival in nearby Cave Creek, he found a wooden carving of a red tail hawk, a Kachina doll.

It seemed magical to Michael and somehow of profound significance, so he spoke to the creator who told him he had had the wood it was carved from for over ten years, but he had never known what to do with it. Then, he said, a few months ago (at precisely the time that the 'Old Man' had been destroyed) the artist suddenly realised it must be a red tail hawk and had started carving it. Of course, Michael bought the carving and it remains a treasured possession.

For me this story can mean many things, but what it says most is that running can reunite you with the natural world. By running you become a wild animal among other wild animals and get access to a dimension you otherwise wouldn't.

That evening Maria Walton kindly gave me a Caballo Blanco badge to cover a hole in my trousers and a great buff, too (a buff is a kind of bandana, worn by runners for protection and fun). They were fantastic mementoes from my evening with Maria and I wear them with pride.

The next day I ran a protest marathon. I was annoyed about Jup and Patrick leaving and wanted to let the race directors know it, so I walked for most of it, finishing in a time of over six-and-a-half hours. My heart wasn't in the running and I was seriously thinking about quitting myself. It was an unsettled period for us all as we struggled to come to terms with the loss of core members of the team.

I decided to stay in the end, and I'm glad I did. I just focused on the horizon and got on with running through the dry, hot Arizona landscape. Then, just as things seemed to be settling down, Chris Knodel dropped out, too. I didn't even get to say a proper goodbye. Apparently he had some family issues that needed immediate attention, so I can only hope it wasn't anything too serious. Chris was a good guy and another face I missed seeing each day.

So, in the space of a week we'd lost a third of the core team, four out of 12. It felt like the whole thing was falling apart and we all wondered what might happen next. I guess it was one of those moments when it could have gone one way or the other. There were lots of conversations in camp, as you can imagine. For the most part the runners were committed to what they had set out to do, and while there was sympathy for Jup and Patrick, I don't think anyone else, apart from me, even contemplated joining them.

Still, it was a strange time in camp. Like a ship in a storm, we all wondered if the next wave would come along and sink us, but fortunately the storm passed and the waters calmed. Whatever brought us to take on this challenge, helped keep us on track. The mood was subdued, but still the remaining runners carried on running, through the outskirts of Phoenix and into the Tonto National Forest, towards the New Mexico border.

I had some family issues of my own. I phoned Joanna every five days or so to chat, but always seemed to get in trouble. She felt I wasn't ringing enough, because she obviously had little idea what was going on, while I felt perfectly happy with what I was doing. She also told me I wasn't responding quickly enough to her texts, which made her feel stressed. The problem was that by the time I'd get them, it was the middle of the night back home and I didn't want to wake her. Deep down, I knew she was proud of me, and I'd have liked to hear her say so, but communication can be really hard in those circumstances.

We had a rest day on 4 February, and while the others were resting I did two marathons that day, the first following the marathon route from the day before, through the Cave Creek area on the outskirts of Phoenix. Then, when I'd finished that, I just carried on running until I got to the end of the second marathon at Rock Creek on Highway 87 (the same marathon we would all run the next day). The two together took me over nine-and-a-half hours to complete, so it was not exactly what you would call a rest day.

It felt good to have done that, and in three days I would have a crack at my 300th marathon, which was pretty amazing, especially after my legs had almost given up on me a couple of months back. I was in great condition, except for a nagging toothache. Before that, I had an interesting experience after having finished my 299th marathon. We were on the outskirts of Phoenix and I'd seen a couple of gun shops in the small towns we had passed through. I wanted to find out how easy it would be to buy a gun, so I went into a store to find out. I looked around for a while before approaching the owner. As an Englishman, it's very strange to be looking around a shop at bullets and rifles, even submachine guns and what looked to me like a rocket launcher. Eventually I spoke to the heavy-set guy at the counter.

'I'm visiting from England, but if I wanted a gun could I get one here?'

'Well. That all depends,' he said.

There was a bit of a long pause as I wondered what complicated hoops and red tape I would have to go through to be able to qualify to buy one. 'On what?' I asked.

'You ever been to prison?' he said.

'Nope.'

'Ever shot at anyone? Tried to kill anyone?'

'Nope.'

'Should be fine, then,' he said. 'Just need to fill out some paperwork, then we'll get you hooked up.'

Surely it couldn't be that simple? I had no intention of buying a gun, but it was amazing to see how easy it would be. I filled out the forms and he went out back with them. A few minutes later, he returned and said I was good to go. I could choose any gun I wanted.

'Even the semi-automatic guns over there?' I asked.

'If you can shoot it, you can buy it,' he said. I couldn't believe it. It just seemed so crazy to me. The guy told me that the further south you got, the easier it was to buy a gun.

'Shoot, in Alabama, they'll practically buy you the gun,' he said.

From about this point on the route, until we got to Dallas, we weren't allowed to camp outside anymore. The desert nights were considered too cold in eastern Arizona, New Mexico and western Texas for that to be a sensible option, so we bedded down in a church in Payson, Arizona. I remember when some poor families came to get a free meal that the church was offering. I saw children, just like I had been once, ashamed yet grateful for a handout. It was very moving and reminded me of the problems even the richest of countries have and the need for the rest of us to do more to help such children wherever they are.

A volunteer at the church told me they gave shoes to the children, as the parents couldn't afford them. I felt like I needed to give something, so I went to my room where I had a bunch of $5 bills and I screwed them all up into little balls and went around giving them to the kids, quietly. Seeing their faces light up when they unfolded it and realised it was money was priceless! Some of them were confused, though; they couldn't understand why I had given them money. I didn't know them, after all. The minister heard about what I'd done and came over to thank me. He said that was more money than anyone had ever given them. EVER.

I saw one girl give her money to her mum, saying: 'Here

Mommy, this is to make you happy again.' Wow! That really touched my heart – the little girl giving her mother the only money she had in the world. Trying to help children was exactly why I had started on my quest, and now I was seeing the impact I could have with even a small gesture. I thought: this is what I want to do – give everything I have to help others. I left that day knowing that 14 children or so had a smile on their face because of my small act of generosity, and a couple had even shed tears of joy. I spent a mile or so on the next day's run wondering what those kids might buy. It was fun to think of them looking around a toy shop for something they'd enjoy.

For the next nine days, we continued on through the forest on the interstate highway of Arizona. We made steady progress and soon we'd finished the Arizona leg of the tour. To celebrate conquering our second state, we went out to eat that night in a rib shack called the Waterhole in Springerville. It was supposed to be the best barbecue joint in the whole of Arizona. They weren't wrong either. The brisket and pulled pork was to die for, and the perfect end to a long day's running.

While everyone else had a rest day, I was back on double marathon duties and so was the first to try out the New Mexico route. I ran the next day's marathon route twice, out and then back again, in a little over eight-and-a-half hours. It took me to 308 marathons/ultras in 307 days.

The next morning we had a nice bonus as two guys, Jesse Riley and David Warrady, visited us for a pep talk. David was a former winner of the 'TransAm' transcontinental race, back in 1992, when he ran the 3,000 miles from LA to New York in 64 days, while Jesse was a two-time race director of the event. They were knowledgeable guys and good to chat with. They assured us that the worst was over, that all we had to do was to keep our heads on and we would make it to the

Atlantic in one piece. They stayed with the race for the next few days, giving us all the benefit of their many years' experience in such races, and it was good having them around.

I had actually met David the day before while I was out running. He'd pulled up alongside me in his car, wound his window down and asked, 'Aren't you meant to be resting?'

'Yes,' I said, 'just going for a few miles.'

'I've heard all about you, Rob,' he said, 'so I know what that means in your world.'

In New Mexico the landscape changed, for sure. Gone were the sand and scrub bushes of the Mohave in California and the cacti and grass of Arizona. Gone were the amazing views in Phoenix, looking down over the valleys and mountains and never-ending trees. Now it was empty land, with no trees to speak of, just a rolling ocean of dry grass and empty space – except for cows. This was grazing country from what I could tell, with more cattle than people, or so it seemed.

Things were certainly getting quieter, and there was more of a feeling of being out in the middle of nowhere each day. Fewer cars passed by on the highway and the towns we ran through were tiny, with just a few shops, and those usually empty. This was the quiet heart of America, and it went on forever. My toothache hadn't gone away and was my only real difficulty at the time. It was always there in the background, throbbing, aching and occasionally sending bolts of pain into my head. It was calling out for some action and in the end I took it.

I'd already decided a dentist would be too expensive so, one evening, while holed up in a school hall for the night, I took a pair of long-nose pliers and got to grips with that tooth. It wasn't the best tool for the job and I struggled to get hold of it to begin with, but in the end I got some purchase and starting shaking that tooth. It hurt like hell, but I knew it would be better out than in. Eventually it cracked, diagonally, and most of it came away, leaving a sharp shard behind. Shit! Not what I was hoping for. After some more clattering around in my mouth, I managed to break what remained down to a nub, so at least I wouldn't perforate my gum while I slept.

I wanted the whole tooth out, but I couldn't get hold of that nub now so that was that. It wasn't a great result, but it bled profusely which seemed to relieve the pressure. While it felt marginally better that night, within a week it had stopped hurting altogether, so I think it worked out overall.

The rest of the team had other aches and pains to worry about: blistered feet, Achilles problems, back problems, cramps, the list goes on. When we weren't running, we were icing our legs and sore muscles, doing what we could to make things better. Jessica Hardy was clearly struggling. I felt for her and let her use my Game Ready machine to help relieve her painful muscles. She was struggling to finish some races and some of the stronger guys were trying to keep her positive, running along with her at times. I was busy thinking about everyone else because I felt fine, physically. I was tired, obviously, but motivated. I didn't have too long to go and I wasn't going to give up easily – which was lucky because I was about to face my toughest marathon yet.

CHAPTER EIGHTEEN
Closing in on the Record

23 February–13 April 2015

The weather changed overnight. Drastically. After a run of 38 fine-weather days with blue skies, we got up one morning and it was different. Not freezing yet, but there was a nip in the air and some scary looking clouds on the horizon. Then we got running and the snow started falling and falling. Soon we were in a near blizzard with the winds gathering pace all the time.

It was awful. It had been fun to begin with, of course, the way snow is. For half an hour we all enjoyed the novelty, but the wind was fierce, practically blowing me off my feet. We were running into the wind for most of the race and I felt like I was making all this effort but going nowhere. It was ridiculous; I was obviously weaker than I'd thought. Still, I finished first, and after Bryce and Barefoot Alex crossed the line, we decided to get some hot chocolates and take them out onto the course to help people get around.

I'll never forget the look on Newton's face at about mile 20 when he got a mug of hot chocolate inside him. He didn't say anything, he was too cold for that, but his face told me it was a lifesaver. It was difficult enough for me to finish that day, let alone for a 73-year-old man. What an inspiration that guy is.

The next few days gave us more of the same, weather-wise. On one day, running through Picacho, it was the coldest it had been yet. For the first 16 miles, it didn't stop raining and the rain was icy cold. Then it started to freeze on my face and on my facial hair. My clothes were covered in ice as the rain froze. I was really struggling and signalled to the support van that I needed more clothes, but they were in the other van. I had been leading the race up to that point, but soon Bryce and Alex caught up with me and then ran on as I was too cold to keep up with them.

I was in trouble now, starting to suspect hypothermia would set in soon. Fortunately Andrea stopped to ask if I was OK and I told her I needed my clothes. She responded fast and soon Sam arrived in the other truck. I jumped inside and got all my clothes on, my foil blanket and my sleeping bag around me, and sat by the truck's heater. It was pumping out hot air but it didn't feel like heat to me. I was still shivering and pains shot all the way up my arms and into my back. It was so bad I cried out, I couldn't help myself. I yelped. I've never been like that before or since. I didn't know quite what was happening.

I felt like quitting that day in the truck, I really did. But then I remembered that lady I had met in Richmond Park whose son had committed suicide, and my promise to her to continue running no matter what. I also had an unspoken promise to all the other kids I had met in schools who had shown me that my story was far from unique. I had to carry on. I wasn't running for myself, but for every other victim of abuse whose story isn't being told.

Eventually the rain stopped and I was able to get out and finish the last few miles of the race. If the rain hadn't let up, I don't think I would have finished that day, and I probably wouldn't have been the only one. It just hurt too much. It was only thanks to the quick actions of the support team – Andrea, Sam and Garrett – and a break in the storm that I was able to chalk up my 320th marathon and keep on track for the race series. Thanks, guys. You kept my hopes alive out there.

The weather continued like that for a few days. It was frozen underfoot and wet and snowy in the air around us. They were tough conditions, especially for the Californians among us, who thought cold weather was when the sun goes behind a cloud for a minute or two.

Running through Roswell, there were almost no cars out on the roads because it was just too icy. The highway was like a barren desert and we could run wherever we wanted on it. We each tried to pick the best route along the road, but it was no good. There was no best route; it was hazardous and perhaps we should have stopped. Even with the best trail running shoes on, there was no grip to be had. I made the ice-skating motion with my legs at times, which was more effective than trying to run, then I slipped and fell over on my face. Ouch! My arm and hip were bruised after that. It was nothing serious, but it takes its toll when you're freezing cold, soaking wet and going nowhere fast.

I fell a few times that day, but the worst of it was the ice in my beard. I've taken some videos of myself running that day and I look like Scott of the Antarctic. It was pretty hardcore, but we knew Texas wasn't far away and I doubted those cowboys would put up with much of this weather. It was surely just a case of enduring it for a little while longer.

*

I was right about Texas. Even as we approached the border, the sun came out and it was back to being warm again, but it didn't last long; soon we had freezing rain and snow again. The Texan hospitality, however, was always warm. There are countless stories from the runners of generosity from strangers throughout the whole race, but in those 23 marathons across the Lone Star State we were treated particularly well. People would stop us regularly and, on the spot, donate money to the 100 Mile Club. On more than one occasion, after chatting to locals in a diner while getting something to eat, we later went to pay for our food only to be informed that it had already 'been taken care of'.

As well as being a welcoming one, Texas is also a tough state, typified by something a local said to Bryce one time. When he told this guy he was running across the USA, he looked mystified. Bryce asked him if he ran and he replied: 'This is Texas. We don't run – we're armed!'

It's tough country in other ways, too. Rattlesnakes were supposedly a constant threat, though I didn't actually see one. Someone rolled down their window at one point in Haskell and said: 'Hey, you better watch it out here. When you get up ahead, there are a lot of rattlesnakes that are gonna jump on y'all.' Fortunately that never happened, but it kept me focused on the ground ahead, that's for sure.

In the beginning we were running through oil country, with oil fields by the side of the freeway as far as the eye could see. At night we usually stayed in churches where we were well looked after and we were always grateful for the warm hospitality at the end of a hard day's running. One evening I remember a local fire station offered us all dinner for the night. After a day's running in the cold wind and a constant drizzle that was really appreciated. More good ole

Texan hospitality. They entertained us with funny stories of
how they raced lawn mowers at speeds of up to 50mph, and
I learnt about mud bogging for the first time (from what I
could tell you drive your car through a muddy pit and the
fastest through it wins). And they thought we were crazy!

We reached the halfway point in the race in Texas, which
was a big moment in camp. I called Jo that evening to try to
celebrate with her, but the call didn't go well. I guess she was
finding it all harder than I realised at the time. To make matters worse, I was running out of shoes and didn't have any
sponsorship. Fortunately, one of my benefactors back in the
UK, known as Financial Bear, stepped up to help me out and
one day a whole load of Brooks trainers were delivered to
camp. It had been another one of those moments when
things got a bit tight but someone came through for me, and
the show was still on the road. However much I wanted to
focus purely on the running, there was always something else
to worry about – or someone else.

On 14 March, Jessica finished in 7 hours 30 minutes. For
much of the last few marathons, she'd been completing the
race close to the cut-off time of eight hours. She was in a lot
of pain and finally realised her time was up. She'd been
trying to run through the agony, but there was no more
denying it. Her body was falling apart and she was no longer
fit to run. I knew exactly how she felt.

We were all really sad to see Jessica leave, but none more
so than her. Scans would later show she had stress fractures
in her leg and also a problem with her spine, so it was amazing she continued as long as she did, and a testament to her
bravery and determination. I have no doubt she'll be back
out doing something epic soon; people like her are unstoppable. So now we were down to just seven core runners.

Again there was sadness in camp, and it took a little bit of getting used to, but we all had to focus quickly on the next day's running. If you don't do that, you can pay the price.

I had a flight back to the UK out of Dallas aiport booked for 18 March. As I had only a visitor's visa, I couldn't be in America for longer than 90 days without leaving the country, however briefly. So the plan was to fly back to the UK for less than 24 hours, do what I needed to do there, and then rejoin the race. My flight was booked for the evening after the Springtown marathon. I ran that quickly, in 3 hours 35 minutes, so I'd have time to run another before catching my flight. I ran that second marathon towards the airport, 26.37 miles on my GPS watch, before Andrea gave me a lift the rest of the way to the airport to catch my flight.

By the time I got back to the UK, it was morning and I had an appointment at St Mary's University in Twickenham for some testing, done in conjunction with the BBC as part of a programme they were doing in the run-up to the London marathon in April. Afterwards, I gave a couple of interviews in Richmond; one was with Lucozade for the London marathon and the other was for Channel 5. Once I'd done them, I ran around the park for another marathon, like old times. It was funny to be back there, among the deer and the cyclists, on the track I knew so well. My life had changed so much since I'd run my first marathon there almost a year ago.

Joanna arrived in the evening, having left Buddy in Poland with his grandparents. It was amazing to see her again. After my marathon, we holed up in the Victoria, our local pub in Sheen, where we had booked a room for the night. Unfortunately, the flight and the running caught up with me and I fell asleep during dinner, but I was still awake enough at other times to enjoy our precious few hours together.

Early the next morning it was straight off to the airport for my return flight to Dallas. When I landed in America, it was the end of the RAUSA rest day. I was picked up from the airport and was soon back in the camp with the team as if I'd never even been away. The next day I finished so quickly, in 3 hours 9 minutes, I decided to run an extra marathon for the heck of it. I was feeling fresh and didn't seem to be suffering from any jetlag.

A week later on 27 March, I was running in our final marathon in Texas, out near Jefferson, and was well out in the lead, as was usual by then. I'd been running consistently under four hours for my marathons that week, so I was in a good place, but then I got to a crossroads on Highway 49 and suddenly everything got a bit confusing. I needed to stay on the same road, but when I saw a sign to Highway 59 I followed that instead. As Forrest Gump would have said, 'I just kept on running.'

After a couple of miles, I realised I'd gone wrong and started walking back. I stopped to ask someone how to get back to the 49 and they told me to keep going and take a left at the McDonald's. That sounded about right, so I carried on for a while, but somehow I felt like I was lost again. This time I asked an old lady where to go and she pointed off down a dusty path. 'Follow this little road and then nip over the rail tracks and the forty-nine is there,' she said. 'You can't miss it.'

Don't be so sure, I thought. You don't know who you're talking to here, lady.

Anyway, I followed her advice and ended up at the tracks as she had said, just as a really long freight train was passing.

Then it stopped and I was standing there, waiting for it to move again, but it didn't seem to be going anywhere. I was in a hurry and figured that if I tried to walk around it that could take ages, so the best option seemed to be to nip underneath it really quickly and get out the other side. I thought it would take a moment to get going anyway, and so as long as it didn't fire into gear while I was under there I should be OK.

I dipped under that huge freight train, scuttled under its rusty belly, on my hands and knees, and got safely out the other side. Mighty pleased with myself, I hopped over the rail next to it, without a moment's thought I just rushed across it. A couple of seconds later, a train hurtled by at full speed. It seemed to have come out of nowhere. I hadn't looked down the line properly before crossing or I would have seen it bearing down on me. That was a bit of a close thing, my second near run-in with a train. If I'd have crossed that track just few seconds later, things might have worked out very differently.

I found the 49 after that and ended up chasing the leaders to try to catch them up. I made up a lot of ground, but ended up finishing in fourth place. I was pretty annoyed with myself; I'd run an extra five miles and got lost again. Getting lost so often was starting to bug me by now, and I was feeling angry with myself. So I wasn't in the best of moods when Sandy came over after the race and started bombarding me with questions. Where had I been? Had I run the entire course? One minute I was in the lead by a couple of miles, then where did I go? I couldn't believe she was actually cross with me.

'I'm giving you a thirty-minute penalty, Rob. You didn't stay on the course,' she said.

'That's because I got lost, Sandy. And ended up running five miles more on top of your bloody marathon.' I didn't say that, but you can bet I was thinking it. Apparently, as soon as I'd finished I should have gone to tell her what had happened. Other people got lost that day, too, as well as on other days, and they hadn't been penalised. At the time, I felt like Darren and Sandy were gunning for me, though that was probably just because I was so tired. It was true that my relationship with them wasn't the best by then, maybe because I'd spoken my mind about a few things already, crucially when Jup and Pat had decided to leave the race. Also I felt that they weren't listening to the runners' feedback, be it on small things or larger issues. And I'd let them know that, too. I don't need to get into the specifics here, but when race organisers ignore runners' feedback then a gulf grows between them, which doesn't make for a happy camp. I like to think I'm pretty amenable and easy going, but some things need airing or they just fester. Now I felt like my frankness had turned me into an easy target.

I was furious, so I handed in my number and said I was through with the race; I quit. It was difficult enough contending with the daily marathon without feeling like your support crew weren't backing you. And of course your tolerance levels dip when you're physically exhausted. At the time it felt like the last straw.

Darren approached me later back at the camp to explain the penalty, but I felt he kept changing his mind about why it had been given. Now I was told it was because I hadn't been carrying a mobile phone with me (which wasn't something stated as compulsory in the event's rules). When I pointed that out, it became because I had an 18oz water bottle instead of a 20oz water bottle. I was being penalised for carrying too little water now! It all seemed crazy to me. 'Check the others' water bottles, too,' I said. 'I'm sure they won't all be twenty ounces either. Don't just single me out.'

It felt clear to me they just wanted to make that penalty stick. I suspected it was because they didn't want a Brit to win the race, but that may have been because I was seething about it at the time. I was so cross I had to get away, and I had energy to spare, so I went out and ran another marathon. They couldn't stop me doing that. The extra running calmed me down and tired me out. I got something to eat that night with the rest of the gang and watched the sunset, then I told Darren I'd changed my mind and I'd continue. They weren't going to stop me winning that race. They'd have to slap a whole bunch of time penalties on me to manage that.

Next up we had two marathons in the state of Louisiana – Bryce pipped me in those for the overall state win. This was followed by a rest day when I ran another couple of marathons. The following week, we ran six marathons in Arkansas and I averaged 3 hours 45 minutes for each one. My body had become noticeably leaner by this stage and I was running faster and with greater ease day by day. My leg was now completely healed from the pre-stress fracture two months earlier, and no hint of that issue remained.

After those Arkansas marathons we effectively had another two rest days. On the first of those, I ran two marathons. One running back into Arkansas, the reverse of the route we had completed the day before, around Lake Chicot and down the 82. Then I turned around and came back. Once again, I finished both marathons in under eight hours, which was solid running for me.

It was a special moment. That day took me to 366

marathons in 360 days. I had finally equalled Ricardo Abad's record, and still I had five days to go before the year was fully up. After chasing that ridiculous number 367 for almost a year, I finally stood next to it. I'd always said it would require something of a miracle to get this far and I think I'd had my share along the way.

The next day was a rest day for the group as we left Arkansas and headed into Mississippi. I decided to hang out with Bryce and Alex rather than chasing a number by running yet another marathon. I ate plenty and called Joanna just as she was going to bed. For once, it was a good phone call and the tension was gone. This year of running was almost over for both of us.

On 10 April, starting from the great Mississippi river, we set off on yet another marathon, my 367th that year – but something was different that day. Bryce had come down with the flu in the night and he was in a really bad way. I decided to try to help him get round, as he looked like he'd need all the support he could get, so I ran with him most of the way; Nancy and Linda were with us, too. Bryce felt nauseous so I tried to get him to be sick. He wasn't keen on that, so I gave him regular sips of water and words of encouragement. Meanwhile, it was good to run with Linda and Nancy, and the three of us ended up finishing together in a little under six hours.

So I had done it: 367 marathons/ultras in the year! All those crazy journeys around the UK, the struggles with money and with being away from my family had amounted to something. I wanted to celebrate, but there was no time for that. Bryce hadn't finished yet, so I went back out on the course to find him. He ended up taking 7 hours 17 minutes to get to the end; every step must have been awful and he was really brave to get through that day. It took a lot of guts. I think he knew how much we were all rooting for him, which must have helped, too.

That night we had a quiet celebration of my achievement, but as Bryce still had a fever it was all a bit muted. Newton, our tour poet, wrote this for me:

> A world record Rob will pursue
> And run marathons with us 'til through.
> In spite of his feat
> You should see this man eat.
> 'Twill be a world record too!

After a couple more days of suffering, Bryce's fever broke and he returned to feeling normal again. It had been quite a few days, but now it was Alex's birthday which gave us all a chance to let off some steam. Everyone got one of his tie-dye t-shirts, making us the most colourful party in the restaurant.

On 13 April it was exactly a year since I'd run my first marathon and that day I finished my 370th marathon/ultra – more than I'd ever hoped I would run. It was a great feeling of satisfaction and, more than that, of relief. I was still running, though, but without the stress now. This whole adventure wouldn't be finished until we got to the Atlantic.

CHAPTER NINETEEN
Journey's End at the White House

14 April–3 June 2015

We ran through Mississippi and into Alabama next. Alabama was warm and very pretty – even the greens of the trees seemed more vivid – everything was lush and the weather was hot and sticky. I'd take that over snow and ice any day of the week. On the second day's running in Alabama, there was an incident involving a dog worth mentioning. We'd had some problems with stray dogs along the way (Newton had even been bitten), so we were all wary of the possible dangers.

It happened when I was near the third aid station in the last half of the race. I was moving well at the time, feeling good, running along a busy highway. All of a sudden I heard a dog barking behind me. I stopped and looked around and saw it running towards me. Not far behind, giving chase, was a little boy no older than six years old. I watched as he tore after the dog into the road. A car swerved noisily to avoid hitting them both. The boy froze, realising where he was for the first time.

It all happened in a matter of seconds. As soon as I'd registered what was going on, I rushed out into the road, narrowly missing a couple of oncoming cars. I reached the boy, who was still frozen to the spot, and scooped him up, then I carried him back to the roadside and safety. Cars were screeching to a halt around us, one behind another. It was chaos. We were lucky no one got injured in a pile-up that day. Then the boy's older brothers and mum turned up – I can only assume they lived in one of the houses I could see nearby – and she thanked me before turning on the boy and telling him how much trouble he was in. I doubt he got any dessert that night.

The next day we visited Talladega Superspeedway racing circuit, made famous by the Will Ferrell movie, *Talladega Nights*. We had a good laugh running around the track, remembering funny moments from the film. It was amazing how steep the bends on those tracks are – you can barely even climb up them.

However, I had another focus that week: I was going back to the event that had inspired me to take up the challenge in the first place – I was going to run in the London marathon. During the week, I tried to unwind as much as possible after getting the record, while also preparing for London. Even though I was thousands of miles away, I had to do a fair amount of interviews on the phone with people back in the UK in the build-up to the race, and I was delighted that my story hadn't been forgotten while I'd been racing across the USA. It wasn't an easy time for me, though. It was so hot and humid during the days that running had become a real challenge, a real uphill battle every day.

The logistics of flying back to the UK for the marathon were tight, which was stressing me a little bit. I needed to get into the UK the day before the London marathon for various press and sponsor commitments, then I'd have to run a quick time in the race itself, in order to do an interview or two, say hi to a few people and make it back to Heathrow airport again for my flight back to America.

I was due to fly out on Friday 24 April, which meant I would miss the Jacksonville marathon that the rest of the guys would be running on the Saturday. Thankfully, the race organisers let me run that one on the Friday, after I'd finished my first marathon with the rest of the guys. As soon as I'd finished that double marathon (52.94 miles in total), it was off to the airport to catch my plane to the UK.

I didn't manage to sleep on the flight, but watched several movies instead. Sitting with my legs bent for those eight hours in an economy-class seat certainly wasn't the ideal way to recover between marathons. I'd put the word out on Facebook that I would need some help getting between Heathrow airport and central London, both before and after the race. Lucky for me, a guy called Rob Hutchings offered to give me a lift both ways – on the back of his motorbike taxi, which I thought should be interesting. He was waiting at Heathrow when I landed and whisked me off to the ExCeL centre in East London for the pre-London marathon day's events. As well as taxiing me for free, Rob found and paid for me to have a hotel room near the race start the next day. What a guy!

Joanna had flown back from Poland to see me, leaving Buddy in Poland with his grandparents. So after doing all the interviews at the ExCeL centre, I got to spend the night in a hotel room with Joanna after months apart. Seeing her again for the first time since January was very emotional, but I was

underslept and physically exhausted so it wasn't exactly quality time. Still, it was something and better than nothing. We
enjoyed a nice dinner together in town and got to bed early.
It was wonderful to be with her again. We both knew this
crazy year was almost over and it wouldn't be long till we
would be able to see each other all the time.

The next morning, after not much sleep, I was up early
and drinking gallons of coffee to keep me awake. I ended up
feeling very strange; I was so caffeinated, jet-lagged and
excited at the same time, I wasn't quite sure what I was feeling. But one thing was for sure: this was a huge day for me.

There was a problem at the beginning, as they'd given me
the wrong coloured race number. The London Marathon has
three starting areas: Blue, Green and Red. Blue is for the elite
runners, Green is for the celebrities and Red is for everyone
else. I'd been given a Red number, which meant I didn't
have access to the press area for the elite athletes, near the
Blue start. I was supposed to be in there to give various interviews. Fortunately, I bumped into Dr Kipps who flashed his
pass and ushered me into the right area for my interviews.
Once inside I spoke to an organiser who said it'd be OK for
me to begin the race from the Blue start once my interviews
were done. So I didn't have to worry about trekking around
to the Red start which was a fair way away.

I met a few people before the race and everyone was really
nice, high-fiving me and telling me how well I was doing. It
was quite a homecoming. People I didn't even know
embraced me that day, along with many of those I'd got to
know well in the running community throughout the year.

This was the event that had started everything for me, my
whole crazy year. And finally I was here, running it. It was
a lot to take in. As with everything else, there was plenty of

time pressure. Because logistics were my number-one preoc-
cupation, I didn't get chance to savour the occasion as much
as I'd have liked, as I was focused on catching my plane back
to the USA. I had a few photos at the start and then it was
time to race. I knew I needed to run really quickly so as not
to miss my flight. That plus the caffeine in my blood and the
24 hours' rest I'd just had, meant I flew to the half-marathon
point. I was really moving and on target for a sub three-hour
marathon.

I stopped to have some hugs with a few people, and did a
couple of interviews at the press areas at miles 21 and 23, as
well as saying hello to the MMUK faithful who were gathered there to see me. It was so good to see everyone and I
was touched at how many had made the effort to be there to
cheer me on. After stopping there for a good 15 minutes, I
rejoined the race and reached the finish in 3 hours 7
minutes.

As soon as I'd finished, I immediately tried to find Rob
so we could head back to Heathrow. I didn't have my phone,
though, so there was no way of getting hold of him.
Eventually I tracked him down, by sheer chance rather than
careful planning, and we set off. I must still have had some
of that Talladega dust in my hair, as we bobbed and weaved
through those corners and arrived at Heathrow in no time
at all.

The London marathon had passed me by in a blur of
colour, noise and excitement. I'd had my five minutes with
Joanna, my five seconds with dear friends and my time with
the press. Now I was moving at speed to the next race a
whole continent away. It was all going according to plan, but
it was a bit fast and furious to appreciate in any significant
way.

At the airport things went smoothly at customs, but by the time I got through I was starving. All I could think about was burgers covered in mayonnaise, but with almost no time before we boarded, I had to make a choice: either eat or take a shower; there was no time for both. It was a tough call, but I ended up taking the shower. Standing under the hot water was worth it, and I think my fellow passengers would have approved of my choice.

I landed in Jacksonville that evening after a rather squashed and uncomfortable journey. US customs officials then proceeded to give me a tough time about how often I was leaving and re-entering the States. I chatted to an immigration officer till they were satisfied with what I was doing and why. It turned out I should have had a work visa for what I was doing. Oh, well, you live and learn. Soon I was allowed through and was back in camp with the rest of the guys, as if the London marathon was some dream I'd had.

The next day we'd all run our first marathon into the state of Georgia. I was back on track and the finish line was only a month or so away. By now the weather had started to become hotter and more humid. The eight Georgia marathons went well and I was taking it easy, enjoying the views and helping my friends get through it. There were more school visits which were always fun. Soon we reached South Carolina, and the temperatures and humidity continued to rise and we all struggled with it. We needed ice on the course to cool us down, otherwise I don't think some of us would have made it.

It was around this time that another issue grew between the runners and the event organisers over how well we were being protected from the heat. I've slept in caves before, so it takes a lot to bother me, but the heat out in the tents at night was something else, and after a day's running it was a little too much. It was 90°F with 90 per cent humidity at times, with the heat radiating off the ground. There appeared to be no escape.

However, when we heard that offers had been made to put us up in air-conditioned accommodation, which had been turned down by the organisers, we wanted to know why. We would have done almost anything for some relief from the heat at that time (I even paid for Newton and me to have an air-conditioned room one night because he was struggling so much). So why were they turning down offers like that?

We were told the race directors wanted to honour the bookings they'd already made. We believed that the camps wouldn't mind if we didn't turn up for our reservations, as long as they'd been paid. Refusing the chance of better accommodation on a small point like that wasn't acceptable. I hope the race directors look at that question for future events. We got through it in the end, just like we had over-come all the other issues we had faced along the way, through discussion and support of one another. It was a shame for the camp to become divided like that, but fortunately the show was still on the road.

There was one moment that stands out from our time in South Carolina. I was way out in the lead one day, with thick forest all around me, busily looking for a turning which I knew should have been coming up, and just starting to worry that I might have missed it. Looking around, I noticed a girl standing on a railway line about 50 metres off, which seemed strange, so I jogged over to see if she was OK and to ask for directions. By the time I got closer, I could see she was upset and had been crying. I thought she might be threatened by my running over towards her, out in the middle of nowhere, so I apologised if I'd startled her.

'No, it isn't you,' she said. 'I'm just a bit upset.'

'Why? What's happened?' I asked.

'Oh it's nothing. I've just got some problems.'

'Heck, we've all got problems,' I said, trying to make her smile. It didn't work.

'Why don't you tell me a bit about your problems? Then I'll tell you about mine,' I said. She didn't look sure about that. So I started telling her about the race and then about my fundraising, then a bit about my own childhood.

She was very pretty, and told me she was a 36-year-old Canadian, and a very accomplished cake–maker. She went on to explain how miserable she was living out here, having moved to the States to be with her boyfriend, who turned out to be a bit of a dick. With no ties and no children, I couldn't understand why she didn't just leave this guy and start anew somewhere else, so I suggested she move to a different city and that she should take up a sport and get out and meet people. Soon enough things will get better that way, I told her. That was my experience at least. We chatted for about 20 minutes out there on the track, before I said good-bye and continued on with the race.

'You're an angel,' she said as we parted, which I didn't really understand. After all, we'd only had a conversation. Anyway, she seemed in much better spirits by the time I left, so I guess I'd cheered her up. About five minutes after leaving her, I heard a train go by in the distance, presumably on the very line where I had seen her. I stopped and wondered if I should go back to see if she was OK. She must be, I thought. Why wouldn't she be?

As I ran on, I couldn't stop thinking about her and that

train. Why was she even out on the track in the middle of nowhere? Had she come out there to throw herself under a train? If so, had she gone along with it? It was too awful to consider. Later, in camp, I asked the other runners if anyone had seen someone out on the tracks, but none of them had. I would have loved to have known for sure that she was safe.

The next night I had a chance to check my Facebook page and I was really pleased to find I had a message from her (I'd told her about my page during our conversation and she'd said she'd check it out). What a relief it was to hear from her. She sounded pretty upbeat about things and was full of gratitude for our little chat. She said I'd made a big impression on her. I was just glad she was alive and grateful that, with nobody else around for miles, I'd managed to bump into her and give her the encouragement she clearly needed.

A few races and school visits later, on 13 May, we arrived in North Carolina before heading into Virginia. It was all about coping with the heat for most of those marathons. I think after all the running we'd done, we all felt we'd make it to the finish at that stage, so it became more relaxed in camp, and people were quite philosophical. Mentally we began to prepare for the end of the journey, when we would be reunited with our loved ones and the lives we'd left behind. It was a time of reflection and preparation. Some were looking forward to getting back to their 'normal' lives while others, like me, were planning the next big adventure. One thing was for sure: the adventure would not end here.

On the morning of 2 June, after four-and-a-half months on the road together, we set off on our penultimate marathon of the Race Across USA series in very good spirits. That day we were running 27.63 miles, all the way to the White House. It wasn't the last race of the series, but it felt like it somehow. There was still another marathon the day after, out to Chesapeake Bay and the Atlantic Ocean, but running to the White House, where I knew I was going to see Joanna, felt like the end for me. It was the end of this particular journey, my race across America and my extended year of intensive marathon running (416 marathons/ultras in 416 days at that point). I was looking forward to a rest, however brief.

We started as 12 and now we were eight (Steve Cooper had flown in to run the last couple of marathons with us, which was a nice touch). During the race we had lost members of the group – Jup, Patrick, Jessica, Chris – who through injury, circumstance or a change of heart had said their goodbyes and left. Morale had been dented and they were missed, but the rest of us had continued on to our goal. And all of those who finished that race will share a bond that will last forever, I think.

I decided to run quickly that day. Since breaking the record, I'd been in third gear for the last few weeks, with nothing to motivate me as I was way out in front in the overall lead in the race. So I had been taking a breather, horsing around more than usual and generally winding down towards the finish line, but that day I decided it was time to clear out the cobwebs.

The end didn't happen quite as I would have planned it. Way out in front, I reached the White House in 3 hours 4 minutes, according to my watch. The only problem was the finish line wasn't there yet, so I had to run around looking for it and eventually someone told me it was in the middle of the square. When I got there, I found a handful of friends and family of the runners, and my own Joanna and Alexander. They had been standing in the cold and the drizzling rain, waiting for me. It was amazing to see them both after so long. We got to hug, but it was all too brief – a journalist and a photographer from the *Sun* were waiting to interview me. Then Sandy arrived and looked surprised to see me.

'How long have you been here?' she asked. I looked at my watch.

'About fifteen minutes,' I said.

'Well, I've only just arrived,' she said. 'So I'll have register your finishing time as now, I'm afraid.'

Apparently, she hadn't expected anyone in that soon, so effectively I had even beaten the finish line. Now you have to be really going some to do that. After that, I wanted to wait to see all the other runners come in, as well as play with Buddy and chat to Joanna. It was a difficult moment in a way. I had become part of a new family in the past five months. We had helped each other through an incredible journey, and now I was rejoining my actual family, Joanna and Alexander. So while I was happy to be back with them, I was a little sad to be saying goodbye to all those wonderful people.

Over the next couple of days we wrapped things up. First, there was the closing party that night which was an okay affair. I didn't feel it was handled incredibly well by the organisers and by now many of us simply wanted to go home. It was a shame. It should have been a riotous party, a celebration that lasted throughout the night, but we had all said our goodbyes throughout the week, person to person. That was where the farewells were done. And of course there was still one final marathon to Chesapeake Bay to run the next day.

That final marathon to the Atlantic was somehow symbolic of the whole race. We had all agreed to run it together as one and to finish, as we had started in January, together, hand in hand at the ocean. It started off that way, but then at one point Darren decided to run on. Perhaps he wanted to win a stage for the first time, but still it felt inappropriate. So he finished on his own and the rest of us finished together in a little under seven hours. At the end, there was management and there was the rest of us, and the lack of unity was evident.

Still, nothing could take away the sense of achievement we all felt seeing that ocean after months of hard running, through ice and searing heat. There had been moments of turmoil as well as great times of fun, hilarity and together-ness. It had been an awesome journey and that journey was now complete.

I had finished 420 marathons/ultras in 420 days, even with my three-week 'pause' in November. But as a group we had run 117 back-to-back marathons over the last four-and-a-half months for a total of 3,080 miles by the group (plus a couple of hundred more for me, as I had done a few extra). You couldn't help but feel like you'd accomplished something pretty special. Most of us would have liked a little time together without running, to reflect on what we'd been through, but the race organisers left swiftly as they had to return to LA for something.

A final note about the race organisers, and Darren in par-ticular. I have expressed my discontent with many decisions that were made and the way in which things were done, and I stand by them, but he's a good guy and did his best under those circumstances. I think if he had been able to focus on the organisation and had the reins to himself, things might have gone a lot better. I hope he isn't too discouraged by my comments and continues next year with a revised version of this race, which has the potential to be something even greater than it currently is.

The next day we had some final tests to do with Bryce and his medical team. Joanna and Alexander had flown all this way to see me, and frustratingly I just couldn't seem to get more than five minutes with them, but eventually we were together again in our hotel room, and got to start making up for all the time we'd spent apart.

That night, lying next to Joanna, with Alexander in the next room, I couldn't sleep. I wondered what my next adventure might be. Running to the North Pole? Swimming the Atlantic? It had to be something epic. But little did I know, my next big adventure had already started. At that moment, a billion of my sperm had set out on their own long-distance race. There would be no aid stations on the way and it may have taken 72 hours before they reached their destination. It would be an epic journey and one sperm would eventually cross the finish line and be crowned champion.

I was going to be a dad again!

Epilogue

Coming back to the UK was great, though a little daunting. I had the immediate issue of trying to find some kind of work and a place for Joanna, Buddy and me to live as we began what was essentially a whole new life. We moved into a flat above a shop in East Sheen and I found a new hobby, assembling Ikea furniture through the night.

Not having to run every day was a new concept, but one I quickly got to grips with. I decided to take a rest from running for a few weeks, to let my body rest and recover. In the meantime, I hired an agent and started hustling to try to make endurance running a career, somehow. I didn't want to go back to an office job, so this was my time to capitalise on my year's running and use it as a launchpad into a new career as an athlete.

There was finally time to reflect on the year that had passed and what it had all meant. I had been forced to push myself beyond my limits and learned a lot about myself along the way. Not all of it was pretty, mind. One of the major things I found out is I'm not the best at communicating (which is ironic when you think I joined the Royal Corps of Signals precisely because of the communications aspect). In fact, I'm one of the worst. I also learned that juggling my love of extreme endurance challenges with a family is going to be pretty tricky. I hope I manage to get the right balance in future.

I also learned that everyone is in such a hurry but where are they actually hurrying to? Running somehow has made me more still, I think. As a result, the rat race with all its accompanying worries and concern to keep-up-with-the-Joneses seems even more absurd to me. Life shouldn't have to be that stressful and I hope to choose a different path for myself.

On that note, I was lucky enough to have won the Sports and Peace award in December. Receiving the honour in Monte Carlo was a chance to meet so many people, big hitters in sport's governing bodies. It was heartening to see how committed so many of them were to making positive change in sport and in the world. There was real passion and stop-at-nothing devotion to creating a brighter future for the world. I hope I can be a part of that movement myself in some small way.

I come from a certain past, with many disadvantages, but the one big advantage it has given me is the chance to connect with young people going through similar things. Young people really are the most important people, because they are pure potential. With the right support they can become heroes, but without it they can become monsters. So we need to inspire and teach them well, particularly the vulnerable, the at-risk and the impoverished. We need to remember that today's street kids can be the champions of tomorrow. No one can be forgotten in society. A chain is only as strong as its weakest link, so we must spend our time and money on helping those most in need. It's in all our interests that we do.

I hope in all my hundreds of school visits that I have had an impact on some children's lives, helped them to steer their lives in different directions. The feedback I have from them reassures me that I have. And after all, as I have said, if I change only one life for the better then it has still all been worth it.

During the course of the year, I have shared tears with some and laughter with many. I have come to love the sport of running with all my heart and that love has expanded to a greater appreciation for the wider community. Everyone is my friend, no matter who you are or where you are from. I love people and I want to help anyone if I can. We often underestimate the power of the smallest act of kindness, a smile, a kind word, a listening ear, a small charitable donation. I have learned they can be the difference between life and death at times.

On the fundraising front, I had managed to raise about £70,000 by the end of the year, which was a lot less than I had hoped for, but I know it has helped change a few children's lives for the better and what could be more satisfying than that? By the time of writing, that figure had gone up to £214,000, which was much more like it, so I'm still making progress and will continue to do what I can. If you want to chuck a pound in the pot then please do, check out my website www.marathonmanuk.com. And thanks in advance.

There are clearly plenty of people without whom I couldn't have done what I did, and there's a thank you section just for them, but one of the most important things I've learned is that we can't achieve anything on our own: co-operation is what gets us to our dreams.

After recovering from the Race Across USA, I haven't returned to the couch again. I took on Dean Karnazes's record of running 350 miles without sleep, and I'm glad to say I managed to run 373.75 miles before the wheels finally came off. Then I spent a few days in Guernsey with some running friends and we broke three treadmill world records and ten British records over there, and had a lot of fun along the way. After that I 'ran for peace' with Adam Holland, carrying a torch all around the country as part of a Kenyan initiative, 'the Champions Walk for Peace'. You can read about all of those stories on my website or, who knows, in my next book.

Thanks for reading this. I hope it's been as thrilling to read as it was to run. And if it's inspired you to go for a run, whether it's around the block or all the way around Mont Blanc, then please just do it. There's an incredible world out there just waiting to be discovered.

After all, it's only a bit of running!

Appendix 1:
The Crazy Running Handbook

My doctor might tell you not to listen to a word I say, that I'm a maverick and following me will only get you into trouble. He probably has a point. That said, I am still alive and well after finishing 370 marathons/ultras in a year – and not all of that is down to dumb luck. So, for those who are interested, here are a few things I've learned about marathon running and how to survive it. I haven't always followed my own advice or what the doctors have told me (and you should really ALWAYS check with them when taking on any kind of extreme endurance event), but one thing I did learn to do in addition was to throw out the rule book and trust my instincts.

Mental focus – Your mental focus is one of the most important things you'll need to accomplish your goal. This applies to anyone and everyone, in any sport, or with any goals. You have to believe in yourself; don't hope to accomplish your goal, *know* you're going to accomplish it.

Running properly – People who have grown up with access to modern running shoes tend to have terrible running form. Most people run on their heels too much, have tense upper bodies, do not control their breathing and have lazy leg mechanics. You need to learn to keep your upper body as relaxed as possible, with your body in an upright position and your arms loose. If you're tense, you are wasting energy. When running, try putting your thumb and one finger together slightly touching; this should stop you from squeezing your hands together and reduce the tension in your arms and shoulders.

One of the best things I've learnt is that I have a perfect mid to forefoot running strike. Without getting too much into the science behind it, it's biomechanically more efficient in terms of energy expenditure versus powering forward, compared with a heel strike.

You can also improve your running by watching any professional runner. Note how they land on the mid part of their foot, with their torsos upright and bent ever-so-slightly forward. There's no need to buy barefoot shoes, as modern running shoes protect your feet, reduce stress on bones and soft tissues, and you can have a natural running form in them. You just need to be conscious of HOW you are running.

Choosing your marathons – Many people have asked me how to go about choosing the right marathon for them. It can be difficult to decide, especially if it's your first. First of all, you need to decide if you want to run in a big city marathon or a smaller local one. Both have their pluses and minuses.

Pretty much every major city around the world has a marathon. These big events are run like well-oiled machines and there will be a massive background crew to make sure the race goes smoothly. You will find thousands of competitors around you and spectators in even greater numbers. Although these events have an amazing atmosphere, they can feel at times a bit overcrowded for some, with too much going on. Most big marathons have a high entry fee, but what it will get you is:

- Drinks stations, usually sponsored by a big brand, every two to three miles consisting of water, sometimes energy drinks and gels.
- Lots of competitors and many spectators who can inspire you to keep going.
- Accuracy – there is nothing worse than finding out that the course was shorter or longer than the said distance. That is why the larger races will be ratified by the national governing body and are almost guaranteed to be pinpoint accurate.

Smaller races tend to have fewer than a thousand competitors and are usually held in smaller towns, cities or villages. They will rarely have many elite runners and the courses are often a little longer, by a tenth of a mile or so. Generally they offer more picturesque routes over many different terrains, with less waiting time to get over the starting line. The entry fees are often much lower, and you'll probably not struggle to get an entry.

You might not get as many spectators, but the whole community often gets behind the race and there's usually an awesome atmosphere on the day. The aid stations are normally stocked up with more food, such as water melon, crisps, sandwiches, cake, chocolate, jelly babies, salted oranges and sausage rolls – the list goes on. You will also find that people look after each other very well at these smaller events, and you'll never be too far away from someone wanting to help you.

Although it's hard to choose my favourite marathons in the UK, the following get a special mention: Coniston, Brighton, Manchester, the Midnight Brutal Run, Loch Ness, Dublin, Hell of a Hill, the Wales marathon, Halstead, Richmond Park, Kent Roadrunner, Beachy Head,

Edinburgh and Chester. I found that any event run by the following organisations should be worth the entrance fee: White Star Running, Saxon-Shore, Endurancelife, VOTWO, Great Barrow Challenge and Hermes Running.

Preparing for a marathon – Ideally, you shouldn't rush out and run a marathon on day one (unless you're impulsive like me). The best way is to pace yourself through a training schedule, slowly building up to taking on the marathon distance. Most people take several months to prepare for one. Below is an ideal 24-week training schedule, in brief:

Weeks 24 to 16 – This is the time where you lay the foundation miles. Gradually build up the distance, adding no more than 10 per cent a week to your weekly mileage. Your long runs should gradually extend in distance until you can run a half marathon comfortably, and preferably 16-18 miles without too much difficulty. If you cut this training section short, you increase the risk of injury later.

Weeks 16 to 4 – Start your tempo runs at six miles in week 15, building up by a mile a week. Your long, slow runs should include some 20 milers, about two weeks apart from each other, for example in weeks 15, 13, 10, 8, 5. During weeks 12 to 8, you will need to cut back on some of your speed work and focus more on strength training.

Week 3 – It is now time to begin to taper down. It is tough to love the marathon taper, but it's vital that you do it. It is the period many aspiring marathoners fantasise about as they finish their long training runs. The few weeks leading up to the race are when a training programme calls for less running and more recovery, otherwise known as the tapering phase. It is a critical part of your marathon training.

Tapering allows your awesome body and mind a chance to rest, repair, replenish and regroup in preparation for your marathon. But even though the break from a tough training schedule can be appealing, it can also be a little daunting to take time off, especially if you are like me. But trust me, a taper will leave you healthy and strong for race day.

As a general guideline, you should do your last long training run or long race three weeks before the marathon. Treat this long run as a dress rehearsal for your race. Wear your planned race outfit and practise your race nutrition and hydration plan. After that last long run, cut your mileage down to about 80 per cent of what you were doing before and run no further than 20 miles. Try to do at least one marathon-pace run of 10km during this week to make sure your goal pace feels comfortable. Doing so will give you a big confidence boost.

Week 2 – With two weeks to go until race day, cut your mileage to about 60-75 per cent of what you had been doing. Beginner runners who want to do a tune-up race during this time should stick to 10km or shorter. More advanced runners can do a half-marathon race up to two weeks before the marathon or a training run of no further than 15 miles. Doing a tune-up race before your marathon can help you predict your marathon time and be a real boost.

You will probably feel tempted to run longer and harder during this time, but you must resist the urge. You will not make any race-fitness improvements with two weeks to go before the marathon. You may feel some new aches and pains during the tapering period, too, but it is a normal part of the process as your body repairs itself from months of training.

If you want to get a pre-race, deep-tissue massage to loosen up your muscles, do it at this point and no closer than a week before your marathon. A deep-tissue massage can have the effect of a hard workout on your muscles, so you don't want to do it too close to the race. You can, however, have a light massage to flush out your legs, but make sure it is only a light one.

Finally, in this period try to remember – LESS IS MORE. Running less reduces your risk of injury, gives you time to rest and recover and allows your muscles to store carbo-hydrates in preparation for the big race.

Week 1 – Cut your mileage down to about one-third of normal during the final week before the marathon, but run at your normal race pace. Slowing too much can alter your stride or make you feel sluggish. Your body loves routine, so try for a 30-minute easy and relaxed run on the same days you would normally run, chatting with other runners or along a favourite route.

Don't chase time or worry about the GPS stats, just run easy and keep relaxed. If you feel strong, then consider a light session five days before the race; for example, 30 minutes including 3 × 5mins at threshold or your marathon pace, with a two-minute jog as recovery. You are just keeping your legs used to a little pace and feeling faster. Avoid spending ages on your feet, walking with family and friends, sightseeing around the city or talking for long periods of time. It's simple: if you don't need to do it, don't – and save your energy. During this week it is vital that you snack on small good meals throughout the day and stay well hydrated.

The day before – I would advise runners to jog for 10–20 minutes the day before the race and stretch. It helps you to feel loose on race day and can calm the nerves. However, always practise what you are used to in race week and the day before. If you usually rest, then definitely do this.

Surround yourself with positive, supportive people and those that enjoy the challenge and are excited by the thought of race day. If you have any negative people around you, then it can play on your mind, leaving you feeling exhausted. As race day approaches, you're likely to be stressed and irritable. So stay relaxed and confident, and know that pre-race nerves are normal.

You always need to sleep and rest well before a marathon; respect this key element as a runner if you want to improve. Try to get a few early nights in race week and definitely protect that immune system in the final weeks, as late nights and picking up a cold will be a disaster come race day. Make sure you stay in your hotel room relaxing the night before, and only come out of it for that small jog or going to eat.

Prepare your race kit and lay it out ready for the morning – if you have your number, pin it to your top. Make sure any clothing has been worn and washed a few times before you race in it – don't try anything new. Trust me, getting your kit sorted in the morning can be a real pain and stressful.

Race day – Wake early, shower and take a few moments lying down – breathe deeply, relax and stay calm. Eat the race-day breakfast you have practised in training two hours before the race start. Keep your kit simple and wear the shoes you ran your last few long runs or half-marathons in. Take a carbohydrate-based snack (for example, a banana or energy bar) and sports drink to snack on between breakfast and the race start and be prepared with fuel in case of a delayed start.

Remember your pace split times and don't rely on your

GPS – they often fail with so many signals in the same area. Have your splits per mile written on your hand or arm in permanent ink or on a wristband. Sip your final mouthfuls of water/sports drink, but don't take on more than normal – you don't need it.

Don't run to warm up or do any high-intensity drills – save your energy and use the first few miles to warm up. Unless you are going straight out from the gun, then a couple of 100–200m jogs is all you need to do. Do remember to stretch if you are used to doing so. Finally: enjoy your race.

Ultras and back-to-back running – Once you commit to taking on an ultra or a multiple marathon series, the first thing you have to do is accept that ultras are about pain. I was going to say they are about suffering, but they aren't. Suffering is the moaning and resistance we put up when we experience pain. How much you suffer is entirely up to you – but it will be painful.

Pain management, then, is a big part of it. Coping with sleep deprivation and the low points that will come along will be your biggest hurdles, so try to stay focused on your goal and have the determination never to give up until you reach it. Remember the pain is what will make the success rewarding and the medal worth hanging around your neck. Without pain there is no glory.

Picking your first ultra – Technically, any distance beyond a marathon is considered an ultra. However, the usual starting distance for ultras is around 50km (32 miles). When deciding which ultra you want to run, stay grounded and realistic and do not rush into the big stuff too soon. I bit off more than I could chew on one or two, even though I managed to finish them.

The temptation is to throw yourself straight into the big races before you have even had chance to build up to them, which is crazy. Think about what you wish to achieve or get from your race. Are you looking for a fast time, or is it simply about the experience? What kind of weather do you want to do this in? Picking an ultra in the summer is not going to be much fun if you're no good at handling the heat. Likewise with the cold too, you may have to carry plenty of mandatory gear in your pack, which adds another dimension to your race.

Among those in the UK and Ireland that I found put on great ultra events are the following: Hardmoors, Team OA, Centurion Running, Lakeland, High Terrain Events, T Series Racing, XNRG, Ultra Running ltd. Do look them up if you want to run an ultra.

Training for ultras – Training for ultras and multiple marathons is very similar to the classic training method for running marathons, with long runs at the weekend and shorter ones in between. You just need to add in bigger long runs at the weekend and some back-to-back runs to make your body more durable. If you are training for a 100-miler, I recommend adding some five-hour runs, with a two- or three-hour run the next day. The more you can get used to that experience of running on tired legs, the better prepared you will be on race day.

Where possible, always practise for a race by running on similar terrain to what you will experience on race day. If it is a trail event, then prepare on trails. If there are hills, then make sure to do lots of hill work (see page 76 for my advice on how to run down hills). Trail races are uneven underfoot, which puts different demands on the body, particularly the feet, knees, calves, hips, upper body and shoulders. Strength training in a gym can help you here, focusing on the quads and the abdomen. Train with the same equipment, clothes and shoes you will be using on race day, and carry a backpack if that's what's required.

If you have a desk job, why not create a stand-up desk for yourself so you are on your feet all day. It will toughen you up if you get used to running after being on your feet for long periods of time. If you are preparing for a 100-miler, or a race that will involve running through the night, then practise running through the night after working that day or at least staying up through the night to get used to what it feels like. Again, you will be better placed to handle the stresses on the day if you have been exposed to them, to some degree at least, beforehand.

Race day – Remember to keep a positive attitude through-out. This is supposed to be a hobby not a punishment. Try to have fun and don't get too serious about anything. It's just a bit of running! Have more than one goal for the race; that way if your primary goal goes out the window you can still chase your secondary goal. Whatever goals you set, finishing the race in whatever time or fashion is a victory, so do everything you can to finish it.

While moving forward is how you reach the finish line, taking a break at the right time can also help you get there in one piece. Stop when you need to, walk when you need to – anything to get you to that finish line!

Focus on one mile at a time. Having long-term goals is important, but you'll have to stay in the moment to reach them. Get through those low points (they will come) using mental techniques. Sing a song, talk to other runners, help them out when you can (this will give you a real boost) or even take a fizzy sweet and concentrate on the taste of that to take your mind off the pain you're in.

LOOK AFTER YOUR FEET. This is important (hence the capitals). They need to be in perfect condition, so address small issues before they become big problems. Put on fresh socks when you need to and keep your feet dry.

If you have a crew, then trust them. They are on your side and you chose them, so trust them to do their jobs. Listen to them and pay attention to their advice. You are tired and sore and probably grouchy; they aren't. Be kind to them and show your gratitude before, during or after the race. Be nice to the race volunteers. Thank them for their help – that's the only payment they get. Most importantly, enjoy the day, have fun and be silly.

Food – Load up with whole foods before a race as much as possible. By the time you're in the race and exhausted, you often lose your appetite and trying to play catch-up then is a doomed strategy (we process sugar and food very poorly during exertions). My advice is to eat whole foods during a race and not gels, which I'd only use as a last resort.

Test different foods during training. Find what works for you while you are on the move. For me, peanut butter, honey and banana sandwiches are good, as is soup. I also like wraps, quinoa, pasta and watermelon. When I'm organised, these are the foods I take with me on an ultra race. Every now and again, it's worth doing a long run without eating anything. This helps increase your fat adaptation, but if you do try this, always remember to take some emergency food with you in case you hit the wall.

If you have the option of having your own drop bags at various points on a course during an ultra, then make sure you use them. Put your food in bite-sized pieces in clear zip-seal bags for quicker access. It can be fun to have someone else make up your food for these drop bags, using ingredients you specify. Then you get a nice little surprise when you find out just what they've made for you and it's a mental boost as well as a physical one.

Have a spare water bottle in the packs that's already filled up, so you don't have to waste time filling up the one you arrive with (also change your socks and top at these times). Your heart rate needs to be below 160 to absorb calories, so slow down to eat. I usually walk while I'm eating. During an ultra, there will be lots of aid stations. Don't dally in all of them as you can waste a lot of time this way. Have a plan for what you are going to eat and when, and try to stick to it.

Back-to-back marathons – Traviss Willcox has a lot of good ideas about multiple days' marathon-running which helped me early on. Back then, I started experimenting with different paces and tried many techniques over a three-month period before finding the right methods for me. On a back-to-back marathon, you need to take the first one easy; the harder you run it, the harder it's going to be to complete the next one. If you usually complete a marathon in three hours, then aim for 3:15; if you take five hours, then try to finish in 5:30.

However, if you're trying ten marathons in ten days or a longer back-to-back series, there are two methods. You can look to drop your pace even more, say from three hours to 3:30, but I found an even better one was to run the first half-marathon at my full race pace or quicker (for me that meant in 75-90 minutes), drinking energy drinks as I go. Then, for the second half-marathon, I would ease off (completing it in about two hours or even 2 hours 15 minutes) while drinking electrolyte-based drinks. This method allows me to start my recovery two hours before anyone else, plus it leaves me with less of a cool-down period after the race and a quicker, higher tolerance of food intake. All this in the end equals about three hours extra a day resting period than any other athlete. If you do not use either of these techniques, I can almost guarantee you will get injured quickly or your race times will plummet as the days go by.

When I finish I am immediately thinking about rest and recovery (as well as cheering others over the line). As soon as I can handle it, I hit the calories hard – usually a milkshake of around 1500/2000 calories with three burgers at 500 calories apiece. It's fast food, so I'm usually hungry again later, and this time I have a nutritional meal, such as chicken and fish, with rice or pasta, and I will also snack on vegetables and fruit.

There are a few other things to bear in mind: make sure you rest in between races – put your feet up and get plenty of sleep if you can. Wear different shoes for each day's race. Your feet may be slightly swollen by the second day, so consider trying a half-size bigger shoe. However you feel in the morning, get to the start of the race, because once you've done that you're halfway there. My legs take a few miles to wake up properly, but by then they are always ready for more.

Appendix 2:
Checklists

When you are taking part in an event, whether it is a marathon or an ultra, you will need to remember to do plenty of things, and to pack for the event. The following should be on your checklists:

My suggested marathon checklist:

- airline tickets
- alarm clock
- bin liner to keep warm and dry
- bottles, hand-straps
- cap (running)
- drop bags & kit set of warm & waterproof clothing, food & drinks
- empty bottle for under bin-bag peeing at the start
- energy bars
- fleece
- gloves
- hotel/camp info
- jackets
- money & wallet
- nipple tape
- old t-shirt for the start
- pace/split times
- race info & maps
- rain shell
- running number & safety pins
- running shorts
- singlets/run vest
- soap & towels
- socks (running)
- space blanket

CHECKLISTS

- sports bra
- stopwatch
- sunglasses
- sunscreen
- t-shirts &
  long-sleeves
- tights
- toilet paper

- tracksuit
- trainers & back-ups
- underwear
- vaseline
- Ventolin (if you are
  asthmatic)
- wet bags

My ultra checklist:

- airline tickets
- alarm clock
- alcohol wipes
- bandanas/buffs
- batteries & bulbs
- blanket
- bottled water
- bottles, hand-straps
- bottles, race pack
- cap (knit)
- cap (running)
- drink powder
- drop bags
- drop kit
- energy bars
- first-aid kit
- flashlights
- flask
- fleece
- food & drink
- gaiters

- gel bottle
- gel holster(s)
- gloves
- headlamp
- hotel/camp info
- hydrocortisone
- ice chest
- jackets
- kilt
- knife/scissors
- maps
- money & wallet
- pace/split times
- race info & maps
- rain shell
- rubber gloves
- safety pins
- shorts (running)
- shorts (street)
- singlets
- soap & towels

- socks (running)
- space blanket
- stopwatch
- sunglasses
- sunscreen
- sweatshirts
- sweatsuits
- t-shirts, long-sleeve
- t-shirts, short-sleeve
- tape (duct, medical)
- tights
- toilet paper
- trainers & back-ups
- underwear (running & street)
- vaseline
- wet bags
- zantac, salt

Some ultra races give you the option to have drop bags at various stages of the race, and this is what I suggest you do with yours: make sure you turn off your mobile phone, as a ringing bag is an invitation to thieves. Do not overload the bag as it can tear and the contents spill out and get lost; also you will not want to lug a heavy bag after the run. The most likely point for the bag to break is the draw-cord neck. Be careful with it, and if necessary consider reinforcing it with tape.

You also need to prepare for an event, and allow time the day before an ultra race to do the following:

- band-aid nipples
- go to briefing and weigh-in if needed
- carbo load and hydrate
- cut up bars and food into zip-seal food bags and place in drop bags
- deposit drop bags
- pin on race number and lay out clothes for the morning
- go over plan with crew and pacer if you have them
- set alarm clock
- mix drink powder and fill water bottles

CHECKLISTS

Things I would do before leaving home:

- toughen up feet to avoid blisters by walking around barefoot. Do this all the time
- prepare feet properly – trim toenails, remove corns, callouses and rough spots on skin to avoid getting pressure points. Do this two to three days before race
- buy food and ice if needed
- carbo load and hydrate
- double check you have chosen the correct socks
- fill and label drop bags with clothing and with the food needed for that section
- fill drop packs with the food needed for that section
- put all kit next to the front door
- phone pacer(s)

Things I usually do once I get to a race:

- apply sunscreen, hydrocortisone, vaseline
- check GPS watch
- eat and drink something
- go to the toilet
- check-in at start line
- check and adjust laces just before the run to ensure shoes feel snug and not loose
- double-knot laces and tuck the ends under crossover lacing to ensure that they do not come undone, otherwise you might catch it on a branch and fall
- ensure race number is pinned on

Things for my crew to remember (if I have one):

- ice and bottled water
- food and drinks for themselves
- petrol
- a clock
- hurry me in and out of aid stations quickly, ideally in less than five minutes
- at each aid station, check pre-recorded crew notes for things I will need there
- arrange gear in car or on a mat so you can find things quickly
- pre-mix and chill drinks if possible
- have two bottles and a hand-strap bottle ready

Things I would do at aid stations if I don't have a crew:

- swap water bottles
- swap zip-sealed food bag
- swap socks (for me only at 50 miles and 75 if needed)
- swap top (for me only at 50 miles and 75 if needed)

Appendix 3:
Training

Easy run – This should be 20–60 minutes in length. Pacing should feel comfortable, with the ability to hold a conversation. A slight variation would be a recovery run, which should not exceed 45 minutes. Easy and recovery runs should make up about 60 per cent of your weekly volume.

Long run – This should be 60–150 minutes in length. As with an easy run, you should be able to hold a conversation during these runs. Some variations on a typical long run would be progression runs. There are several versions of a progression run, but essentially it's where you start out slowly and then at some point run quicker. These are helpful in improving your stamina and your overall fitness as well as in aiding recovering times.

Tempo run – Tempo running really improves a crucial physiological variable for running success, which is our metabolic fitness. Most runners train their cardiovascular system to deliver oxygen to the muscles, but not how to use it once it arrives there. Tempo runs teach the body to use the oxygen for metabolism more efficiently. This involves running harder and faster than is comfortable, pushing yourself

303

beyond the point where you can hold a conversation, for example. The better trained you are, the better your muscles become at using the by-products of exercise, the lactate and hydrogen ions. The result is less acidic muscles – in other words muscles that have not reached their new threshold, so they keep on contracting, letting you run further and faster.

There are many ways to do tempo or threshold runs, but here are a few of them. The most common is a 20–40 minute run, done at a pace you could sustain for an hour-long race. For slower runners, this may be close to your 10km pace and for faster runners this would be around your half-marathon pace. For this type of tempo run, do a few miles at an easy pace then pick it up for 20–40 minutes at your tempo pace, followed by a few miles at easy pace.

Another common form of the tempo run is to run intervals. I tend to do a lot of interval work, where I run at a faster pace than my standard marathon tempo, probably the sort of speed I'd run a 3km or 5km race, with short periods of rest between intervals. For example, I might do a one-mile warm-up, followed by 6 × 1000 or 3 × 2000 metres at 5k + 20 seconds pace, with 200 metres jogging/walking rest in between, and then with a one-mile cool down. Interval work like this is essential if you want to reach your full potential as a distance runner. You can of course vary the distances where you run fast or slow, but this sort of exercise should comprise about 10 per cent of your weekly volume.

Hill intervals – Hill training is a highly specific form of strength/resistance training that has many benefits for the endurance runner, including improvements in stride frequency and length, muscle strength and power, neuromuscular co-ordination, running economy, fatigue resistance, muscular endurance, speed, aerobic and anaerobic power, and it also protects leg muscle-fibres against damage and delayed-onset muscle soreness. Hill training also increases both aerobic and anaerobic power, placing a much greater emphasis on anaerobic energy metabolism than is the case when running across flat terrain.

A good example of this type of workout is 10 x 30-90 second hill repeats at a hard effort, with a walk or jog back down the hill for recovery. As a runner, you can do squats, lunges and hamstring curls until your muscles scream and burn, but nothing compares exactly to running. The forceful contractions caused by the lifting of the hips, glutes and quads when you are running up the hill utilises the same principal mechanics as many plyometrics exercises. Also, if you do long hill repeats, these are often very intense and are a great VO2 max workout. To be honest, hill intervals work nicely as part of a full training programme.

Cross-training activities that complement running – Cross-training activities use your main running muscles in many different ways, and engage many additional muscles that you may never use while running. Performing these activities will allow you to gain greater strength and balance, therefore reducing your risk of injury and helping you to perform better.

Cycling, either indoors on a stationary bike at the gym in a spinning class, or outdoors on the road or trail, is another low-impact activity that can give your body a break from the high impact of running. It will also help build your engine – your lungs, capillary network and heart strength. You can keep off unwanted pounds and maintain a pretty good fitness baseline even if you're just cycling.

Cycling also targets the quadriceps and shin muscles, which are slower to develop in runners and helps strengthen the connective tissue of the knees, hips and ankles, which may reduce your risk of injury. However, some running experts advise against cycling on non-run days because it can still be strenuous and exhausting to your muscles. So what do you do? If you want to cross train with biking, include it on your running days by running first and then cycling later in the day. If you're replacing a running session with a cycling workout, 10–15 minutes on the bike is about the equivalent of one running mile.

Swimming can be a beneficial cross-training activity for all runners because swimming is a non-weight-bearing exercise, serving as an ideal form of active recovery for runners. Swim sessions allow you to increase endurance and oxygen capacity, while it gives the joints and connective tissues a break from the impact of running while maintaining aerobic fitness. Not only that, but it also targets all the major muscle groups (quadriceps, hamstrings, glutes, abs, lower back and upper body). Swimming allows your legs a break while developing the upper body musculature that is often neglected in runners.

Deep-water running, also known as pool running, is just running in deep water. This is achieved by slipping on a flotation device around the waist, such as an AquaJogger, so that your legs are suspended off the bottom of the pool. This activity most mimics running on land without the impact on the joints. It also makes a perfect cross-training activity for injured runners.

The rowing machine provides an amazing workout. Rowing is great for runners who want to develop strength in their quadriceps and hips, while also improving upper-body strength. Good form is necessary when using the rower, so do ask a certified trainer for some pointers, but if you get this right then it is a perfect tool to have.

Whether you choose to climb stairs in your office building, at home or at the gym on the stair-stepping machine, heading up stairs provides an excellent workout for the quads and hip flexors. Because runners tend to have stronger hamstrings, stair climbing targets the quadriceps which can help you achieve better muscle balance, therefore reducing injury risk.

Plyometrics may look a bit like child's play, as it involves lots of hopping, skipping, bounding and jumping drills. Jumping onto a box, step or a raised surface is ideal for plyometrics. These activities can help improve a runner's overall strength, speed, range of motion, push-offs and stride length, but they are best suited for conditioned athletes. Basic forms can be introduced for beginners; however, you must perform the explosive drills correctly. Because of their high impact, landing improperly can lead to a greater incidence of injury. If you are not familiar with plyometrics, you may want to work with a personal trainer for several sessions until you have the techniques down to a T.

The elliptical trainer is one of the most popular cardio machines in the gym, and because it mimics running action without the impact, it makes an excellent cross-training activity. Even though the elliptical is a weight-bearing activity, it is low-impact for the joints. The elliptical also helps develop a runner's core and leg muscles, and if you use one with the arm levers, the pushing and pulling motion allows you to develop a stronger arm swing therefore helping make you a more efficient runner.

An indoor cross-country ski machine can help improve

running economy (the amount of oxygen used during a run). Because the hips, quadriceps, core and upper body are all utilised in performing this workout, it allows for development of the weaker quadriceps without the impact. And one of the greatest benefits is the high-calorie expenditure that comes from doing this activity.

Please remember that cross-training should not replace a scheduled day off from running. Rest is just as vital to your training as running is.

~~THE END~~

JUST THE BEGINNING

Acknowledgements

Over my year's running I have been lucky to have had the support of so many different people from all walks of life. I'm aware that I cannot do everything myself, so I have not been afraid to ask for the help from others to achieve my goals. And almost everyone has come through for me. I love you all. Thanks for having given me your time, expertise, money, petrol, home-made energy bars, company and friendship this last year. The list below contains those I'd most like to thank. If I have missed anyone off, I am sorry (and I love you, too).

Illana Adamson, Vivienne Alexander, Sam & Andrea, Andrew & Nicola Bald, Sarah Bate, Dominika Brooks, Dustin Brooks, Helen Caddy, Martin Campbell, Angela Cluff, Lucy Ann Collins, Alex Cooke, Paul Cooke, Sam Cousins, Penny Demetriou, Matt Dickinson, Tiago Dionisio, Christopher Dixon, Colin Dow, Matt Dowse, Michael & Boo Dwyer, John & Ceri Edmonds, Sarah & Mark Etienne, Mo Farah, David Fernando, Sir Ranulph Fiennes, Abby Flanagan, Rukiye Forshaw, Sue Fowler, Brett & Issy Garrard, Nick & Chris Giffen, John & Theresa Gilding, Duncan Goose, Ewan Forrest Gordon, Emily Hannon, Clive & Jackie Hearn, Adam Holland, Vicky Horne, Rob Hutching, Khalil Ibrahimi, Eddie Izzard, Ted Jackson, Zara Jaffrey, Kate Anna-Louise Jayden, Karen Kay, Dr Courtney Kipps, Amanda Kirtley, John Leach, Lloyd Lecuona, Neil Leonard,

Kate Leonard-Morgan, Juliette Lloyd, Joanne Lumb, David Luxton, Joanne McCaffery, Rob McCargow, Stuart Mackenzie, Ian Marshall, Denzil Martin, Warren Mauger, Lucas Meagor, Michael Miller, Lara Milward, Justine Neville, Sarah Nisbet, Kevin O'Rourke, Timmy Osborne, Simon Oxley, Lorna & Alistair Parkes, Andy Persson, Nicola & Jay Prehn, Clare Broadbent Purcell, Garrett Quathamer, Dunstan Rickard, Nigel Robinson, Pippa Rollitt, Shirley Rollitt, Dave Ross, Adam Smith, Philip & Louise Smith, Juliet Stallard, Lua Stifani, Paul Swindles, Ben Thornton, James Thurlow, Matthew Tonks, Chris Twiselton, Samantha Upton, Gillian Verdin, Paul Walton, Oliver Weingarten, Pip Wilson, Chris Winter, Oli Winton, Ricky Wood, Ellan Yak, Lisa Yates, Ewa Maria Zareba, Andrea Zuchora.

The following companies and organisations also helped me: Lucozade Sport, British Airways, Virgin Airways, Brooks, Bellwether, Coldplay, David Luxton Associates, Firefly recovery, Game Ready, Sense Core, Up & Running, Sheen Sports, Terra Ferma Medi@, Virgin Trains, Skins.